"Now I will tell you stories of what happened long ago. There was a world before this. The things that I am going to tell about happened in that world. Some of you will remember every word that I say, some will remember a part of the words, and some will forget them all—I think this will be the way, but each man must do the best he can. . . . You must keep these stories as long as the world lasts; tell them to your children and grandchildren generation after generation. . . ."

⊞

from *The Storytelling Stone*

The Storytelling Stone

Traditional Native American Myths and Tales

Edited and with an Introduction by
Susan Feldmann

DELTA TRADE PAPERBACKS

A Delta Book
Published by
Dell Publishing
a division of
Random House, Inc.
1540 Broadway
New York, New York 10036

ISBN: 0-385-33402-8

Reprinted by arrangement with Dell Publishing

Manufactured in the United States of America

Published simultaneously in Canada

February 1999

10 9 8 7 6 5 4 3 2 1

BVG

Acknowledgments

The editor and publisher wish to make acknowledgment to the following:

"The Man Who Holds Up the Sky" from *Tsimsyan Myths*, by Marius Barbeau. Bulletin No. 174, Anthropological Series No. 51, Ottawa: National Museum of Canada, 1961.

"The Emergence," "The Flood," "The Monster Slayers," "The Sky Has Fallen," "The Rolling Skull," and "Who Is the Strongest?" from *Zuni Mythology*, by Ruth Benedict. New York: Columbia University Press, 1935.

"In the Beginning of the Nisqually World," "How Raven Helped the Ancient People," and "Coyote and Eagle Visit the Land of the Dead" from *Indian Legends of the Pacific Northwest*, by E. E. Clark. Berkeley: University of California Press, 1933.

"The Earthdiver," "The Origin of the Pleiades," "The Girl Who Married a Dog," and "Water Jar Boy" from *Indian Tales of North America*, by Tristam P. Coffin. *(Journal of American Folklore)* Philadelphia: American Folklore Society, 1961.

"Olelbis," and "The Two Sisters" from *Creation Myths of Primitive America*, by Jeremiah Curtin. Copyright 1898 by Jeremiah Curtin. Reprinted by permission of Jeremiah Curtin Cardell.

"How Old Age Came into the World" and "Bat" from *Myths of the Modocs*, by Jeremiah Curtin. Copyright 1912 by Mary Alma Curtin. Reprinted by permission of Jeremiah Curtin Cardell.

"The Story Telling Stone" and "How Chipmunks Got Their Stripes" from *Seneca Indian Myths,* by Jeremiah Curtin. Copyright 1923 by E. P. Dutton & Co., Inc. Renewal © 1951 by Jeremiah Curtin Cardell. Reprinted by permission of the publishers.

"Blackfoot Genesis" and "The Theft from the Sun" from *Blackfoot Lodge Tales* (1892), by George Bird Grinnell. "Blackfoot Genesis" and "The Theft from the Sun" also appear in *Pawnee, Blackfoot and Cheyenne: History and Folklore of the Plains* from the writings of George Bird Grinnell, edited by Dee Brown, N.Y.: Charles Scribner's Sons, 1961.

"The Winnebago Origin Myth" and "The Faster" from *Primitive Man as a Philosopher,* by Paul Radin. Copyright 1957 by Dover Publications, Inc., New York, 14, N.Y. at $2.00, and reprinted through permission of the publisher.

"The Twins Alter the Book of Life," "From the Winnebago Trickster Cycle," "Hare's Adventures," and "The Man Who Brought His Wife Back from Spiritland" from *Winnebago Hero Cycles,* by Paul Radin. Memoir No. 1 of Indiana University Publications in Anthropology and Linguistics, July, 1948. Reprinted by permission of the publisher.

"Raven" from *Tlingit Myths and Texts,* by J. R. Swanton. Washington, D.C.: Bureau of Ethnology, 1909. Reprinted by permission of the Bureau of American Ethnology of the Smithsonian Institution.

"The Woman Who Fell from the Sky," "Sun Sister and Moon Brother," "Sedna, Mistress of the Underworld," "The Theft of Light," "The Bird Whose Wings Made the Wind," "The Release of the Wild Animals," "The Empounded Water," "The Lizard Hand," "The Deceived Blind Men," "The Eye Juggler," "Big Turtle's War Party," "The Sun Tests His Son-in-Law," "Lodge Boy and Thrown Away," "Dirty Boy," "The Jealous Uncle," "The Man Who Acted as the Sun," "Orpheus," "The Arrow Chain," "The Girls Who Wished To Marry Stars," "The Girl Enticed to the

Contents

II   Trickster

III   Tales of Heroes, Supernatural Journeys, and Other Folktales

The Storytelling Stone

Introduction

"They were living in the fourth world," begins the Zuni genesis. "It was dark. They could not see one another. They stepped upon one another, they urinated upon one another, they spat upon one another, they threw refuse upon one another. They could not breathe. . . . The Sun took pity upon them. He saw that the world was covered with hills and springs but there were no people to give him prayersticks. He thought, 'My people shall come to the daylight world.'" Aided by their priest-gods the people emerge from their womblike underworld to the earth's surface and the light of day. These are the First People, who precede the coming of man: they are queer creatures with short, hairless tails, long ears, webbed feet and hands; their bodies and heads are covered with moss whose tufts form horns, they give off a foul odor of burning sulphur. They are obviously prehuman and unequipped for life in the upper world. Their divine helpers must cut mouths in their faces that they may eat, separate their fingers to enable them to work, cut off their tails and horns to give them a more human aspect. The process of civilization begins in the underworld and is represented by the detailed account of the people's ascent through several intermediary worlds. These worlds correspond to successive ages or stages of development, bearing both on the race and on the individual, evoking a grand evolutionary scheme at once cosmic and cultural.

In the Zuni account the First People must be transformed to make them fit to inhabit a good world. In many other myths the world must be made or reshaped to serve as a suitable dwelling place for the coming of the people. In both instances creation represents an effort at establishing harmony between man and his environment, and native tales recount the great struggles of the mythical age with a keen sense of drama, a love for detail, and often with pathos and humor.

For the North American Indian the coming into being of the world does not mean the disruption of an original state of harmony. The pathos of the loss of paradise, so prominent in other mythologies, is remarkably subdued. We find a suggestion of the loss of paradise theme in the Navaho version of the emergence. The first people, the Navaho relate, were happy in the underworld—however unattractive their condition might appear to us. But they were driven out by a great flood as a punishment for their promiscuities. In the Navaho account, the breaking of a tabu precedes at each station the people's progression from world to world until they reach the surface. The myth conveys the reluctance of the First People to move on and in its telling points out that the world submits to progress both unwillingly and unwittingly, and further, that any advance is precipitated by some act of lawlessness.

North American mythology is rich in the great variety of cosmogonic tales. Aside from the Trickster and Hero tales, the main interest is in the evocation of primeval struggles in preparation for the present world and its inhabitants. The Eskimos of the north possess the most fragmentary traditions relating to origins, while the tribes of the Southwest and California are most remarkable for their highly developed cosmogonies, elaborate in detail and rich in ceremonial associations.

According to Eskimo tradition, "the earth was always there." There are independent tales telling of the origin of man, of thunder, lightning, and rain and of day and night. One widespread story of particular interest is about the transformation of an incestuous brother and sister pair into the sun and the moon.[1] The basic myth of the Eskimo serves to account for the origin of the goddess of the underworld and of the food supply.[2] Sedna, a girl who has refused all her suitors, is enticed into marriage by a bird who takes her to his own land. She gives birth to bird children, and is distressed when she discovers that the life of birds differs from that of men. Her father comes to the bird country to rescue her, kills the bird husband and takes his daughter and her children into his boat. A storm rises, and in way of sacrifice he throws Sedna overboard and, when she clings to the boat, cuts off her fingers. These fingers fall into the sea and become various kinds of fish. Sedna sinks in the ocean and becomes the goddess of the underworld.

Navaho traditions contain the most complete and detailed account of the emergence-type myth common to the tribes of the Southwest. The myth falls into four episodes. The first, the Age of Beginnings, tells of the ascent of the First People from the underworld from story to story and their final emergence upon earth. The second, the Age of Animal Heroes, describes how the earth was set in order, the creation of light, and the adventures of its early inhabitants. The third, the Age of the Gods, recounts the slaying of the giants, ogres, and other monsters by the twin brothers. The fourth, the Patriarchal Age, deals with the growth of the Navaho nation in the years of its early wanderings; to this age, too, belong most of the revelations visionaries bring back in the form of rites.[3]

---

[1] *Cf.* tale 10.
[2] *Cf.* tale 11.
[3] The Hopi emergence contained in this volume corresponds in many important details to an episode of the Navaho myth and probably derives from the same stock.

Some fifty native groups account for their presence on earth by a myth relating how their ancestors ascended from the underground to the surface of the earth. The myth contains many elements that serve to validate religious beliefs and is often connected with tribal rituals. It

4   Introduction

The story of the hero brothers, in many instances twins, who subdue the giants and monsters of the primeval age, appears in a great number of cosmogonic myths; the episodes in the story of the testing of the Sun's children recur in the hero tales of the Pacific Northwest and other areas. The brothers usually live with their grandmother, a personification of Earth, who equips them with various charms whereby they withstand trials and reach the end of their quest. In the Navaho myth, the Great Goddess and her sister give birth to the heroes Thobadzistshini, Son of the Waters, and Nayanezgani, Son of the Sun. The boys journey to the House of the Sun and, with magic aids, pass through clashing rocks, which, like the Symplegades, close upon those who go between them, a plain of knifelike reeds and another of cane cactuses that rush together, and finally a desert of boiling sands. By means of spells they overcome the guardian animals who bar their way to the Sun's House. Sun submits them to a number of tests with the intention of killing them, but, failing, finally accedes to their request for weapons with which to fight the monsters that are devouring mankind. The brothers return to earth and in a series of adventures, as in the labors of Hercules, rid the world of man-devouring monsters. On a second visit to the Sun, they receive four hoops by means of which their mother raises the great storm that brings to an end the Age of Monsters. The Goddess reshapes the world anew, but permits three monsters to survive—Old Age, Poverty, and Hunger; for "should they be slain, men would prize neither life nor warmth, nor goods, nor food."

In the mythology of the Woodland tribes, genesis opens with a sky world, usually peopled with familiar beings from the earth world yet to be created.[4] The action begins with the

is presented in dramatized form as an integral part of the Navaho "Up-ward-Reaching-Way," and the Hopi "Bean" and "Snake" ceremonies.
[4] Cf. tale 4.

fall of the heaven-born Titaness, who, since the world is still covered by the primeval waters, is caught by waterfowl. The birds set about making the earth serve as her permanent resting place. They dive for soil at the bottom of the sea and spread it on the back of a turtle.[5] The myth continues, narrating the birth of twin brothers who create forests, lakes, and animals. Here, as in the Navaho myth, the brothers represent the upper and the underworld, powers of nature. Significantly, they quarrel in the mother's womb. The twins, Flint and Sapling, each proceed to create a world independently and then inspect and modify each other's work. Sapling finds Flint's world too inimical to man; he softens the landscape full of cliffs and ledges and reduces the giant mosquito created by Flint to its present size. Flint, on the other hand, finds that Sapling has made a world too easy for man, so he shakes the animals Sapling made so fat that they could hardly move, causing them to be small, changes the trees that originally bore fruit, and causes the rivers to flow only in one direction.

The notion that the hardships of life were intended by the beings of the First Age is commonly expressed in American myths. Often it is attributed to the wish of a trickster figure who opposes the creator. According to the Maidu myth, the creator Earth-Maker wanted men to live in ease and to live forever, but Coyote, his helper, brings it about that men must toil and die. Other accounts, however, seem to express the view of the Goddess in the Navaho emergence myth, that the dispensation of toil and death is really for the good of man.

American Indian accounts of the origin of death show, on the whole, a greater acceptance of this fact than the myths of most other peoples. The myth often takes the form of a debate between two demiurgic beings, one of whom pleads for eter-

---

[5] For a striking parallel to the Iroquois myth of the woman who falls from the sky and is caught by birds, is lowered to the surface of the water and becomes the creator, see the Finnish *Kalevala*.

nal life for man while the other argues for death. The issue is usually decided either by divination or by reason. If the latter, the two most common winning arguments are both of a practical nature: to prevent overpopulation and to insure man's appreciation of life. In a Winnebago tale, Hare's grandmother points out to him that she, the earth, is not broad enough to accommodate an unlimited population.[6] Old Woman in the Blackfoot myth argues that men should die forever on the grounds that the living would cherish and mourn their loved ones less if death were not final.[7] In an Eskimo myth the choice is between living in darkness without death or having light and death. Two old women debate the issue and decide to have both light and death. Sometimes the debate is finally decided by magic.[8] In a number of myths the demiurgic trickster introduces death simply to oppose the creator, who decreed eternal life for man, and apparently in ignorance of what death means; for when his own son dies he wants to revoke the edict of death, but his first word remains law.

Where the notion of death as a punishment occurs, the guilty one is always a mythical culture hero rather than man. Thus Hare, the Winnebago culture hero–trickster, brings about death by breaking a tabu.[9] Similarly, in a Wishram tale, it is due to Coyote's laziness that the dead cannot be brought back to life.

The episode of diving for soil is widely diffused and constitutes the creation myth of several tribes.[10] Probably of shamanistic origin, it belongs to one of the most ancient strata of myth and is known in parts of Asia and Polynesia as well as on the North American continent. In southern California creation generally begins with primordial waters before the earth

---

[6] *Cf.* tale 23.
[7] *Cf.* tale 7.
[8] *Cf.* tale 7.
[9] *Cf.* tale 23.
[10] *Cf.* tales 5, 17.

was shaped, over which dwell Coyote and the birds. In some versions they perch on a mountain peak that pierces the waves, where they wait for the waters to subside. In others they float on a raft, or rest upon a pole or tree that rises above the waters. In the latter case the birds dive for soil from which to build the earth. Usually the Duck succeeds, floating to the surface dead but with a bit of soil in its bill, which is magically expanded and becomes the earth floating upon the original waters. Birds—Eagle, Hawk, Crow, and Hummingbird—figure chiefly in these tales. Coyote generally appears as creator and transformer although sometimes his place is taken by the birds, and the person of the creator reverts to the original shamanistic bird-man.

The earth-diver episode is frequently told in connection with deluge stories. In many accounts the flood destroys the first world and the myth of creation describes the restoration of the world by the culture hero. Stories of a primeval deluge that destroys the world and most of its inhabitants are found throughout the continent.[11] The flood is sometimes brought about by the people's wickedness, as in the Biblical account of Noah.[12] But often we find quite different explanations for the world deluge. A tale popular among the Plateau tribes, the North Pacific Coast and Siberia, attributes the flood to tears, often those of a disappointed suitor. Another tradition extending from California to Nova Scotia tells about a monster who drinks up a lake; when he is killed, water flowing from his pierced belly causes the flood.

In the Californian Wintun cosmogony the First World is destroyed successively by fire and by flood. Olelbis (He-Who-Sits-Above) presides as chief over a preexistent Sky World and, with the aid of his two grandmothers, constructs a paradisic sweathouse in Olelpanti, the upper side, as a refuge

---

[11] *Cf.* tales 2, 6, 17.
[12] *Cf.* tales 2, 17.

for the First People during the violent upheavals of the Primeval Age. The elements subdued, Olelbis puts the earth in order and sends down to the lower world all those among the First People who are not needed in Olelpanti, turning them into beings useful to mankind. A detail of particular interest is the failure of Olelbis to modify the primordial nature of Grizzly Bear, Rattlesnake, and Flint. The first two refuse to wear braces on their teeth. Flint in turn vows to keep his teeth, in order to punish the evil sisters. His hate, however, cannot admit any restraint. "I am stronger than both of you, he tells his sisters. You . . . will hate people only, but I shall hate all living things. I shall hate you, hate everyone; kill you, kill everyone. I want nothing of anyone. I want no friend in any place." And Olelbis replies, "Well, you go as you are." Thus, Flint goes to the lower world, the symbol of primordial belligerence and hate personified in the form of the killing point of the arrow. All the others, "let their teeth be made innocent."[13]

It is among the Californian tribes that the idea of a single creator is most popular. Whether animal or human in form, he is usually presented as dignified and benevolent, and there is a tendency to humanize his character. Unlike the Biblical creator, he is seldom if ever unbegotten. Many creators have elaborate birth legends. Hupa tradition tells of their creator springing into existence from the earth behind the inner house wall. The lofty Olelbis himself was not unbegotten since many of the stories refer to his two grandmothers. The Zuni myth of Awonawilona and the Winnebago myth of Earthmaker offer the nearest analogy to the Biblical conception of the creator.[14] Of these, however, the Winnebago origin myth recorded by Paul Radin belongs to a rather recent tradition and represents an attempt toward systematization on the

---

[13] *Cf.* tale 6.
[14] *Cf.* tale 8.

part of an esoteric group of priest thinkers. The Zuni myth of Awonawilona seems in its broad outlines to constitute an integral part of Zuni ceremony. The account taken down by Cushing, however, is considerably colored by monotheistic ideas. Even so, its details betray creation by magic rather than fiat. Awonawilona, who alone has being in the beginning, assumes by sheer force of concentration the form of the sun. The Sun father then proceeds to make balls of his cuticle by rubbing his skin, which he casts upon the waters. From these are created the primal pair, Earth Mother and Sky Father from whose union all life issues. Earth Mother then repulses Sky Father and they become respective guardians of Earth and Sky. The theme of the union and separation of the primeval World Parents can be found in the mythologies of the ancient worlds, of Africa and Polynesia. On the North American continent it is also told among the Pima, the Mohave, and the Yuma. In the Winnebago myth Earthmaker's first creative act is to cry; to his surprise his tears turn into seas. Next he discovers that whatever he wishes comes into existence, and by wishing creates light, the earth, and man in his own likeness.

The creation of the human race usually marks the close of the Primeval Age, and even though the gods of the first age had put themselves to all the trouble of creating a world for man's sake, accounts of the creation of man in most tribes do not approach the conception of the Winnebago myth. In most myths mankind is fashioned from clay, sticks, feathers, grass, or ears of maize. Sometimes they are earth-born or issue from a spring or a swamp, or from the bones of the dead. In Northwestern traditions carved images are vivified to become human ancestors. Sometimes the most primitive accounts are not wanting in touching details, as in the Maidu story of Earthmaker lying down beside the two clay figurines he made and sweating day and night to bring life into them. In the Blackfoot genesis, Old Man, who creates all sorts of things while casually walking around in the world, does not depend on a primal couple to populate the earth but keeps on creating people wherever he goes.[15] A Kato story is quite graphic, telling how the creator made a trachea of reed and pounded ochre to mix with water and make blood. In contrast, the creator of the Wishosk of the same area used no tools but formed things by spreading out his hands.

> ▶ *When Gudatrigawitl wanted to make people, he said, "I want fog."*
>
> *Then it began to be foggy, Gudatrigawitl thought: "No one will see it when the people are born." Then he thought: "Now I wish people to be all over, broadcast. I want it to be full of people and full of game." Then the fog went away. No one had seen them before, but now they were there.*[16]

While the Biblical account of creation achieves its sublime effect by sheer suppression of any concrete detail, what is so appealing in this "naive" native tale is that here the need to veil the actual modus operandi of the creator is expressed and concretely rendered by the device of a fog-screen.

The tribes of the North Pacific Coast have no creation myths in the strict sense, but various incidents usually connected with such a myth, such as the forming of the mountains and the creation of light, are told as part of the legend of the culture hero.[17] The events of the primeval age revolve around the great deeds of the culture hero, conceived in animal form as Mink, Blue Jay, or Raven by the various tribes, who makes available to mankind the elemental resources of fire, water, fish, and wild game and regulates the seasons and the winds.

The legend usually begins with the birth of a child, either from supernatural conception or from an adulterous relation,

---

[15] *Cf.* tale 7.
[16] H. B. Alexander, *North American Mythology* (N.Y.: Cooper Square Publishers, 1963), p. 229.
[17] *Cf.* tales 9, 12, 13, 14.

and proceeds to his supernatural growth and boyhood adventures. As a young man he seduces his uncle's wife or, in some tales, the daughter of the Sky Chief. His misdeed brings on a flood, and the boy flies to the sky. His child drops from the sky on some drifting kelp and is found and adopted by a chief. The child will not eat at first, but once he is instructed in the use of food he becomes so voracious that he threatens to exhaust the provisions of the tribe and must be sent away. This child is the culture hero and the myth continues with a series of his demiurgic deeds. Having secured various necessities for mankind, the culture hero travels about and transforms animals and objects into their present form. This, in bare outline, is the basic pattern of the North Pacific Coast origin myth. The best examples of the Raven cycle as a creation story are found among the Tsimshian and the Tlinkit.

An important function of many American Indian culture heroes is the stealing of light or fire or water from some monster who keeps them from men. The tale of the Theft of Light occurs all over the continent but is most persistent as a legend on the Pacific Coast. The culture hero, usually in his animal form, goes to the monster's house and succeeds in carrying off the vessel or basket containing light while the monster's attention is drawn away. On his return he releases the light so that it scatters all over the earth. In another story, the culture hero turns himself into a stick or otherwise transforms himself so that he is swallowed by the ogre's daughter and reborn. As the young child of the house he simply runs away with the light. [18] The same motifs frequently appear in stories of the Theft of Fire.

The Promethean myth is one of the most universal in America. Although sometimes it is daylight that is stolen and sometimes the sun, in the great majority of cases it is fire.[19] The legend often has a practical turn, describing the kinds of wood

---

[18] *Cf.* tales 13, 14.
[19] *Cf.* tale 12.

in which the fire is deposited. Usually the flame is guarded by a celestial being, but in some instances, as in the Northwest versions, it is derived from ghosts or the ocean, suggesting a volcanic origin. In the most common form of the myth the theft of fire is followed by its distribution by relays of animals and may refer to the ritualistic preservation and kindling of fire, with the distribution of the new fire by relays of torch bearers, rites of which there are traces in both North and South America.

Two other stories of thefts, popular particularly along the coastal areas, are concerned with the release of water and of wild animals.[20] In the beginning all the water is held back by a monster, often a giant frog; the hero succeeds in slaying the monster and liberating the water. In the analogous story of the release of the wild animals, all the game are kept originally in one place, frequently in a cave, until they are released finally and made available to mankind by the culture hero.

A common motif in the mythology of the North Pacific Indians is the story of the primeval flood after which the world must be restored.[21] As in the Californian myths, after the deluge the survivors of the First Age are transformed into animals, human beings are created with their several languages, and the present order of the world is established. An interesting inversion of this pattern is presented by a Kwakiutl story, which tells how the antediluvian wolves took off their wolf masks after the waters subsided and became human beings.

II

For the natives their myths represent a true account of their origins and, in many instances, sanction institutions and rites. At our removal from the context in which these myths

---

[20] *Cf.* tales 15, 16.
[21] *Cf.* tale 9.

flourished we are bound to ask, in the manner of outsiders, what do these stories mean? The study of a large sample of the traditions of various peoples shows that myths have a wide range of reference, embracing all relevant areas and dimensions of human experience, and that, therefore, any interpretation of myth that tries to reduce it to one of these, the psychological, the social, or the natural, is bound to be hopelessly inadequate. To begin with, we should ask what these stories say, and read them attentively. For a complete elucidation of any myth the student would need to penetrate the native's closed world and acquire thorough familiarity with its language, clan organization, and ceremonial life as well as its oral literature.

Preliterate people live in an elaborately symbolic universe where all that makes up man's reality, whether physical or social, is charged with traditionally fixed associations. In the Hako ceremony of the Plains Indians, the priest draws a circle with his toes and places a feather within it. According to the Plains priest's own explanation,

➤ *the circle represents a nest and is drawn by the toes, because the eagle builds its nest with its claws. Although we are imitating the bird building its nest, there is another meaning to the action; we are thinking of Tirawa making the world for the people to live in. If you go on a high hill and look around, you will see the sky touching the earth on every side, and within this circular enclosure the people live. So the circles we have made are not only nests, but they also represent the circle Tirawa-atius has made for the dwelling place of all the people. The circles also stand for the kinship group, the clan, and the tribe. [22]*

----

[22] H. B. Alexander, *op. cit.*, p. 97. The Hako = *sacra* or sacred objects employed in the ceremony, as the Pawnee rite is called, is a dramatic prayer for life, children, health, and prosperity directed to the powers of sky and earth.

Mythic ideas are embodied in ritual, architecture, and social organization as well as in stories. Myths, therefore, cannot be treated as independent creations of fancy. They are fictions not in our sense of the word, but insofar as any traditional culture may be regarded as an elaborate artifice.

The tendency to personify qualities, forces, states, and relations as well as objects is one of the most obvious characteristics of myth. It springs from a dramatic view of reality wherein all process is seen as an action and all things, whether men, beasts, stones or stars, figure as actors in a single ceremony. The Beginners, even when theriomorphic, or cosmic like Earth or Sky, are always called the First People. To the native the division between things and people or men and animals is not so absolute as it has become for us. In the mythical age there were only "people"; in setting up the present world some of these were changed into "things"—but under special circumstances they can regain their animate character. The same holds true for the division between men and animals. As mythologies evolve the *dramatis personae* tend to become more fixed in their identities and systematically related. The more primitive a myth the greater the fluidity of its world of personages. In many of these tales men and women turn into parts of the scenery, and sticks, stones, weapons, and utensils join the ranks of the actors with bewildering rapidity.

Magic plays a primary role in North American myths. Indeed, the creation of the world is represented in most myths as an act of magic, and the sorcerer emerges as the most likely prototype of the American Indian creator. In the Piman emergence myth the creator appears clearly in the form of a shaman:

> ➤ *In the beginning there was nothing where now are earth, sun, moon, stars and all that we see. Ages long the darkness was gathering, until it formed a great mass in which developed the spirit of Earth Doctor, who . . . drifted to and fro without support or place*

to fix himself. Conscious of his power, he determined to try to build an abiding place, so he took from his breast a little dust and flattened it into a cake. Then he thought within himself, "Come forth, some kind of plant," and there appeared the creosote bush." Three times the earth-disk upset, but the fourth time it remained where he had placed it. When the flat dust cake was still he danced upon it singing:

> *Earth Magician shapes this world.*
> *Behold what he can do!*
> *Round and smooth he molds it.*
> *Behold what he can do!*[23]

The chant continues. Earth Magician, still dancing on the flat dust cake, makes the earth grow large, flings sun and moon into the heavens, and sprays stars into the sky from his mouth.

Magic pervades hero tales as well as cosmogonic myths. Ogres are more often transformed into harmless beings than slain; trials are withstood less through strength or cunning than by means of sorcery. Of the numerous magical devices employed in these stories, simple transformation is perhaps the most common. These transformations range from the great metamorphosis of the People of the First Age into present day animals, to incidental changes of form, disguises assumed by heroes to ensnare or to flee an adversary. They include transformation of human beings into stones, trees, plants, animals, and meteorological phenomena.[24]

In many instances changes are wrought through songs and spells. The power of words or even thoughts to produce real effects is a strong native belief. It is shown also by the importance of song in ritual and the tabus that forbid songs to be

---

[23] H. B. Alexander, *op. cit.,* p. 177.
[24] *Cf.* tales 10, 44.

sung out of season. The use of charms is as frequent and probably more ancient than that of spells. In a story found all over the world, the hero pursued by an ogre creates successive obstacles by charms, which the ogre in turn overcomes.

The notion of magical increase is also common, especially in creation myths. The underlying idea, probably suggested by plant and animal growth, is that, given a little of a substance, it can be magically increased by rubbing, blowing, or singing over it.

The predominance of magic as well as the tendency to treat the mythic scene in familiar terms often gives these tales a fairy-tale quality. Also, many of the characters we encounter on the primeval scene remind us of märchen types rather than the figures of classical mythology. As in fairy tales, the obstacles the hero encounters and the ogres he must conquer clearly belong to the sphere of infantile and puberty experiences. In contrast to the fairy-tale treatment of infantile sexual fears, the American Indian tale tends to be less abstract and symbolical, and on the whole quite literal, as in the story of the women with toothed vaginas and the witch with the sucking womb.

III

The great personage in North American mythology is the hero-transformer-trickster, a being who combines both human and animal traits and is at once demiurge, culture hero, marplot, and buffoon. The trickster-demiurge belongs to the oldest strata of myth and is probably related to the prehistoric animal-god, from which more specialized types have evolved. In the mythology of some tribes the trickster nature of the demiurge still predominates, while in others his heroic and divine qualities are stressed. The primitive traits of the trickster-god are best preserved in the Raven cycles of the North Pacific Coast and the Coyote cycles of the Great Plains.

In a great number of stories popular among the tribes of the Great Plains, Coyote appears as the personification of unbridled appetite and a conglomeration of all the vices. Cruel, deceitful, and licentious, he is depicted in many tales as seducing his own daughter or grandmother by trickery. Coyote is famed for his gluttony. A favorite motif is his transformation into a dish so that he may receive the food people place on it. A gullible fool, Coyote is often outwitted by the animals he tries to trick and dives into rivers after the reflection of fruit and pretty women. His lack of mercy and his ingratitude to those who help him make him almost monstrous. Yet in other tales Coyote figures as the mighty magician who brings order into the world and bestows great benefits on mankind. It is true that these benefits are less a result of his altruism than an indirect outcome of his efforts to satisfy his own selfish appetite.

Raven, like Coyote, is a transformer and trickster, part demiurge and part clown. His insatiable food quest sends him wandering through all the world in search of things to eat. As he travels from place to place he encounters various animals, which he kills and eats or cheats out of their food supply. His lust is only second to his voracity. In a number of tales he is depicted as posing as a doctor in order to seduce women. Tales showing him as a lecherous father and brother are also frequent. In a story popular from the Great Lakes westward, he attempts to have intercourse with a woman on the opposite side of the stream, but fish bite off his member reducing it to its normal size. In some versions of this tale parts of the trickster's penis are transformed into various edible plants.

For all his clownishness the acts of Raven are creative. A Haida epithet for Raven is He-Whose-Voice-Is-Obeyed. The cycle usually begins with the wanderings of Raven. The world is covered with water and Raven is seeking a resting place. He alights on a bit of flotsam and from this creates the earth. His adventures, creative in their consequences rather than in intention, follow. He steals daylight, the sun, moon and stars from an old man who keeps them in chests or sacks. He steals water from its guardians and creates rivers and streams. He captures fire from the sea and puts it in wood and stone for the use of man. He seizes and opens the chest containing the fish that are to inhabit the sea and further creates fish by carving their images in wood and vivifying them. The Haida distinguish between the first portion of the Raven story, which narrates his creative acts, and the amoral adventures of the later anecdotes. The former are called the "old man's" story, and the young men are forbidden to laugh while it is told.

In the mythology of other tribes the primordial trickster-god has split in two, and the roles of demiurge and foolish deceiver are apportioned to two distinct personages. Thus in the Maidu myth, Coyote appears in a subsidiary part as the antagonist of Earth-Maker, the creator.[25] Similarly, in the Wintun creation myth, Coyote is given the role of the temptor beside the high god Olelbis.[26] Where the creative deeds of the original trickster-demiurge are performed by some other being, only the trickster character remains in a group of fairly constant adventures. These reveal the trickster as a combination of stupidity and cunning. Trickster's stupidity conforms to the popular saying of biting off one's nose to spite one's face, only in his case it is his buttocks he scorches as a punishment for failing to guard his game while he slept.[27] On other occasions his inability to distinguish between animate and inanimate, or his environment and his own body leads him into foolish mishaps. This dualism of sly-stupid is brought out in a common episode where his left hand quarrels with his right hand.[28]

---

[25] *Cf.* tale 7.
[26] *Cf.* tale 6.
[27] *Cf.* tale 23.
[28] *Cf.* tale 22.

A number of tales illustrate Trickster's cleverness in cheating or destroying his enemies or in killing game. In a tale that combines cunning with wanton cruelty, Trickster, left to guard the young of another animal, kills and cooks them and serves them as a meal to their parents. Three incidents relating to the capture of game are especially well known: the tricking of birds into a bag, the enticing of animals over a precipice, and the feigning of death in order to catch game.[29] Trickster's cruelty is revealed in the tale of "The Deceived Blind Men," and his silliness in the somewhat foolish story of the "Eye Juggler," both widely distributed over the continent.[30] Perhaps most trickster tales are too rambling and pointless to suit our Western taste. Some, however, like "The Big Turtle's War Party" and "The Sky Has Fallen," rank with the best European and African folktales.[31] What the stories lack in taste and polish they amply compensate for by a Rabelaisian vitality.

The popularity of trickster stories is one of the characteristics of North American folklore. In certain areas we find anecdotes told about Trickster strung together in a cycle and occasionally, as in the Winnebago cycle, with some attempt to show development of character.

Owing to its length it has not been possible to reproduce in this volume the trickster cycle in its entirety. An excerpt from Paul Radin's summary and discussion of the Winnebago Trickster Cycle will give the reader some idea of its plot development:

➤ *In the first twelve episodes frustration follows frustration without any benefit accruing to him, to any other individual or to society. He cannot even return kind for kind. Beginning with the thirteenth where he is imprisoned in an elk's skull there is, however, a visible*

---

[29] *Cf.* tale 22.
[30] *Cf.* tales 24, 26.
[31] *Cf.* tales 27, 28.

change. He does not get into his predicament to gratify any appetite. He sees other people enjoying themselves and he wishes to do the same. . . . Here, too, he has to use all his ingenuity in order to be extricated. But when he is freed he does not simply laugh at those who have freed him. . . . Instead, he rewards them in a positive and beneficent fashion. It is his first generous act. In the next episode he revenges himself. . . . There then follows the incident in which his penis is eaten away and the transformation of its pieces into objects beneficial to mankind. . . . The visits to the four animals, although evidence of Trickster's laziness and trickery, are here motivated by the desire to feed his family. For his laziness and his unscrupulousness he is punished; for his thoughtfulness about his family he is rewarded. In the next two episodes he revenges himself upon two old enemies and, in the grand finale, he becomes a person with the conscious mission of helping mankind.

The plot of the Trickster cycle is quite clear. . . . A normal individual, the chief of the community, takes it upon himself to defy all customs, sacred and profane. As a result, he finds himself deserted and alone and is thrown back, externally, upon the vaguest type of relationship with nature as symbolized by the birds who taunt and mock him. Internally, he is thrown back upon his primitive undisciplined appetites, hunger and sex. Instead of embarking upon the warpath, a highly socialized, cooperative enterprise, he finds himself proceeding aimlessly from place to place to satisfy his hunger and an undifferentiated sex drive, in the course of which he destroys and kills wantonly and sins against all human values. When he attempts once more to establish a connection with other human beings he has to do it indirectly, through animals . . . , and on the basis of hunger, and of sex inversion. It is a rogue's progress; a picaresque novelette.

Since he is basically the male principal, a kind of Priapus, the cynical transformation of himself into a woman and his bearing of children, brings him to a sudden realization of what has happened. This has been skillfully indicated by having him run away from his last exploit after he has attained his objective, food and sexual gratification. In other words, he does not, as in his previous exploits, stop to laugh at the discomfiture of others and then proceed to walk aimlessly into another adventure. Instead, he flees from it and returns to his family. . . .

This first return to socialization is of short duration and inadequate. He cannot, after all, undo the harm he has done himself quite so quickly. Moreover, he still retains one of his physical characteristics, his gargantuan sexual organs. The incident that follows his departure from his home is the most Rabelaisian in the whole cycle. He is overwhelmed and almost suffocated by falling into mountains of his own dung. Extricating himself, he proceeds onward. . . . He cannot attain complete socialization again until his sexual organs have been reduced to normal size. Once this has been accomplished . . . , he can return to his family and human normalcy again. At the very end, . . . he rises to a still higher level by being transformed into a divine personage with a mission to help mankind.

Paul Radin believes that Trickster serves to demonstrate what happens when man's instinctual side is given free reign.

➤ *He is the symbol for that instinctual side and, overtly, as we have just seen, he can serve either as an object lesson or made to be ridiculous, and become a source of laughter and amusement. If we follow instincts, so runs the ethical, philosophical meaning of the myth, we lose our sense of proportion and we kill others as well as ourselves.*

Trickster . . . is likewise the symbol for the irrational and the non-socialized. For the Winnebago, for all primitive peoples, in fact, they all belonged together. They dreaded all three and tried to create as many safeguards against them as possible. Yet they recognized only too well that man could relapse into all three at a moment's notice. Every man, they felt, possessed a Trickster unconscious which it was imperative for both the individual concerned and, even more so, for society, to bring to consciousness lest it destroy him and those around him. No man can do this for himself. He must call his fellow-men and society to his aid. In the career of Trickster all this is depicted.[32]

In contrast to the uncreated Trickster, Hare, the "First-born" who lives in a special universe of his own, already represents an approximation of, and possibly a step toward, the culture-hero type.[33] The scene of Trickster's adventures in the Winnebago myth is a still unformed world inhabited by vague beings. There are neither men nor monsters. By contrast the universe over which Hare presides is preparatory to our own. It is peopled by animals, monsters, and men. Hare is born of a god and a human mother. His mother dies in childbirth and he is raised by his grandmother, the earth, who, in the stories, figures now as the actual earth, now as a woman.

➤ *Although Hare emerges at the end of his adventures as the transformer of the world and the founder of culture, he is only secondarily moral and purposive. Toward human beings, represented as weak and helpless and the prey of all the evil forces in the world, Hare is ambivalent, a trait he shares with his grandmother Earth. But, while he is ambivalent because he is the eternal child who has no knowledge of good or evil, Earth is ambivalent because, being conceived of originally as antagonistic to man, she must be taught to be friendly.*[34]

The theme of the Hare cycle, according to Paul Radin, is the education of Hare and, by inference, "the first correction of instinctual man" as he is portrayed by Trickster. The concluding episodes of the Hare cycle contain two of man's most persistent phantasies: to obtain food without work and to pos-

---

[32] P. Radin, *The World of Primitive Man* (N.Y.: Abelard-Schuman, Ltd., 1953), pp. 337–39.
[33] *Cf.* tale 23.
[34] P. Radin, *op. cit.,* p. 310.

sess any woman he desires. Hare in the story asks and is given magic control over everything, provided he does not cohabit with the woman who controls the magic food supply. By breaking the one tabu he loses magical control over food. For this reason, men must work today in order to eat.

IV

The hero who overcomes seemingly invincible adversaries is a universal theme in myth and one abundantly developed in North American mythology. In certain areas, like the Southwest and California, the heroes tend to be demigods and their adventures relate the ridding of the earth of primeval monsters in mythical times. For the greater part of the continent, however, we have an extensive body of hero tales that deals with the exploits of extraordinary mortals in a world roughly conforming to its present shape. Many of these center around the theme of the hero subjected to various ordeals. Often, as in the Greek hero cycles, the hero is deliberately sent out on fatal errands with the idea of having him killed either by a jealous male relative or his prospective father-in-law. While the particular trials to which the hero is subjected and the tasks he must perform vary from culture to culture, we find the basic motifs of the Greek hero myths in tales like "The Sun Tests His Son-in-law" and "The Jealous Uncle."[35]

In "The Sun Tests His Son-in-law," a youth goes to the land of the sun or the sky chief and, after passing through a number of tests, marries his daughter. Characteristic of this tale, popular in many areas, is the hero's supernatural growth, the incidents of the snapping door through which he must pass, the guardian animals he must evade or placate by food or gifts, the path between two monsters through which he

[35] *Cf.* tales 29, 32.

must steer, the dangerous animals he must kill or capture, and the adventure with the woman who kills all her husbands by means of her toothed vagina. Tests by heat, burning food, drowning, and being pushed over a precipice figure in these tales and it is common for the hero to escape death by charms and magic transformations. Thus, in many stories the hero pushed over a cliff survives by changing himself into a feather.

In a tale told by the tribes of the North Pacific Coast, the Southeast, the Iroquois, and the Eskimos, a jealous uncle kills all his nephews. The youngest escapes by passing as a girl but is discovered and sent on perilous quests by his uncle. Each time he returns unharmed. Set afloat on the sea in a sealed box in a final attempt to eliminate him, the hero is found, like Moses, by the daughter of the chief of the land of Eagles, whom he marries. Returning to his home and finding how his uncle has abused his parents, he dresses in his eagle skin and drops the wicked uncle into the sea. Tales of mistreated children, frequently orphans and poor boys who avenge themselves on their persecutors, form a whole body of literature second in popularity only to trickster stories. The hero's flight, his return after a journey to some benevolent god who often turns out to be his father and his subsequent elevation to power, are some of the recurrent motifs in this story.[36]

In a number of hero tales the hero is subjected to difficult tasks not with the intention of eliminating him but simply to test his mettle or magic powers.[37] Tales of this sort may reflect in idealized form actual customs relating to the winning of the bride and to initiation ordeals. Almost invariably magic rather than physical strength or cunning enables the hero to perform superhuman feats of skill and endurance.

Finally, the hero may set out voluntarily on a self-appointed quest. There is a genre of hero tales found especially

---

[36] *Cf.* tale 50.
[37] *Cf.* tale 31.

in the Northwest Coast area in which the test theme is absent altogether, and the hero and his companions set out somewhat in the spirit of medieval knights to seek peril for the sake of adventure. Heroes of the "dreadnought" variety repeatedly go in the direction of dangers against which they are explicitly warned.[38] These tend to form a rather fixed repertory of incidents and characters. Typical are the old woman with a pot that sucks people in as she points it at them, and sucking giants and caves; the swallowing monster the hero kills from within, killing trees and snakes that enter the hero's rectum, and finally the ogre with moccasins that set fire to everything around which he walks. Dreadnought tales usually feature twin brothers, one of whom, like "Thrown-away" in tale 30, is a rejected child who grows up wild and spurs his less daring brother to dangerous exploits.

Strange and miraculous births are a constant feature of hero tales. As a rule, the hero's mother is impregnated by wind, rain, sunlight, or contact with various objects. Often the hero is born of tears, wounds, or mucus. In a popular Californian tale a woman digs up a root that turns into a child. Dug-from-the-Ground grows up to engage in various contests and climbs the stretching tree to the sky. A Plains story, known also to the Woodland tribes, tells how an old man abused by his son-in-law finds a clot of blood from which a child is born. Blood Clot boy avenges the old man and also goes on adventures. A particularly weird tale, in which the main interest is not in vengeance or in the hero's exploits, has the hero born in the form of a jar to a girl who has refused to get married. One day, when Water Jar boy is chased by rabbits, the jar breaks and out comes the boy. He goes out to seek his supernatural father by a spring and joins him.[39]

A favorite theme of a great number of tales is to show how

---

[38] *Cf.* tales 3, 30.
[39] *Cf.* tale 46.

an unpromising hero achieves unexpected success. It sometimes appears in the form of the "Loathly Bridegroom" found in European fairy tales, who, once he is accepted by a beautiful maiden in a disagreeable or animal shape, turns into a handsome young man. In "Dirty-boy"[40] a supernatural being assumes the disguise of a poor, sickly boy. He enters in the contest for the chief's daughter, wins the girl, and reappears in his original form.

The quest of the American Indian hero usually takes him on journeys to other worlds. In tales involving the test motif, this is usually the sky world, the house of the sun or the sky-chief. Another group of tales, remarkably similar to the Greek legend of Orpheus and Eurydice, centers around the hero's journey to the land of the dead to bring back a loved one. In some versions the return of the dead wife is prevented because of the breaking of a tabu, as in the Greek instance. In others the dead wife is successfully restored to life, as in the Winnebago tale, which in contrast to the Cherokee version gives the story a happy ending. Finally, there are macabre tales in which the revivication of the wife is only apparent, and the seeker awakes to find himself clutching a corpse or a skeleton.

In the Winnebago version, the Orpheus story has been adapted to serve as the origin myth of the Ghost Dance.[41] While the Orpheus story enjoys a wide circulation as a folktale quite detached from rites of bringing back the dead, it is possible that the version in which the husband succeeds in restoring the dead wife by the proper ritual observances is the more ancient. There is evidence, moreover, that the story in its happy-ending form was known to the ancient Greeks.

The Cherokee Orpheus, with its tragic finale, offers a general explanation of why we cannot bring our loved ones back

---

[40] *Cf.* tale 31.
[41] *Cf.* tale 35.

from the land of the dead.[42] Similarly, in a Wishram myth, Eagle and Coyote go to the World of Spirits to bring back their wives, but Coyote wearies of carrying the basket in which he has enclosed the spirits and lets them fly back. If he had not opened the basket, the dead would come to life every spring as grass and flowers do.[43] The afterworld is generally described as a place of happiness, dancing, and feasting on inexhaustible supplies of food. The dead are disturbed by these visits of the living and, in particular, object to their odor.

Other worlds may be reached by the most varied means: by crossing a tempestuous river or sea, or by descending underground; by stretching trees and a magic chain of arrows, or merely by uttering a wish. In a story of particular interest because of its wide distribution, two girls sleeping under the open sky make wishes to marry certain stars. When they awake the next morning they find themselves in the upper world, married to sky husbands. The girls are soon disappointed; one of them breaks the tabu against digging and makes a hole in the sky through which she can see her old home. The rest of the myth relates her return to earth, usually along a rope.[44] In another version of the tale a sky man selects a wife from the earth people and, in the form of a beautiful porcupine, lures her up a stretching tree to the sky.[45] In other tales girls wish upon themselves bird, beast, fish, and stone husbands, from whom they must be rescued. In a number of instances the unnatural wish proves to be fatal: the girl who married a sea scorpion is never found again, and the girl who wished for a stone husband turns piecemeal into stone.

In another group of tales concerned with girls who marry animal husbands the interest lies chiefly in their offspring. A tale of wide distribution about a woman deceived into mar-

---

[42] *Cf.* tale 34.
[43] *Cf.* tale 36.
[44] *Cf.* tale 38.
[45] *Cf.* tale 39.

rying a dog who first rejects her dog children and then seeks in vain to recover them, shows affinities to the Sedna myth and the tale of the deserted children.[46] The Cheyenne tale of "The Girl Who Married a Dog" has been adapted to serve as an explanatory myth for the origin of the Pleiades. Explanations of both customs and natural phenomena are scattered throughout North American myths. In most cases, however, the explanations are merely incidental and are tagged on to a tale that has an independent existence. The same explanations combine freely with a number of different tales and the same tale is found with and without the explanatory ending.

Miscegenations, unnatural relations between children and parents, incest, and adultery constitute some of the favorite motifs of these tales and figure prominently in myths accounting for the origin of heavenly bodies. In a particularly weird and beautiful story, which recounts the passion of Loon for her brother Wild-Cat, the guilty sister is not, as in other tales of incest, transformed into a stone or a star, but put in a sweathouse whence she emerges purified with no more evil in her.[47]

Popular throughout the continent is the haunting and barbarous tale of the pursuing head. A husband discovers that his wife has committed adultery with a snake. He kills the snake and, in some versions, serves the snake's genitals to his wife. Then he kills the wife and cuts off her head. The head rolls after the man and his family, and they escape only with the greatest difficulty. The story of the rolling head, which is here worked in as part of the punishment, is also found in other contexts over a large part of the continent.[48] In some instances it has obvious significance, but the incident is probably older than the meaning. It may be connected with the custom

---

[46] *Cf.* tale 43.
[47] *Cf.* tale 44.
[48] *Cf.* tale 45.

of decapitation, which prevailed on the American continent until scalping replaced it. Or it may have been suggested by the analogy of the sun and the moon viewed as traveling heads or masks. In a number of cases we find cosmogonic suggestions in the myth. The Iroquois relate how the severed head and body of Ataentsic ("The Woman Who Fell from the Sky") are transformed into the sun and moon. There is also a Pawnee tale of a rolling head that is split by a hawk and turns into the sun and the moon.

An atmosphere of magic, the constant intrusion of the supernatural, a love for elaboration, and a taste for the weird give the tales of the North American Indians their distinctive flavor. Present-day adventures no less than the events of the primordial age are played out in an enchanted world of fairy-tale transformations and visits to wonderlands. These tales may lack the sophistication, subtlety, and elegance we appreciate in the best of African oral literature. In compensation, however, they lead us through more ancient strata of human experience and phantasy, into the regions of primordial wonders and terrors.

V

No people has been so thoroughly studied as the American Indian. During the past century the labors of scores of fieldworkers have gathered from the native tribes of the North American continent the most extensive body of oral literature representative of any primitive people. These tales are available in government reports, folklore journals, publications of learned societies and a few, mostly out-of-print, collections. Even given a good anthropological library the reader seeking an initial acquaintance with Indian myths is apt to find himself overwhelmed by the sheer mass of the material.

The present volume has been prepared to serve such an introductory purpose and to make available to the general public as well as to students of myth, psychology, and comparative literature some of the most characteristic tales of the North American Indian oral tradition.

The tales in this volume have been grouped by type rather than by tribe or region; at the same time an attempt has been made to include representative specimens from the major cultural groups. The abundance and variety of American Indian native traditions has made serious omissions almost inescapable. The length of some of the most important cosmogonic myths (Creek, Pawnee, Navaho) has made their inclusion in this volume impossible.

In reading the folktale collections from various parts of the continent, one is impressed by the prevalence of certain fundamental types of narrative. Prominent among these are mythological stories or tales that account for the way the world received its present shape and include stories of the origin of the earth and mankind, the theft of fire, stories of the flood, division of humanity and the confusion of tongues, and the establishment of human institutions. Tales of the trickster's adventures, while sometimes mythological in character, take place in a special world and seem to form a class by themselves. Finally, it is convenient to group together all those tales of heroes and orphans, animal wives and husbands, and journeys to other worlds that take place in what appears to be more or less the present world. The organization of the volume in three parts is roughly along these lines.

The American Indian oral tradition does not lend itself to a strict division between myths and tales. Most tribes make a distinction between stories that relate to the present world and those which recount events supposed to have happened in a previous mythological era. Moreover, the distinction often corresponds to the division between sacred and profane traditions. But these classes of tales flow freely into one another, and the difference between folktales and myths characteristic of Western cultures breaks down almost completely for the North American Indian. The content of myths and folktales being largely the same, collectors have published their material sometimes as "tales," sometimes as "myths," and sometimes simply as "traditions."

I
In the Days
of Creation

1
The Emergence

They were living in the fourth world. It was dark. They could not see one another. They stepped upon one another, they urinated upon one another, they spat upon one another, they threw refuse upon one another. They could not breathe. They lived there four days [years]. The Sun took pity upon them. He saw that the world was covered with hills and springs but there were no people to give him prayersticks. He thought, "My people shall come to the daylight world."

The earth was covered with mist. He threw his rays into the mist and there in the world his sons stood up. Their hair was tangled, they had long noses, long cheeks. Next day they played together. The third day the younger brother said to the elder, "Let us go and look for beautiful places. I will go to Corn Mountain[1] and you shall go to the south Where the Cotton Hangs.[1] The third day they went. The younger looked over the world and he saw that nobody lived there. He said to himself, "Tomorrow we shall be old enough to work." When the next day came he called his brother. Elder Brother came and said, "What is it that you have to say that you have called me?" Younger Brother said, "We are four days old and we are old enough to work. This is a good world and nobody lives in it. Let us go to the southwest. There below the people are living in the fourth world. They are our fathers and mothers, our sons and daughters. There is no light there, no room to move about. They cannot see one another. They step on one

---

[1] These are shrines.

another, they urinate upon one another. They should come to this world where they can see our father Sun." Elder Brother answered, "It is as you say. We will go and try."

The two went to the southwest and they came to the entrance to the fourth world. They went in and came to the first world. There was just a little light there. They came to the second world. It was dark. They came to the third world. It was darker still. They came to the fourth world. It was black. The people could not see each other. They felt one another with their hands and recognized their faces. They said, "Some stranger has come. Where is it that you have come from? It is our fathers, the bow priests." They ran to feel them and they said, "Our fathers, you have come. Teach us how to get out of this place. We have heard of our father Sun and we wish to see him." The two answered, "We have come to bring you to the other world where you can see him. Will you come with us?" The people answered, "Yes, we wish to go. In this world we cannot see one another. We step upon one another, we urinate upon one another, we spit upon one another, we throw refuse upon one another. It is nasty here. We wish to see our father Sun. We have been waiting for someone to show us the way, but our brothers must come too. As the priest of the north says, so let it be." The two "needed" the priest of the north. He came and said, "I have come. What is it that you wish to ask?" "We want you to come into the daylight world." "Yes, we shall be glad to come. We want to see our father Sun, but my brothers must come too. As the priest of the east says, so let it be." [Repeat for east, south, west.]

They said to them, "Do you know how we can get to the daylight world?" Younger Brother went to the north. He took the seeds of the pine tree and planted them. He turned about and, when he looked where he had planted, the pine had already grown. He turned again and, when he looked at the tree, the branches were grown to full size. He tore off a branch and brought it back to the people. He went to the west and planted the seeds of the spruce. He turned about and, when he looked where he had planted, the spruce had already grown. He turned again and, when he looked at the tree, the branches were grown to full size. He tore off a branch and brought it back to the people. He went to the south and planted the seeds of the silver spruce. He turned about and, when he looked where he had planted the seeds, the silver spruce had already grown. He turned again and, when he looked at the tree, the branches were grown to full size. He tore off a branch and brought it back to the people. He went to the east and planted the seeds of the aspen. He turned about and, when he looked where he had planted the seeds, the aspen had already grown. He turned again and, when he looked, the branches had grown to full size. He tore off a branch and brought it back to the people. He said, "This is all.[2] We are ready to go up to the upper world. My people, make yourselves ready. Take those things that you live by."

The bow priests took the long prayerstick [elbow length] they had made from the pine of the north. They set it in the earth. The people went up the prayerstick and came into the third world. There was rumbling like thunder. It was lighter in that world and the people were blinded. The bow priests said, "Have we all come out?" They answered, "Yes. Is it here that we are going to live?" They answered, "Not yet. This is not the upper world." They lived there four days [years]. The bow priests took the crook of the west that they had made from the spruce. They set it in the earth. There was rumbling like thunder and the people came up into the second world. It was twilight there and the people were blinded. The bow priests said, "Have we all come out?" "Yes. Is it here that we shall live?" "Not yet." They remained there four days [years] and the two took the long prayerstick that they had made from

---

[2] From the branches long prayersticks, *telane*, were made for the ascent, and prayerstick-making instituted.

the silver spruce of the south and set it in the earth. There was rumbling like thunder and the people came up into the first world. It was light like red dawn. They were dazzled and they said, "Is it here that we shall live?" They answered, "Not yet." The people were sad. They could see each other quite plain. Their bodies were covered with dirt and with ashes. They were stained with spit and urine and they had green slime on their heads. Their hands and feet were webbed and they had tails and no mouths or exits. They remained there four days [years]. The bow priests took the long prayerstick they had made from the aspen of the east and they set it in the earth. There was rumbling like thunder and the people came up into the daylight world. The two bow priests came first and after them those who carried the medicine bundles, the *ka'etone, tcu'etone, mu'etone* and *le'etone*. When they came into the sunlight the tears ran down their cheeks. Younger Brother said to them, "Turn to the sun and look full at our father Sun no matter how bright it is." They cried out for it hurt them and their tears ran to the ground. Everywhere they were standing the sun's flowers [sunflowers and buttercups] sprang up from the tears caused by the sun. The people said, "Is this the world where we shall live?" "Yes, this is the last world. Here you see our father Sun." They remained there four days [years] and they went on.

They came to Slime Spring. They lived there four days [years] and the bow priests said, "It is time our people learned to eat." They took the corn of the witch and they put it in the fields to *itsumawe*.[3] When it had grown they harvested it and the men took it home to their wives. They smelled it, but they had no way to eat. The bow priests were sad and Younger Brother said, "Elder Brother, the people have made *itsumawe*

---

[3] Increase by magic. Putting clay sheep on an altar and planting big clay peaches are acts of *itsumawe*. Planting a garden falls in the same category.

and I am sorry for them that they cannot eat. Let us cut them so that they can enjoy food." Elder Brother agreed and his brother said, "When everyone is asleep we shall go to each house and cut mouths in their faces." That night after the people were asleep the bow priests took their [ceremonial] stone knives and sharpened them with a red whetstone. They went to each house. They cut each face where the skin of the mouth was puffed up. The knife made the lips red from the red of the whetstone. They went home. When the sun rose the people found that they had mouths. They said, "What makes our faces so flat?" They began to get hungry and the men brought in corn and water and they ate. That night they were uncomfortable because they had no exits. They could not defecate. Younger Brother thought, "We should cut the anus so that they can defecate." He went to his brother and he said, "These people should have the anus. Let us cut it tonight when they are asleep." Elder Brother agreed and they took the [smaller] stone knives and sharpened them on a soot whetstone. They cut the anus for all the people and the soot colored those parts black. Next morning the people were uncomfortable and they went outside. They thought they had broken open in their sleep.

They tried to break up the corn so that they could eat it better. They took whetstones in their webbed hands and rubbed the corn on the hearthstone.[4] They mixed porridge and made corncakes. After they had made it, it was hard to clean their hands for they were webbed, and the Younger Brother said to Elder Brother, "I am sorry for my people that their hands are webbed. Let us cut their fingers apart." Elder Brother agreed and that night they took the [larger] stone knife and cut the webbed hands and feet of the people.[5] In the

---

[4] The wide grinding stones found in the ruins are said by the people to prove that their ancestors once had webbed hands.
[5] There was no blood for the tissue was like cartilage. "They had not been eating long enough to have blood running through it."

morning the people were frightened but when the sun had risen they did not notice any more. They worked better with fingers and toes. The next day Younger Brother said to the older, "Our people have been cut. They still have tails, and horns. Let us cut them away." Elder Brother agreed and they took the [smaller] stone knife. They went to each house and cut the tails and horns from their people. In the morning the people were frightened but when the sun rose they did not mind any more. They were glad that they were finished.

(Zuni, Southwest)

2
The Flood

The people were living at Itiwana. The corn clan was the largest of all the clans. The young people of corn clan were handsome, and they played with each other and lay together. Only one man could not overlook their wrongdoing and he was a priest's son and a member of corn clan. He thought to himself: "I will call my uncle, who was killed by the Navaho, and I will ask him for help." He made four prayersticks and took them to Hawiku. He sat down and dug a hole and sprinkled prayer meal in it. He held his prayersticks in his hand and prayed, "Help me, my uncle, you who were killed in the Navaho fight; come to me. My clan does wrong and I am calling on you for help." He put down the prayersticks and covered them. Presently he heard his uncle coming. He heard the moaning and rattling of a dead man in the distance. He was not frightened because it was his uncle. He saw his body rolling toward him. They went together toward Itiwana. It was dark, and when they reached Pinawa the uncle brushed against the boy and he became a dead man. He was sorry at this for he had an old grandmother, and he lived with her and with his sister who had a little boy and a little girl.

The dead man came down close to Itiwana. In all the *kivas*[1] the corn clan was carrying on its shameful practices. The apparition went from *kiva* to *kiva*. People were terrified, and they cried out for they were afraid of the earthquake. Especially those who had been taking their pleasure in the *kivas*

---

[1] A Pueblo Indian structure, usually round, used as ceremonial, council, work, and lounging room for men.

started to run toward Corn Mountain to save themselves. Everybody in the village began to run for refuge there.

All the others had left the village when at last the sister [of the priest's son] and her little children heard of what had happened. They went to their old grandmother and told her they were going to Corn Mountain to take refuge from the earthquake. The grandmother climbed the ladder and they all set out as fast as they could toward Corn Mountain. The boy carried his little sister on his back. When they came to Mat-saka, they felt the earth rumble, and the boy who was now the apparition turned into Kolowisi. They said to their grand-mother, "Stay here, Grandmother, and we will go on to Corn Mountain; it is too dangerous to wait for you." The grand-mother said, "It is well. I have only a little while to live. Let the young ones go on quickly; I must die one of these days." They went on to Corn Mountain without her, and Kolowisi kept back the floods until they had reached the mountain. Then he let loose the waters and they filled all the valley.

One of the priests said to the people, "This flood has come upon us because of the shameful practices of the corn clan. You were always taking your pleasure in the *kivas*. For this reason the apparition came to us and to all the *kivas*, and he has caused this flood. You who are of one clan should be as brothers and sisters, and never desire one another." All the people repeated what he had said, and they stopped these practices. They agreed that no one must have sexual relations within his own clan but always with those of others. That is why we have learned not to have intercourse with those of our own clan even if they do not live with us. And if one of them has a baby or dies in the farthest corner of the pueblo, we go there and help, and if they are pro-viding a feast we grind for them.[2]

---

[2] Children are told that there will be an earthquake if members of one clan mate with one another; also, if children begin sexual practices be-fore they are of age.

[Other incidents of the Zuni emergence story tell of the origins of institutions and cults near the place of emergence, of the hardening of the earth, of the search for the center of the world and of the cities and shrines discovered on the way. Incidents along the journey include the creation of the mountain home of the ancestral gods, where the dead may dance before proceeding to the underworld whence they came, the assignment of languages, and the dispersal of tribes. *Editor's note.*]

(Zuni, Southwest)

3
The Monster Slayers

Long ago the people were living in Itiwana. Cloud Swallower stood in the east. He swallowed each cloud as it came up and there was a great drought. He was like a giant elk; his neck was half a mile long. The Ahaiyute lived with their grandmother on Corn Mountain. One morning she said to them, "In the east there is a monster who eats the clouds; therefore there is no rain. You must not go there, he is dangerous." "All right." Next day the Ahaiyute went to the east. They heard someone speaking to them. It was Gopher coming out of his hole. Gopher said, "Wait a little." They stood still. "Where are you going?" "Oh, we are going to kill Cloud Swallower." "Come into this hole." The Ahaiyute went in. Gopher dug a hole deep down into the ground for those two boys. Gopher said, "Over there Cloud Swallower is asleep. I will make a way for you." He tunneled till his hole was directly over Cloud Swallower's heart. He began to gnaw his hair. Cloud Swallower started up. "No, wait, Grandfather. I want your hair for my nest." Gopher shaved a circle over his heart and went back. He said to Ahaiyute, "I have shaved the hair over his heart; go through my hole and shoot him quickly where I have shaved. He will fall dead." They went. They drew their bow and shot him. Cloud Swallower started up and put his antlers down. The Ahaiyute ran back, Younger Brother ahead and Elder Brother behind. The antlers grazed his back, but just as it touched him the monster fell dead. His great head is there yet where he died.

They came back to Gopher and said to him, "Come and see if he is dead." Gopher went up and touched him. He called to them, "He is dead." The Ahaiyute came up. They said, "Now there will be rain. He will not eat the clouds any more." They said, "We will cut open his breast." They took his heart and threw it to the east and it became the morning star. They took his liver and threw it and it became the evening star. They took his lungs and threw them and they became the Seven Stars. They took his entrails and threw them and they became the Milky Way. They went home to Corn Mountain.

Next day their grandmother said to them, "Do not go to the south, there are owls there. They are dangerous." "All right." Next morning the Ahaiyute went to the south. In their house there were great owls sitting in rows and rows. They never winked. They sat staring straight ahead. Back in the corner there was one girl owl and one boy owl. The Ahaiyute came in. The owls said, "Sit down by the fire." Younger Brother had brought salt [from the Salt Lake] in his hand. When he sat down he threw it into the fire. The owls were staring with their eyes fixed and open. When the salt began to pop it popped into their eyes. It killed them all. The Ahaiyute cut them up and plucked their feathers. Over in the corner little girl owl and little boy owl were still alive. They said, "If you kill us there will be no more owls." The Ahaiyute said, "If we let you go, do not live as human beings [in houses]. Do not kill men. If you do, we will come and kill you. Kill jackrabbits, cottontail rabbits. Live in trees and caves." "All right." They flew off. The Ahaiyute took their big bundle of owl feathers and went home to Corn Mountain.

Next morning their grandmother said to them, "In the southwest there lives an old giant who has a horn in the middle of his forehead. He always kills people. You must not go to Noponikwi." "All right." Next morning the Ahaiyute went to the southwest. They took the trail along the cliff of Noponikwi. The giant's children lived in a cave at the foot of the cliff. They were all girls. When people went by on the trail Hakisuto [Forehead Horn] raised his leg and kicked. He knocked them over the cliff and his children ate them. The Ahaiyute got there. They greeted him and said, "We are passing by." "All right, you can go past without any danger." They started. Just as they were opposite he said, "Ouch, I have a cramp in my leg." His leg kicked. Younger Brother said, "I suppose you want to push me off." "No, I have a cramp." They started again. Just as they got there the giant said, "Ouch, I have a cramp in my leg." He kicked, but they jumped back. Again they started and the giant said, "Ouch, I have a cramp in my leg." He kicked, they jumped back. The fourth time Younger Brother said to Elder Brother, "Next time he does that I will catch him and throw him over." They came up. The giant said, "Ouch, I have a cramp in my leg." Younger Brother got him by the leg and threw him over the cliff. He dropped down where his children lived. They ran up and began to eat. They ate his foot and his thighs and his body and his arms. They came to his head and they saw the horn on his forehead. They cried, "Our father, we have eaten our father." The Ahaiyute came down and killed the children. They went home to Corn Mountain.

Next morning their grandmother said to them, "Away up in the north a woman and her granddaughter live. They kill people. Don't go there." "All right." Next morning the Ahaiyute went to the north. They got there. They saw nice girls. They went in. The girls said, "Which is the elder?" Younger Brother said, "This is my elder brother. Why did you want to know?" "I am the younger sister and this is my elder sister. I shall marry the elder brother and she will marry the younger brother." They went into the house to sleep. The girls tied on red headbands. The Ahaiyute said, "What do you do that for?" "We always do that when we get married." "All right.'' When the girls were sound asleep Younger Brother spoke to them. They did not answer. He knew they were asleep. He got up and took the girls' headbands off. He took the white headbands from around his own head and his brother's and put them on the girls' heads. He tied the red headbands on his own head and his brother's. The girls' father came with a sharp stone knife. He saw the white headbands in the dark. He said, ''These are the husbands.'' He cut the girls' heads off and threw them outside and put their bodies in the cellar. The Ahaiyute said, ''Let's go home.'' They went home to Corn Mountain. Next morning they told their grandmother, ''We killed those girls.'' She said, ''Thank you. Those girls have killed lots of people.''

Their grandmother said, ''Nearby in the west there are eight girls living with their grandmother. Don't go there. They have teeth in their vaginas. They will cut you and you will die.'' ''All right.'' In Tsukipa [Big Belly] the Lehaci lived. They were six young men and they lived with their grandfather. The Ahaiyute went there. They told the six boys to get oak wood and make themselves each a false penis. Then they told them to get hickory wood and each make themselves a second. When they had finished Younger Brother went down west where those women lived. He said, ''Do you girls want us to come and dance tonight.'' ''Yes, how many are there of you?'' ''There are eight of us and our grandfather.'' ''That is just right. There are eight of us and our grandmother.'' ''We shall come tonight.'' Younger Brother went back. He told them, ''They want us to go to dance late tonight.'' They went down. Their grandfather carried the drum. The girls said, ''Come in.'' They went in and danced and sang their songs:

> ''The Lehaci don't know girls.
> The Lehaci don't know girls.
> They just sleep here.''

The eldest sister said, "Which is the smallest boy?"
Masewi[1] said, "I am." Elder Brother said, "I am." They quarreled. All the boys paired with the girls. The youngest took the
youngest. The grandmother said to the girls. "These Lehaci
are going to die soon." The girls said, "Poor boys, pretty soon
we shall kill them." They lay with the girls. The grandmother
took the grandfather. All the men took out their false members. They used them cohabiting. They broke the teeth from
the women's vaginas. The blood ran. When the oak members
were worn out, they put them aside and took the hickory
ones. By daylight the teeth of these women were all worn out.
They were broken in pieces. The grandfather told the boys,
"We shall beat the drum all the way home." No one of them
was killed. They went back home to Tsukipa, and Ahaiyute
went back to Corn Mountain.

They left the eight girls and their grandmother sleeping.
When they had gone Coyote came. He had intercourse with
each of the girls. He pulled a hair out of his moustache and
planted it between the legs of the first girl and breathed on it.
He pulled another hair out of his moustache and planted it on
the second girl and breathed on it, and he did the same to the
third girl and the fourth. When he had given a hair to each of
the girls he went back home. The girls woke. They scratched
themselves. They said, "What is the matter?" They each had
pubic hair. They said, "Why does it smell?" It was Coyote's
odor. These women never killed men any more.

Next morning as they were eating breakfast their grandmother said, "Don't go near Twin Buttes because an old
woman lives there who is mean and kills many people." The
two Ahaiyute said, "All right, we won't go there." They went

---

[1] The little-used personal name of Younger Brother. It is the name always used in Keresan tales.

out and, after they had gone a little way to hunt rabbits, Younger Brother said to Elder Brother, "Let us go where that old woman is. Let us see what kind of woman she is." So the two Ahaiyute went to Hecoktakwi, this side of Twin Buttes. They went up to the top of the mesa and hid, and after a little while one of them looked down and saw the old woman. The old woman was working, fixing her dress. Then one of them took up a piece of rock and threw it at the old woman. The little stone dropped down and the old woman just turned and looked around. The two boys hid, and she did not see anyone. About an hour later they picked up another stone and threw it at the woman again. The old woman turned and looked up, but the two boys had hidden behind the rocks. After a while one of them looked over the edge and the woman was working again, fixing her dress. He picked up a stone and hit her again for the third time. The rock dropped down and the old woman turned and looked up, and the two boys hid again. Then the woman said, "I want to know who hit me." The younger boy said, "Well, next time when we hit that old woman, don't hide." The old woman went back to her work, and a little later the boy picked up a stone and threw it down. The stone fell and the woman turned and looked up, and the two boys were standing there on the top of the mesa. Then the woman said, "Well, my boys, come down. What is the matter? Why did you hit me?" The two Ahaiyute said, "Let's go down and see her."

The two Ahaiyute went down and the woman spoke to them. "Well, my grandsons, I am glad to see you. Sit down here." She made the elder sit on her right side and the younger on her left side, and she held their heads in her lap and combed their hair. She told the two boys, "Now, grandsons, go and get some wood and we shall make a fire and cook some dinner." The two Ahaiyute knew that they would die in a little while, and one of them picked up a stick of wood and said, "This wood will cook my body." Then the other picked up a stick and said, "This wood will cook my body," and they joked about it.

A little later the two boys came back, each with an armful of wood, and the old woman made a fire and put lots of stones in the fire to make them hot. She put a big cooking pot on the fire and filled it with water. The two boys piled wood on the fire to make it burn hard, and the stones got red-hot and the water boiled. Then she said to Elder Brother, "Sit here on my right side, and, Younger Brother, sit here on my left side." She combed their hair again, and after a while she bit the neck of the elder brother, and he died, and then she bit the neck of the younger one and killed him too. Then the old woman said, "You foolish boys, now you are going to die." Then the soul of the elder one came out of his body and went into the water jar, and the soul of the younger one came out and went into the cooking pot. She took the elder and put him into the cooking pot and boiled him, and then she took a red-hot stone from the fire and laid the body of the younger on it and put another red-hot stone on top of his body. She went out.

After a while the old woman said, "I guess I will get something to eat now. I shall eat the younger one as my first course." She went in and put the boiled meat in a dish, and took the younger one from between the red-hot stones and put him in a basket. She ate some of the meat, and while she was eating, the elder Ahaiyute, who was in the water jar, said, "Too bad! I made the meat dirty with my excrement." Then the old woman was angry and she said to the water jar, "Why do you talk like that?" and she took a stone and threw it at the water jar and broke it to pieces. Then the elder Ahaiyute came out and went into the mixing bowl. After a while she sat down to eat the boiled meat. Then the younger one, who was in the cooking pot, said, "Too bad, I urinated in the stew!" Then the old woman was angry and she took a piece of wood and broke the cooking pot, and the younger Ahaiyute went out of the cooking pot into a small bowl. After a while she ate again, and the elder one said something. She took up a stick and broke the mixing bowl. Then, later, while she was eating, the younger one said the same thing, and the old woman was angry and took a piece of wood and broke the small bowl. The elder brother went into her right nostril and the younger brother went into her left nostril. The old woman ate some more and the two boys began to scratch the inside of her nose and she began to sneeze and cough, and after about an hour she died.

After she was dead the two Ahaiyute came out of her nose. The old woman lay there dead. Then they took an arrow point and skinned her from her feet up, and left the body in the house. They went out and got grass and weeds and brought them back to the house and stuffed them into the old woman's skin. They stuffed it full and sewed up the feet. Then they put her dress on it, and it was just like the old woman. They put a stick in each leg and tied a belt around the waist. They went back into the house and they saw lots of food there, corn and wheat and pumpkins. They went into the second room and it was full of wheat. They went into the third room and it was full of melons and pumpkins. They went into the fourth room and it was full of beans. After they passed through the fourth room they were in the other world. They went out and saw a trail. They followed it. They walked about three miles to the other side of a mountain, and there they saw a village where people were living.

After sunset they came into the village and stood looking at the houses. After a while people came out of their houses and went into the *kivas.* After they had been in there a little while lightning came out of the door, and they heard a sound like thunder. After a couple of hours the two Ahaiyute looked into the window of the *kiva* and they saw two men. One of them had a smooth round stone which he rolled and which made a noise like thunder, and the other man had an instrument for making lightning. It was something like a board, and it made lightning. The two Ahaiyute watched them, and late at night the people put away their things on a shelf in the corner of the *kiva*. After a while the men who stayed in the *kiva* went to sleep. Then the two Ahaiyute went into the house quickly, and the younger took the lightning under his arm, and the elder took the thunder. As he took it up it made a little noise, and all the people woke up. The boys ran away, and all the people ran after them. They went to the east and the people almost caught them. They found the house where they had killed the old woman and went in. The people could not catch them, but they said, "Never mind, we will get you someday."

They went through the house and came out to where the old woman's body was standing. The elder put the old woman's belt around his waist and ran as if the old woman were chasing him. They came over the hill and called to their grandmother. Then Younger Brother tied the woman to his belt. Elder Brother called out, "Oh, someone is chasing my younger brother! Grandmother, someone is chasing my younger brother! He has almost caught him!" The old woman heard them and went into the house and picked up a big stick, and a grinding stone in the other hand. She put ashes on one side of her face, and soot on the other side, and ran out as fast as she could. She crossed the Zuni river. The two boys were coming down the hill. Elder Brother was about ten yards away and the younger one a little way behind, with the old woman coming after him. Their grandmother stood there, and Elder Brother came up and said, "Grandmother, someone is trying to catch my brother; you had better hurry!" The old woman ran as fast as she could. She picked up some pebbles and spat on them and waved them around the head of her grandson.[2] She took the stick and hit the old woman as hard as she could, and the old woman fell down. Then she took her

---

[2] To remove misfortune.

grinding stone and mashed her head with it, and the two Ahaiyute laughed and laughed at their grandmother. Their old grandmother was angry and wanted to kill the old woman. The elder one said, "Well, Grandmother, you had better stop. That old woman is dead, she is not alive." Then their grandmother saw that the old woman had died the day before. The Ahaiyute just laughed and said, "That old woman was mean, so we killed her. We kill everyone who kills people and now the people do not need to be afraid any more, because we have killed all the monsters in this country." Then their grandmother said, "Thank you. You have killed all the mean people. Now there are no more dangerous people here any more."

Then they went home and their grandmother gave them something to eat, and she ground flour while the two boys played in the house. The elder brother used the lightning sticks and shot lightning from the door, and the younger brother rolled the thunder stone and made a noise. Soon their grandmother said, "Where did you get those things? You had better throw them away or give them away. You have no right to them. They belong to the Uwanami." "No, they don't," they said and they began to argue with their grandmother. Soon they said, "Let's go out." They went out. Clouds were coming up all over, from the east and the north and the west and the south. The clouds were all over. Soon it began to rain. It rained hard. The two boys used their lightning sticks and their thunder stone. Soon their grandmother began to cry out. The whole house was flooded. There were about two feet of water in the house, and their grandmother cried. The younger one said, "You had better put Grandmother someplace where she will keep quiet." The elder one went into the house and the water came up to his knees. In the corner was a big open cooking pot. He took his grandmother and threw her into the pot. Then he went out and played again. He laughed all the time. Soon the water came high up in the house, and soon the house would be full of water. Then their grandmother cried out again. Soon the water came up to where their grandmother was, and their grandmother was drowned. Soon the water came up over the roof and their grandmother was washed out. Then the younger one saw her and said, "Look, our grandmother is dead." Then the elder one stopped playing with the lightning, and the younger one with his thunder. They got a stick and sharpened one end and made a hole in the wall of the house. The rain had stopped and the water ran out of the house. Then the Ahaiyute dug a hole and buried their grandmother, and the Ahaiyute were alone for about four days. After the four days Elder Brother said, "Now we had better go away. We cannot stay here in this house." They went to Corn Mountain. He put his younger brother in Corn Mountain, and the elder brother went to Twin Buttes. They threw away their thunder and lightning, and the Uwanami came to get them back.

The Ahaiyute killed all the monsters. That is all.

(Zuni, Southwest)

4
The Woman Who Fell from the Sky

A long time ago human beings lived high up in what is now called heaven. They had a great and illustrious chief.

It so happened that this chief's daughter was taken very ill with a strange affliction. All the people were very anxious as to the outcome of her illness. Every known remedy was tried in an attempt to cure her, but none had any effect.

Near the lodge of this chief stood a great tree, which every year bore corn used for food. One of the friends of the chief had a dream in which he was advised to tell the chief that, in order to cure his daughter, he must lay her beside this tree, and that he must have the tree dug up. This advice was carried out to the letter. While the people were at work and the young woman lay there, a young man came along. He was very angry and said: "It is not at all right to destroy this tree. Its fruit is all that we have to live on." With this remark he gave the young woman who lay there ill a shove with his foot, causing her to fall into the hole that had been dug.

Now, that hole opened into this world, which was then all water, on which floated waterfowl of many kinds. There was no land at that time. It came to pass that as these waterfowl saw this young woman falling they shouted, "Let us receive her," whereupon they, at least some of them, joined their bodies together, and the young woman fell on this platform of bodies. When these were wearied they asked, "Who will volunteer to care for this woman?" The great Turtle then took her, and when he got tired of holding her, he in turn asked who would take his place. At last the question arose as to what they should do to provide her with a permanent resting place in this world. Finally it was decided to prepare the earth, on which she would live in the future. To do this it was determined that soil from the bottom of the primal sea should be brought up and placed on the broad, firm carapace of the Turtle, where it would increase in size to such an extent that it would accommodate all the creatures that should be produced thereafter. After much discussion the toad was finally persuaded to dive to the bottom of the waters in search of soil. Bravely making the attempt, he succeeded in bringing up soil from the depths of the sea. This was carefully spread over the carapace of the Turtle, and at once both began to grow in size and depth.

After the young woman recovered from the illness from which she suffered when she was cast down from the upper world, she built herself a shelter, in which she lived quite contentedly. In the course of time she brought forth a girl baby, who grew rapidly in size and intelligence.

When the daughter had grown to young womanhood, the mother and she were accustomed to go out to dig wild potatoes. Her mother had said to her that in doing this she must face the west at all times. Before long the young daughter gave signs that she was about to become a mother. Her mother reproved her, saying that she had violated the injunction not to face the east, as her condition showed that she had faced the wrong way while digging potatoes. It is said that the breath of the West Wind had entered her person, causing conception. When the days of her delivery were at hand, she overheard twins within her body in a hot debate as to which should be born first and as to the proper place of exit, one declaring that he was going to emerge through the armpit of his mother, the other saying that he would emerge in the natural way. The first one born, who was of a reddish color, was called Othagwenda, that is, Flint. The other, who was light in color, was called Djuskaha, that is, the Little Sprout.

The grandmother of the twins liked Djuskaha and hated the other; so they cast Othagwenda into a hollow tree some distance from the lodge.

The boy who remained in the lodge grew very rapidly, and soon was able to make himself bows and arrows and to go out to hunt in the vicinity. Finally, for several days he returned home without his bow and arrows. At last he was asked why he had to have a new bow and arrows every morning. He replied that there was a young boy in a hollow tree in the neighborhood who used them. The grandmother inquired where the tree stood, and he told her; whereupon then they went there and brought the other boy home again.

When the boys had grown to man's estate, they decided that it was necessary for them to increase the size of their island, so they agreed to start out together, afterward separating to create forests and lakes and other things. They parted as agreed, Othagwenda going westward and Djuskaha eastward. In the course of time, on returning, they met in their shelter or lodge at night, then agreeing to go the next day to see what each had made. First they went west to see what Othagwenda had made. It was found that he had made the country all rocks and full of ledges, and also a mosquito that was very large. Djuskaha asked the mosquito to run, in order that he might see whether the insect could fight. The mosquito ran, and sticking his bill through a sapling, thereby made it fall, at which Djuskaha said, "That will not be right, for you would kill the people who are about to come." So, seizing him, he rubbed him down in his hands, causing him to become very small; then he blew on the mosquito, whereupon he flew away. He also modified some of the other animals that his brother had made. After returning to their lodge, they agreed to go the next day to see what Djuskaha had fashioned. On visiting the east the next day, they found that Djuskaha had made a large number of animals which were so fat that they could hardly move; that he had made the sugar-maple trees to drop syrup; that he had made the sycamore tree to bear fine fruit; that the rivers were so formed that half the water flowed upstream and the other half downstream. Then the reddish-colored brother, Othagwenda, was greatly displeased with what his brother had made, saying that the people who were about to come would live too easily and be too happy. So he shook violently the various animals—the bears, deer, and turkeys—causing them to become small at once, a characteristic that attached itself to their descendants. He also caused the sugar maple to drop sweetened water only, and the fruit of the sycamore to become small and useless; and lastly he caused the water of the rivers to flow in only one direction, because the original plan would make it too easy for the human beings who were about to come to navigate the streams.

The inspection of each other's work resulted in a deadly disagreement between the brothers, who finally came to grips and blows, and Othagwenda was killed in the fierce struggle.

(Seneca, Iroquois)

5
The Earthdiver

In the beginning, Prairie Falcon and Crow were sitting on a log which projected above the waters that covered the world. They asked Duck what number he had dreamed of, and Duck replied, "Two." Prairie Falcon assigned him the number three and told him to dive into the water and bring up some sand from the bottom. Duck dived to get the sand, but before he reached the bottom, the three days he had been allotted expired. He awoke from his dream, died, and floated to the surface. Prairie Falcon brought him back to life, however, and asked him what the trouble was. Duck said that he had come out of his dream, died, and then floated to the top.

Prairie Falcon now asked Coot what number he had dreamed of. Coot replied, "Four." Then Prairie Falcon assigned him the number two and ordered him to dive for sand. Before Coot reached the bottom, two days elapsed, and he came out of his dream. He too died, and his body floated to the surface of the waters. Prairie Falcon saw the corpse, recovered it, and brought Coot back to life. He asked Coot what had been the trouble, and Coot replied that he had passed out of his dream.

Then Prairie Falcon asked Grebe what number he had dreamed of. Grebe replied that he had dreamed of five. Prairie Falcon assigned him the number four, and told him that was the number of days he had to bring sand from the bottom of the waters. Grebe was successful. He dived all the way to the bottom of the waters and secured some sand in each hand. As he was returning to the surface, he passed out of his dream, died, and floated to the surface. Prairie Falcon brought him back to life and asked if he had secured any sand. Grebe said that he had, so Prairie Falcon wanted to know what he had done with it. Grebe explained that it had all slipped from his grasp when he died. Prairie Falcon and Crow both laughed at him and said that they didn't believe him. Then they looked at his hands and found sand under the fingernails. They took that sand and threw it in every direction. This is the way in which they made the world.

(Mono, California)

6
Olelbis

PERSONAGES

After each name is given that of the beast, bird, or thing into which the personage was changed subsequently. Names on which accents are not placed are accented on the penult. . . . Kiemila and Herit mean "old" and "young," respectively; they are applied to male persons. Pokaila and Loimis are applied to females; the first means "old," the second "young."

Bisus, mink; Chálilak, goose; Chuluhl, meadowlark; Dokos, flint; Hau, red fox; Héssiha, tomtit; Hilit, housefly; Hlihli, white oak acorn; Hus, turkey buzzard; Kahit, wind; Kahsuku, cloud dog; Kaisus, gray squirrel; Kar, gray heron; Karili, coon; Katkatchila, swift; Katsi, chicken hawk; Kau, white crane; Kiriú, loon; Klabus, mole; Klak, rattlesnake; Kuntihlé, fish hawk; Lutchi, hummingbird; Mem Loimis, water; Mem Tulit, beaver; Min Taitai, sapsucker; Móihas, bald eagle; Pákchuso, the pakchu stone; Patsotchet, badger; Poháramas, shooting star; Sas, sun; Sedit, coyote; Sosini, a small web-footed bird; Sútunut, black eagle; Tede Wiu, a small bird; Tilichi, a water bird; Tilikus, fire drill; Titchelis, ground squirrel; Toko, sunfish; Tórihas, blue crane; Tsárarok, kingfisher; Tsaroki Sakahl, green snake; Tsurat, woodpecker; Wehl Dilidili, roadrunner; Wima Loimis, grizzly bear; Wokwuk, a large bird, extinct; Yilahl, gopher; Yoholmit, frog; Yonot, buckeye bush.

The first that we know of Olelbis [He-Who-Sits-Above] is that he was in Olelpanti. Whether he lived in another place is not

known, but in the beginning he was in Olelpanti [on the upper side], the highest place. He was in Olelpanti before there
was anything down here on the earth, and two old women
were with him always. These old women he called grandmother, and each of them we call Pakchuso Pokaila.

There was a world before this one in which we are now.
That world lasted a long, long time, and there were many
people living in it before the present world and we, the present people, came.

➤ *A long narrative leads up to the destruction of the first world by*
fire. The cataclysm is caused by the theft of Flint from the Swift
(Katkachila), who for revenge induces Shooting Star, Fire Drill,
and Buckeye Bush to set the world on fire.

Olelbis looked down into the burning world. He could see
nothing but waves of flame; rocks were burning, the ground
was burning, everything was burning. Great rolls and piles of
smoke were rising; fire flew up toward the sky in flames, in
great sparks and brands. Those sparks became sky eyes, and all
the stars that we see now in the sky came from that time
when the first world was burned. The sparks stuck fast in the
sky, and have remained there ever since the time of the world
fire. Quartz rocks and fire in the rocks are from that time.
There was no fire in the rocks before the world fire.

Before the fire began Olelbis spoke to the two old women
and said: "My grandmothers, go to work for me and make a
foundation. I wish to build a sweathouse."

They dug out and cleared a place for the sweathouse the
day before the world fire began. Olelbis built it in this way:
When the two women had dug the foundation, he asked:

"What kind of wood shall I get for the central pillar of the house?"

"Go far down south," said the old grandmothers, "and get a great young white oak, pull it up with the roots, bring it, and plant it in the middle to support the house."

He went, found the tree, and brought it.

➤ *The text continues, giving detailed directions for the building of the sweathouse.*

The old women gave him all kinds of beautiful plants now, and flowers to form a great bank around the bottom of the sweathouse. All kinds of flowers that are in the world now were gathered around the foot of that sweathouse, an enormous bank of them; every beautiful color and every sweet odor in the world was there.

When they went into the sweathouse, the perfume was delightful. The two old women said then:

"All people to come in the world below will talk of this house, and call it Olelpanti Hlut when they tell about it and praise the house on high."

Olelbis said: "I want to lay something lengthwise on each side of the door. What shall I get?"

The two said: "We will get *sau*" [acorn bread made in a great round roll like a tree trunk].

They got *sau*, and put a roll at each side of the door; these rolls were put there for people to sit on.

Olelbis walked around, looked at everything, and said:

"I want this house to grow, to be wide and high, to be large enough for all who will ever come to it."

Then the house began to extend and grow wider and higher, and it became wonderful in size and in splendor. Just as daylight was coming the house was finished and ready. It stood there in the morning dawn, a mountain of beautiful flowers and oak-tree branches; all the colors of the world were on it, outside and inside. The tree in the middle was far above the top of the house, and filled with acorns; a few of them had fallen on every side.

That sweathouse was placed there to last forever, the largest and most beautiful building in the world, above or below. Nothing like it will ever be built again.

"Now, my grandson," said the old women, "the house is built and finished. All the people in the world will like this house. They will talk about it and speak well of it always. This house will last forever, and these flowers will bloom forever; the roots from which they grow can never die."

The world fire began on the morning after the sweathouse was finished. During the fire they could see nothing of the world below but flames and smoke. Olelbis did not like this.

➤ *On the advice of his grandmothers, Olelbis sends the Eagle and the Hummingbird to prop up the sky in the north, and to summon thence Kahit, the Wind, and Mem Loimis, the Waters, who live beyond the first sky.*

The great fire was blazing, roaring all over the earth, burning rocks, earth, trees, people, burning everything.

Mem Loimis started, and with her Kahit. Water rushed in through the open place made by Lutchi when he raised the sky. It rushed in like a crowd of rivers, covered the earth, and put out the fire as it rolled on toward the south. There was so much water outside that could not come through that it rose to the top of the sky and rushed on toward Olelpanti.

Mem Loimis went forward, and water rose mountains high. Following closely after Mem Loimis came Kahit. He had a whistle in his mouth; as he moved forward he blew it with all his might and made a terrible noise. The whistle was his own; he had had it always. He came flying and blowing. He looked like an enormous bat, with wings spread. As he flew south toward the other side of the sky, his two cheek feathers grew straight out, became immensely long, waved up and down, grew till they could touch the sky on both sides.

➤ *The fire is quenched and at the request of Olelbis, Kahit drives Mem Loimis, the Waters, back to her underworld home. Now, there are only naked rocks under Olelbis, with a single pool left by the receding waters. The myth goes on to tell of the refashioning of the world by Olelbis, assisted by such survivors of the cataclysm of fire and flood as have managed to escape to Olelpanti. A net is spread over the sky, and through it soil, brought from beyond the confines of the sky-capped world, is sifted down to cover the boulders. Olelbis marks out the rivers, and water is drawn to fill them from the single lake that remains. Fire, now badly needed in the world, is stolen from the lodge of Fire Drill and Buckeye Bush, the parents of flame, without their discovering the loss—an unusual turn in the tale of the theft of fire. The earth is fertilized by Old Man Acorn and by seed dropping down from the flower lodge of Olelbis in the skies. Many animals spring into being from the feathers and bits of the body of Wokwuk, a fabulous bird, while numerous others are the result of the transformations wrought by Olelbis, who now changes the survivors of the first world into the animals and objects whose nature they had in reality always possessed.*

Hlihli was like an old worm-eaten acorn outside; inside he was like meal or snuff, and when he moved this inside sifted out of him. He had a daughter, Hlihli Loimis, and she had many sons.

Tsurat carried Hlihli all over the world, and when he had carried him five days, little oak bushes were springing up everywhere from the dust which fell from him. They took seeds of clover growing around the sweathouse in Olelpanti and scattered them; clover grew up in every place. Olelbis threw down all kinds of flower seeds from the flowers blossoming in Olelpanti.

A little way east of Olelbis's sweathouse lived Sedit. At the time of the fire he ran through under the sky in the south and went up on the sky to Olelpanti. He stayed there with Olelbis until the fire and water stopped. Then he went east a short distance, and made a house for himself. During the great water Sedit caught Wokwuk, and afterward built a house near his own for him.

Wokwuk at the time of the great water lost the middle and longest finger on one hand; it went far north, and after a time became a deer, and from that deer came all the deer in the world after the fire. When Kahit and Mem Loimis went east on the way home, Wokwuk lost a small feather from above one of his eyes. It went west and was turned into the beautiful shells *tsanteris.* He also lost two neck feathers. They went west and became *kalas,* and from that came all pearl shells. He lost the tip of his little finger. It went west and became the Wokwuk bird down here. He lost some spittle. It went east on the water and turned to blue beads, such as people wear now around their necks. Wokwuk lost a small bit of his intestines. It went south on the water and became *mempak;* from that come all *mempak* [water bone]. He lost a piece of his backbone. It went east on the water and became an elk, and from that elk came all elks.

One day Sedit said to Olelbis, when all were telling Olelbis what they were going to do: "Grandson, I am going to take off my skin and let it go to the world below."

"Do so," said Olelbis.

Sedit took off his skin as he would a coat, and threw it down to this world.

"Now there will be Sedits all over down there," said he.

While Olelbis was gathering into Olelpanti all the people

from every place outside this sky above us, Min Taitai and Hessiha were disputing and throwing red mud at each other.

Olelbis gathered people from every side till he had gathered them all at his house. They were there in crowds and in thousands, singing and talking inside and outside everywhere in Olelpanti.

> ➤ *There follows an account of the snaring of the clouds. These had sprung into being when the waters of the flood struck the fires of the conflagration, and they were seeking ever to escape back to the north, the home of Kahit and Mem Loimis. Three of them—a black, a white, and a red one—are captured. The skin of the red cloud is kept by the hunters, who often hang it up in the west, though sometimes in the east; the black and white skins are given to the grandmothers of Olelbis.*

"Now," said the two old women, "we have this white skin and this black one. When we hang the white skin outside this house, white clouds will go from it—will go away down south, where its people began to live, and then they will come from the south and travel north to bring rain. When they come back, we will hang out the black skin, and from it a great many black rain clouds will go out, and from these clouds heavy rain will fall on all the world below."

From that time the old women hang out the two skins, first the white, then the black skin, and when clouds enough have gone from them they take the skins into the sweathouse again; and from these two skins comes all the rain to people in this world.

"The cloud people who went north will stay in the northwest," said Olelbis, "and from them will come snow to people hereafter."

All this time the people in Olelpanti were singing and talking. Anyone could hear them from a distance. Olelbis had brought in a great many different kinds of people, others had come themselves, and still others were coming. After the tanning of the two cloud skins, a man came and took his place above the sweathouse door, and sat there with his face to the east. This was Kar Kiemila. Right after him came Tsararok, and took his place at the side of Kar. Next came Kau; then the two brothers Hus came, and Wehl Dilidili. All these people in the sweathouse and around it asked one another:

"What shall we do? Where shall we live? We should like to know what Olelbis will do with us."

"You will know very soon where we are going," said Toko and Sula. "Olelbis will put us in our places; he is chief over all."

Next morning Olelbis said: "Now, my grandmothers, what do you think best? What are we to do with the people here? Is it best for them to stay in Olelpanti?"

"Our grandson," answered the old women, "send all that are not needed here to the lower world; turn them into something good for the people who are to come soon—those fit for this place up here. The great people, the best ones, you will keep in Olelpanti, and send down only a little part of each of them to turn into something in the world below and be of use to people there."

Olelbis called all who were in the sweathouse to come out, and he began to send them to their places.

To Kar he said: "Go and live on Wini Mem. Be a gray heron there; that is a good country for you." [Before white people came there were many of these birds on that river.]

To Toko he said: "Go to Kawiken on Pui Mem. Be a sunfish and live there always. You, Sula, go to the south of Bohem Puyuk on Wini Mem. Be a trout, and live at Sulanharas."

To Torihas he said: "You will be a blue crane," and to Chalilak: "You will be a goose. You both will have two places to live in, one in the south and the other in the north. You will go north in the spring and live there all summer; you will go south in the fall and live in the south all winter. Do this always; travel that way every year."

To Kiriu he said: "Go and live along the water. You will be a loon, and you will go up and down great rivers all your life."

To Katsi he said: "You will be a fish hawk, catch fish and eat them, live along rivers."

Olelbis plucked one small feather from the neck of Moihas. This he threw down and said, "Be an eagle and live on high mountains." All bald eagles on earth came from that feather, but the great Moihas remained above with Olelbis, where he is now.

From Lutchi Olelbis plucked one feather, threw it down, and said: "You will be a hummingbird. Fly around in spring when the green grass comes and the trees and flowers bloom. You will be on blossoms and dart from one to another everywhere." Lutchi himself stayed in Olelpanti.

Olelbis pulled a feather from Kau, threw it down, and said: "You will fly along rivers, be a white crane, and live near them always." The great Kau stayed in Olelpanti with Olelbis.

From the elder Hus brother Olelbis plucked a feather from the right side, sent the feather down on this earth, and said:

"You be a buzzard down there, and in spring go up on Wini Mem and look for dead salmon and other fish along Pui Mem, Bohema Mem, and other rivers, eat dead salmon and other fish. When people kill a snake or something else which they do not like, you will go and eat the snake or other dead thing. The Wintu, the coming people, will feed you always with what is dead."

Tilitchi had been sent for three persons, and now he brought the first.

"Who is this?" asked Olelbis of the old women.

"This is Dokos," said they; "he is bad."

Dokos was placed a little northeast of the sweathouse. He sat looking toward the west. Tilichi brought in a second and third person.

"Who are these?" asked Olelbis.

"These are both bad people," said the old women. "These are Wima Loimis and Klak Loimis."

"Put them with Dokos," said Olelbis. After he had called all the people out of the sweathouse to send them to their proper places, Olelbis had put something on their teeth to make them harmless.

"Come here, Wima Loimis," said Olelbis. "I have something to put on your teeth so that they may harm no one."

"I want nothing on my teeth," said Wima Loimis. "If something were put on them I could not eat." He asked again, but she shook her head, saying: "I want nothing on my teeth, I could not eat if anything were put on them."

"If she will not come, come you, Klak Loimis." Klak Loimis would not go to him.

"Why not come when I call you?" asked Olelbis.

"My sister Wima will not go. She says that she could not eat if her teeth were touched. I want nothing on my teeth. I am afraid that I could not eat."

"Very well," answered Olelbis, "you, Wima, and you, Klak, want to be different from others. Come, Dokos, I will touch your teeth."

"My sisters, Klak and Wima, want nothing on their teeth. I want nothing on mine. I am angry at my sisters; my heart hates them. I do not wish to be good. I am angry at my sisters. I will be wicked as well as they." Then turning to his sisters he said: "After a while people will employ me against you whenever they are angry at you. Whenever you bite people or hurt them, they will call me to fight against you, and I will go with them. I will go into your bodies and kill you. Then you will be sorry for what you have done today. Olelbis asked you to be good. He wants you to be good, but you are not willing. I will be bad to punish you."

When the two women heard these words they cried, and Wima said, "Well, my brother, we can put something on our teeth yet."

Dokos placed his head between his hands and sat awhile in that posture. Then he straightened himself and said:

"You two have talked enough; you would better stop. You are not like me; I am stronger than both of you, and I shall be so always. You, Wima, and you, Klak, will hate people only, but I shall hate all living things. I shall hate you, hate everyone; kill you, kill everyone. I want nothing of anyone. I want no friend in any place."

"Well," said Olelbis, "you go as you are."

"I will go first," said Dokos.

"Go," said Olelbis, "to Koiham Nomdaltopi, be flint there, and spread all around the place. You, Klak Loimis, will go to Klak Kewilton, be a rattlesnake there, increase and spread everywhere. I will send you, Wima, to Wima Wai Tsaratton; you will be a grizzly bear there. After a while a great family will come from you and spread over all the country. You will be bad; and, Klak, you will be bad, but, Dokos, you will be the worst, always ready to hurt and kill; always angry, always hating your sisters and everyone living.

"You, Klak, and you, Wima, when you see people you will bite them, and people will take Dokos to kill you, and Dokos will go into your bodies, and you will die. Wima, you will be sorry that you would not let me change your teeth. You, Klak, will be sorry. You will bite people, and they will kill you because you cannot run away from them. Your dead body will lie on the ground, and buzzards will eat it.

"Dokos, you will go to your place and increase. People will go there and get you to kill your sisters and others for them, and when you have pleased them and killed all the people they wished you to kill, when they want you no longer, they will throw you down on a rock and break you to pieces, then you will be nothing. You will be dead forever. Now go!"

To all those who let their teeth be made innocent, Olelbis said: "You will go to where I send you—one here, another there." And he gave their places to all. To some he said: "After a while the new people will use you for food," and to the others he said: "The new people will use your skins, and you will be of service to them, you will be good for them."

The first person taken up to Olelbis's sweathouse was Tsurat; and now Olelbis spoke to Tsurat last of all and said:

"Pluck one feather from your back."

Tsurat plucked it.

Olelbis threw the feather to the earth and said:

"The place where this falls will be called Tsuratton Mem Puisono. This feather will become woodpeckers, and their place will be there. Their red feathers will be beautiful, and everyone will like their red scalps and will use them for head-bands. The woodpeckers will be also called Topi chilchihl" [bead birds].

All people that were good on this earth only, of use only here, Olelbis sent down to be beasts, birds, and other creatures. The powerful and great people that were good in Olelpanti and useful there he kept with himself, and sent only a feather or a part of each to become something useful down here. The good people themselves, the great ones, stayed above, where they are with Olelbis now.

(Wintun, West Coast, California)

7
The Blackfoot Genesis

All animals of the plains at one time heard and knew him, and all birds of the air heard and knew him. All things that he had made understood him when he spoke to them—the birds, the animals, and the people.

Old Man[1] was traveling about, south of here, making the people. He came from the south, traveling north, making animals and birds as he passed along. He made the mountains, prairies, timber, and brush first. So he went along, traveling northward, making things as he went, putting rivers here and there, and falls on them, putting red paints here and there in the ground—fixing up the world as we see it today. He made the Milk River [the Teton] and crossed it, and, being tired, went up on a little hill and lay down to rest. As he lay on his back, stretched out on the ground, with arms extended, he marked himself out with stones—the shape of his body, head, legs, arms, and everything. There you can see those rocks today. After he had rested, he went on northward, and stumbled over a knoll and fell down on his knees. Then he said, "You are a bad thing to be stumbling against"; so he raised up two large buttes there, and named them the Knees, and they

---

[1] The personage usually called Old Man is known to the Blackfeet and Arapaho, the western Algonquians as well as the Siouan and Salish tribes. The Crow (Siouan) name for the creator, "Old Man Coyote," is an interesting identification of this character with Coyote. Sometimes a personification of the Great Spirit, Old Man belongs to trickster-transformer family. In Arapaho myth Old Man is the hero of raft story and diving animals.

are called so to this day. He went on farther north, and with some of the rocks he carried with him he built the Sweet Grass Hills.

Old Man covered the plains with grass for the animals to feed on. He marked off a piece of ground, and in it he made to grow all kinds of roots and berries—camas, wild carrots, wild turnips, sweetroot, bitterroot, sarvis berries, bull berries, cherries, plums, and rosebuds. He put trees in the ground. He put all kinds of animals on the ground. When he made the bighorn with its big head and horns, he made it out on the prairie. It did not seem to travel easily on the prairie; it was awkward and could not go fast. So he took it by one of its horns, and led it up into the mountains, and turned it loose; and it skipped about among the rocks and went up fearful places with ease. So he said, "This is the place that suits you; this is what you are fitted for, the rocks, and the mountains." While he was in the mountains, he made the antelope out of dirt, and turned it loose, to see how it would go. It ran so fast that it fell over some rocks and hurt itself. He saw that this would not do, and took the antelope down on the prairie, and turned it loose; and it ran away fast and gracefully, and he said, "This is what you are suited to."

One day Old Man determined that he would make a woman and a child; so he formed them both—the woman and the child, her son—of clay. After he had molded the clay in human shape, he said to the clay, "You must be people," and then he covered it up and left it, and went away. The next morning he went to the place and took the covering off, and saw that the clay shapes had changed a little. The second morning there was still more change, and the third still more. The fourth morning he went to the place, took the covering off, looked at the images, and told them to rise and walk; and they did so. They walked down to the river with their Maker, and then he told them that his name was Na'pi [Old Man].

As they were standing by the river, the woman said to

him, "How is it? Will we always live, will there be no end to it?" He said: "I have never thought of that. We will have to decide it. I will take this buffalo chip and throw it in the river. If it floats, when people die, in four days they will become alive again; they will die for only four days. But if it sinks, there will be an end to them." He threw the chip into the river, and it floated. The woman turned and picked up a stone, and said: "No, I will throw this stone in the river; if it floats we will always live, if it sinks people must die, that they may always be sorry for each other." The woman threw the stone into the water, and it sank. "There," said Old Man, "you have chosen. There will be an end to them."

It was not many nights after that the woman's child died, and she cried a great deal for it. She said to Old Man: "Let us change this. The law that you first made, let that be a law." He said: "Not so. What is made law must be law. We will undo nothing that we have done. The child is dead, but it cannot be changed. People will have to die."

That is how we came to be people. It is he who made us.

The first people were poor and naked, and did not know how to get a living. Old Man showed them the roots and berries, and told them that they could peel the bark off some trees and eat it, that it was good. He told the people that the animals should be their food, and gave them to the people, saying, "These are your herds." He said: "All these little animals that live in the ground—rats, squirrels, skunks, beavers—are good to eat. You need not fear to eat of their flesh." He made all the birds that fly, and told the people that there was no harm in their flesh, that it could be eaten. The first people that he created he used to take about through the timber and swamps and over the prairies, and show them the different plants. Of a certain plant he would say, "The root of this plant, if gathered in a certain month of the year, is good for certain sickness." So they learned the power of all herbs.

In those days there were buffalo. Now the people had no

arms, but those black animals with long beards were armed; and once, as the people were moving about, the buffalo saw them, and ran after them, and hooked them, and killed and ate them. One day, as the Maker of the people was traveling over the country, he saw some of his children, that he had made, lying dead, torn to pieces and partly eaten by the buffalo. When he saw this he was very sad. He said: "This will not do. I will change this. The people shall eat the buffalo."

He went to some of the people who were left, and said to them, "How is it that you people do nothing to these animals that are killing you?" The people said: "What can we do? We have no way to kill these animals, while they are armed and can kill us." Then said the Maker: "That is not hard. I will make you a weapon that will kill those animals." So he went out, and cut some sarvis berry shoots, and brought them in, and peeled the bark off them. He took a larger piece of wood, and flattened it, and tied a string to it, and made a bow. Now, as he was the master of all birds and could do with them as he wished, he went out and caught one, and took feathers from its wing, and split them, and tied them to the shaft of wood. He tied four feathers along the shaft, and tried the arrow at a mark, and found that it did not fly well. He took these feathers off, and put on three; and when he tried it again, he found that it was good. He went out and began to break sharp pieces off the stones. He tried them, and found that the black flint stones made the best arrow points, and some white flints. Then he taught the people how to use these things.

Then he said: "The next time you go out, take these things with you, and use them as I tell you, and do not run from these animals. When they run at you, as soon as they get pretty close, shoot the arrows at them, as I have taught you; and you will see that they will run from you or will run in a circle around you."

Now, as people became plenty, one day three men went out onto the plain to see the buffalo, but they had no arms.

They saw the animals, but when the buffalo saw the men, they ran after them and killed two of them, but one got away. One day after this, the people went on a little hill to look about, and the buffalo saw them, and said, "Saiyah, there is some more of our food," and they rushed on them. This time the people did not run. They began to shoot at the buffalo with the bows and arrows Na'pi had given them, and the buffalo began to fall; but in the fight a person was killed.

At this time these people had flint knives given them, and they cut up the bodies of the dead buffalo. It is not healthful to eat the meat raw, so Old Man gathered soft, dry, rotten driftwood and made punk of it, and then got a piece of hard wood, and drilled a hole in it with an arrow point, and gave them a pointed piece of hard wood, and taught them how to make a fire with fire sticks, and to cook the flesh of these animals and eat it.

They got a kind of stone that was in the land, and then took another harder stone and worked one upon the other, and hollowed out the softer one, and made a kettle of it. This was the fashion of their dishes.

Also Old Man said to the people: "Now, if you are overcome, you may go and sleep, and get power. Something will come to you in your dream that will help you. Whatever these animals tell you to do, you must obey them, as they appear to you in your sleep. Be guided by them. If anybody wants help, if you are alone and traveling, and cry aloud for help, your prayer will be answered. It may be by the eagles, perhaps by the buffalo, or by the bears. Whatever animal answers your prayer, you must listen to him."

That was how the first people got through the world, by the power of their dreams.

After this, Old Man kept on, traveling north. Many of the animals that he had made followed him as he went. The animals understood him when he spoke to them, and he used them as his servants. When he got to the north point of the

Porcupine Mountains, there he made some more mud images of people, and blew breath upon them, and they became people. He made men and women. They asked him, "What are we to eat?" He made many images of clay in the form of buffalo. Then he blew breath on these, and they stood up; and when he made signs to them, they started to run. Then he said to the people, "Those are your food." They said to him, "Well, now, we have those animals; how are we to kill them?" "I will show you," he said. He took them to the cliff, and made them build rock piles . . . ; and he taught them how to drive buffalo over a cliff.

After he had taught those people these things, he started off again, traveling north, until he came to where Bow and Elbow rivers meet. There he made some more people, and taught them the same things. From here he again went on northward. When he had come nearly to the Red Deer's River, he reached the hill where the Old Man sleeps. There he lay down and rested himself. The form of his body is to be seen there yet.

When he awoke from his sleep, he traveled farther northward and came to a fine high hill. He climbed to the top of it, and there sat down to rest. He looked over the country below him, and it pleased him. Before him the hill was steep, and he said to himself, "Well, this is a fine place for sliding; I will have some fun," and he began to slide down the hill. The marks where he slid down are to be seen yet, and the place is known to all people as the "Old Man's Sliding Ground."

This is as far as the Blackfeet followed Old Man. The Crees know what he did farther north.

In later times once, Na'pi said, "Here I will mark you off a piece of ground," and he did so. Then he said: "There is your land, and it is full of all kinds of animals, and many things grow in this land. Let no other people come into it. This is for you five tribes [Blackfeet, Bloods, Piegans, Gros Ventres, Sarcees]. When people come to cross the line, take your bows and arrows, your lances and your battle axes, and give them battle and keep them out. If they gain a footing, trouble will come to you."

Our forefathers gave battle to all people who came to cross these lines, and kept them out. Of late years we have let our friends, the white people, come in, and you know the result. We, his children, have failed to obey his laws.

(Blackfoot, Plains)

8
The Winnebago Origin Myth

In the beginning Earthmaker was sitting in space. When he came to consciousness, nothing was there anywhere. He began to think of what he should do, and finally he began to cry and tears flowed from his eyes and fell below him. After a while he looked below him and saw something bright. The bright object below him represented his tears. As they fell they formed the present waters. When the tears flowed below they became the seas as they are now. Earthmaker began to think again. He thought, "It is thus: If I wish anything it will become as I wish, just as my tears have become seas." Thus he thought. So he wished for light and it became light. Then he thought: "It is as I thought, the things that I wished for have come into existence as I desired." Then again he thought and wished for the earth, and this earth came into existence. Earthmaker looked at the earth and he liked it; but it was not quiet. It moved about as do the waters of the sea. Then he made the trees and he liked them but they did not make the earth quiet. Then he made some grass but it likewise did not cause the earth to become quiet. Then he made rocks and stones but still the earth was not quiet. It was however almost quiet. Then he made the four directions and the four winds. At the four corners of the earth he placed them as great and powerful people, to act as island weights. Yet still the earth was not quiet. Then he made four large beings and threw them down toward the earth, and they pierced through the earth with their heads eastward. They were snakes. Then the earth became very still and quiet. Then he looked at the earth and he liked it.

Then again he thought of how it was that things came into being just as he desired. Then for the first time he began to talk and he said, "As things are just as I wish them I shall make a being in my own likeness." So he took a piece of clay and made it like himself. Then he talked to what he had created but it did not answer. He looked at it and saw that it had no mind or thought. So he made a mind for it. Again he talked to it but it did not answer. So he looked at it again and saw that it had no tongue. Then he made it a tongue. Then he spoke to it but still it did not answer. He looked at it and saw that it had no soul. So he made it a soul. Then he talked to it again and it very nearly said something, but it could not make itself intelligible. So Earthmaker breathed into its mouth and then talked to it and it answered.

(Winnebago, Central Woodland)

9
In the Beginning of the Nisqually World

Long, long ago, some of the Puget Sound Indians used to say, people on the earth became so numerous that they ate all the fish and game. Then they began to eat each other. Soon they became worse than the wild animals had been. They became so very wicked that Dokibatl, the Changer, sent a flood upon the earth. All living things were destroyed except one woman and one dog. They fled to the top of Tacobud and stayed there until the flood left the earth.

From the woman and the dog were born the next race of people. They walked on four legs and lived in holes in the ground. They ate fern roots and camas bulbs, which they dug with their fingers because they had no tools. Having no fire and no clothing, they suffered from both the heat and the cold.

Their troubles were made worse when a giant bear came up from the south. The bear was huge and strong and also had special powers. With his eyes he cast a spell upon whatever creature he wanted to eat. Then that creature was unable to move, and the bear ate him. The people had no weapons. So the bear was about to eat all of them.

At last the Changer sent a Spirit Man over the mountains from the east. His face was like the sun. His voice was like the voice of Thunderbird. He came armed with bow, arrows, and spear. And he had great powers.

"Why do you weep?" he asked the people.

"We weep because of the bear," they answered. "The beast is about to destroy us. None of us can escape from him."

The Spirit Man did not promise to help them, but he did show them how to walk on two feet. And he told them that there were two powerful spirits. "One of them is good; the other is evil. The Good Spirit sent me to you."

Then he returned to the mountains to talk with the Good Spirit, the Changer. When the Spirit Man came to the people a second time, he brought many strange gifts and stayed for many moons.

First he called all the people together for a big potlatch, the first potlatch of all the Indians. He told them that a potlatch is a big feast and gift-giving celebration. To the young men, the Spirit Man gave bows, arrows, and spears, and he taught all the young men how to use them. To the old men, he gave canoes. He showed them how to make canoes from cedar trees, how to make fishing spears and nets, and how to fish from the canoes.

The Spirit Man taught the girls how to make skirts from the inner bark of the cedar tree, how to paint their faces and oil their hair so that they were more beautiful, and how to sing. He showed the older women how to dig camas roots with the sticks he brought them, and how to make baskets out of cedar bark and seaweed. He showed them how to make fire by rubbing two sticks together, how to cook, how to carry burdens by strapping them across the head. "You will serve man and be useful to him in these ways," the Spirit Man told the women. "He will be your master."

Then the Spirit Man filled himself with strong powers, for his next task was to kill the giant bear. First he put seven arrows into his bag. He called together the men of the tribe, and for one whole sun the group chanted over the arrows to make them strong with spirit power.

Then the Spirit Man took one arrow and pushed it into the ground in the center of the plain west of Tacobud. After walking half a day toward the lodge of the great bear, he pushed a second arrow into the ground. He walked for another half day toward the bear's den and pushed a third arrow into the ground. Thus he kept on until he had placed six arrows erect and in a straight line.

With the seventh arrow in his hand, the Spirit Man went up to the bear. The beast tried to cast a spell from his eyes, but the Spirit Man's spirit powers were so strong that the bear could have no effect on him. He shot the seventh arrow into the beast and then ran back to the sixth arrow. The bear followed him. He shot the sixth arrow and then ran back to the fifth. The bear followed him.

They kept running until they reached the first arrow. The Spirit Man shot the first arrow into the heart of the beast and killed him. There the great bear died, in the middle of the Nisqually plain.

All the people were glad when they gathered together near the dead beast that had frightened them for so long. They removed the skin and divided it equally among the different branches of the tribe. The bear was so huge that the skin of one ear covered the whole of Mound Prairie.

The last thing the Spirit Man did for the people on this journey to their land was to make a large building with just one opening. In this big house he placed all the diseases and evil deeds known to the world since then. Then he called a certain family to him and made them guardians of the building. What was in the house he told only to the head of the family.

"You and your children and grandchildren will take care of this house forever," the Spirit Man said. "Remember that the door must never be opened. And remember that only the head man of the family is ever to know what is in the building."

After many years, the only members of the family left were an old man and his wife and daughter. One day, when her father and mother went away from the house, the daughter saw her chance to peek into the Spirit Man's house. She had long wanted to see what was behind that door.

So she undid the fastenings and pushed back the door a little distance. Out rushed all the creatures of the house—all the diseases and evil deeds and sorrows that have been in the world ever since.

The Changer was so angry with the daughter that he created the demon Seatco. Seatco's home is among the rocks in the distant mountains. He sleeps by day. At night he flies over the earth to seize any woman found away from her home.

(Puget Sound, Northwest Coast)

10
Sun Sister and
Moon Brother

In olden times a brother and his sister lived in a large village in which there was a singing house, and every night the sister with her playfellows enjoyed themselves in this house. Once upon a time, when all the lamps in the singing house were extinguished, somebody came in and outraged her. She was unable to recognize him; but she blackened her hands with soot and when the same again happened besmeared the man's back with it. When the lamps were relighted she saw that the violator was her brother. In great anger she sharpened a knife and cut off her breasts, which she offered to him, saying: "Since you seem to relish me, eat this." Her brother fell into a passion and she fled from him, running about the room. She seized a piece of wood (with which the lamps are kept in order) which was burning brightly and rushed out of the house. The brother took another one, but in his pursuit he fell down and extinguished his light, which continued to glow only faintly. Gradually both were lifted up and continued their course in the sky, the sister being transformed into the sun, the brother into the moon. Whenever the new moon first appears she sings:

Aningaga tapika, takirn tapika qaumidjatedlirpoq;
   qaumatitaudle.
Aningaga tapika, tikipoq tapika.

➤ *My brother up there, the moon up there begins to shine;*
he will be bright.
My brother up there, he is coming up there.

(Eskimo)

11
Sedna, Mistress of the Underworld

Once upon a time there lived on a solitary shore an Inung with his daughter Sedna. His wife had been dead for some time, and the two led a quiet life. Sedna grew up to be a handsome girl, and the youths came from all around to sue for her hand, but none of them could touch her proud heart. Finally, at the breaking up of the ice in the spring, a fulmar flew from over the ice and wooed Sedna with enticing song. "Come to me," it said; "come into the land of the birds, where there is never hunger, where my tent is made of the most beautiful skins. You shall rest on soft bearskins. My fellows, the fulmars, shall bring you all your heart may desire; their feathers shall clothe you; your lamp shall always be filled with oil, your pot with meat." Sedna could not long resist such wooing and they went together over the vast sea. When at last they reached the country of the fulmar, after a long and hard journey, Sedna discovered that her spouse had shamefully deceived her. Her new home was not built of beautiful pelts, but was covered with wretched fishskins, full of holes, that gave free entrance to wind and snow. Instead of soft reindeer skins her bed was made of hard walrus hides and she had to live on miserable fish, which the birds brought her. Too soon she discovered that she had thrown away her opportunities when, in her foolish pride, she had rejected the Inuit youth. In her woe she sang: "Aja. O father, if you knew how wretched I am you would come to me and we would hurry away in your boat over the waters. The birds look unkindly upon me, the stranger; cold winds roar about my bed; they give me but miserable food. O come and take me back home. Aja.''

When a year had passed and the sea was again stirred by warmer winds, the father left his country to visit Sedna. His daughter greeted him joyfully and besought him to take her back home. The father, hearing of the outrages wrought upon his daughter, determined upon revenge. He killed the fulmar, took Sedna into his boat, and they quickly left the country that had brought so much sorrow to Sedna. When the other fulmars came home and found their companion dead and his wife gone, they all flew away in search of the fugitives. They were very sad over the death of their poor murdered comrade and continue to mourn and cry until this day.

Having flown a short distance, they discerned the boat and stirred up a heavy storm. The sea rose in immense waves that threatened the pair with destruction. In this mortal peril the father determined to offer Sedna to the birds and flung her overboard. She clung to the edge of the boat with a death grip. The cruel father then took a knife and cut off the first joints of her fingers. Falling into the sea they were transformed into whales, the nails turning into whalebone. Sedna holding on to the boat more tightly, the second finger joints fell under the sharp knife and swam away as seals; when the father cut off the stumps of the fingers they became ground seals.

Meantime the storm subsided, for the fulmars thought Sedna was drowned. The father then allowed her to come into the boat again. But from that time she cherished a deadly hatred against him and swore bitter revenge. After they got ashore, she called her dogs and let them gnaw off the feet and hands of her father while he was asleep. Upon this he cursed himself, his daughter, and the dogs. They have since lived in the land of Adlivun, of which Sedna is the mistress.

(Eskimo)

12
How Raven Helped
the Ancient People

Long ago, near the beginning of the world, Gray Eagle was the guardian of the sun and moon and stars, of fresh water, and of fire. Gray Eagle hated people so much that he kept these things hidden. People lived in darkness, without fire and without fresh water.

Gray Eagle had a beautiful daughter, and Raven fell in love with her. At that time Raven was a handsome young man.[1] He changed himself into a snow-white bird, and as a snow-white bird he pleased Gray Eagle's daughter. She invited him to her father's lodge.

When Raven saw the sun and the moon and the stars and fresh water hanging on the sides of Eagle's lodge, he knew

---

[1] Raven was the benefactor of the mythological people along the shores of Puget Sound and the beaches of the Olympic Peninsula, much as Coyote was of the ancients east of the Cascade Range. Among many other deeds, according to Quillayute mythology, Raven brought the blueback salmon to the rivers along the Washington coast. Having eaten some in the underground home of his father-in-law, Mole, young Raven determined to take a blueback salmon home with him. Pursued, he hid the scales of the fish in his mouth and nostrils. He came up to the south. He threw one scale of the salmon into the Quillayute River, one into the Hoh, and two into the Queets. He washed off all the rest of the scales into the Quinault River. That is why there are a few blueback salmon in the Quillayute and Hoh rivers today, many in the Queets, and very many in the Quinault. "So much for that."

In the following story told by a Puget Sound tribe, Raven is again the benefactor. Two themes universal in mythology are combined in this little tale—the origin of daylight and the origin of fire.

what he should do. He watched for his chance to seize them when no one was looking. He stole all of them, and a brand of fire also, and flew out of the lodge through the smoke hole.

As soon as Raven got outside, he hung the sun up in the sky. It made so much light that he was able to fly far out to an island in the middle of the ocean. When the sun set, he fastened the moon up in the sky and hung the stars around in different places. By this new light he kept on flying, carrying with him the fresh water and the brand of fire he had stolen.

He flew back over the land. When he had reached the right place, he dropped all the water he had stolen. It fell to the ground and there became the source of all the freshwater streams and lakes in the world.

Then Raven flew on, holding the brand of fire in his bill. The smoke from the fire blew back over his white feathers and made them black. When his bill began to burn, he had to drop the firebrand. It struck rocks and went into the rocks. That is why, if you strike two stones together, fire will drop out.

Raven's feathers never became white again after they were blackened by the smoke from the firebrand. That is why Raven is now a black bird.

(Puget Sound, Pacific Northwest)

13
Raven

No one knows just how the story of Raven really begins, so each starts from the point where he does know it. Here it was always begun in this way. . . . When Raven was born, his father tried to instruct him and train him in every way and, after he grew up, told him he would give him strength to make a world. After trying in all sorts of ways Raven finally succeeded. Then there was no light in this world, but it was told him that far up the Nass was a large house in which someone kept light just for himself.

Raven thought over all kinds of plans for getting this light into the world and finally he hit on a good one. The rich man living there had a daughter, and he thought, "I will make myself very small and drop into the water in the form of a small piece of dirt." The girl swallowed this dirt and became pregnant. When her time was completed, they made a hole for her, as was customary, in which she was to bring forth, and lined it with rich furs of all sorts. But the child did not wish to be born on those fine things. Then its grandfather felt sad and said, "What do you think it would be best to put into that hole? Shall we put in moss?" So they put moss inside and the baby was born on it. Its eyes were very bright and moved around rapidly.

Round bundles of varying shapes and sizes hung about on the walls of the house. When the child became a little larger it crawled around back of the people weeping continually, and as it cried it pointed to the bundles. This lasted many days. Then its grandfather said, "Give my grandchild what he is crying for. Give him that one hanging on the end. That is the bag of stars.'' So the child played with this, rolling it about on the floor back of the people, until suddenly he let it go up through the smoke hole. It went straight up into the sky and the stars scattered out of it, arranging themselves as you now see them. That was what he went there for.

Some time after this he began crying again, and he cried so much that it was thought he would die. Then his grandfather said, "Untie the next one and give it to him." He played and played with it around behind his mother. After a while he let that go up through the smoke hole also, and there was the big moon.

Now just one thing more remained, the box that held the daylight, and he cried for that. His eyes turned around and showed different colors, and the people began thinking that he must be something other than an ordinary baby. But it always happens that a grandfather loves his grandchild just as he does his own daughter, so the grandfather said, "Untie the last thing and give it to him." His grandfather felt very sad when he gave this to him. When the child had this in his hands, he uttered the raven cry, "Ga," and flew out with it through the smoke hole. Then the person from whom he had stolen it said, "That old manuring raven has gotten all of my things."

Journeying on, Raven was told of another place, where a man had an everlasting spring of water. This man was named Petrel [Ganù'k]. Raven wanted this water because there was none to drink in this world, but Petrel always slept by his spring, and he had a cover over it so as to keep it all to himself. Then Raven came in and said to him, "My brother-in-law, I have just come to see you. How are you?" He told Petrel of all kinds of things that were happening outside, trying to induce him to go out to look at them, but Petrel was too smart for him and refused.

When night came, Raven said, "I am going to sleep with

you, brother-in-law." So they went to bed, and toward morning Raven heard Petrel sleeping very soundly. Then he went outside, took some dog manure and put it around Petrel's buttocks. When it was beginning to grow light, he said, "Wake up, wake up, wake up, brother-in-law, you have defecated all over your clothes." Petrel got up, looked at himself, and thought it was true, so he took his blankets and went outside. Then Raven went over to Petrel's spring, took off the cover and began drinking. After he had drunk up almost all of the water, Petrel came in and saw him. Then Raven flew straight up, crying "Ga."

Before he got through the smoke hole, however, Petrel said, "My spirits up the smoke hole, catch him." So Raven stuck there, and Petrel put pitchwood on the fire under him so as to make a quantity of smoke. Raven was white before that time, but the smoke made him of the color you find him today. Still he did not drop the water. When the smoke-hole spirits let him go, he flew around the nearest point and rubbed himself all over so as to clear off as much of the soot as possible.

This happened somewhere about the Nass, and afterwards he started up this way. First he let some water fall from his mouth and made the Nass. By and by he spit more out and made the Stikine. Next he spit out Taku river, then Chilkat, then Alsek, and all the other large rivers. The small drops that came out of his mouth made the small salmon creeks.

After this Raven went on again and came to a large town where were people who had never seen daylight. They were out catching eulachon in the darkness when he came to the bank opposite, and he asked them to take him across but they would not. Then he said to them, "If you don't come over I will have daylight break on you." But they answered, "Where are you from? Do you come from far up the Nass where lives the man who has daylight?" At this Raven opened his box just a little and shed so great a light on them that they were nearly thrown down. He shut it quickly, but they quarreled with him so much across the creek that he became angry and opened the box completely, when the sun flew up into the sky. Then those people who had sea-otter or fur-seal skins, or the skins of any other sea animals, went into the ocean, while those who had land-otter, bear, or marten skins, or the skins of any other land animals, went into the woods, becoming the animals whose skins they wore.

(Tlingit, Northwest Coast)

14
The Theft of Light

Giant flew inland [toward the east]. He went on for a long time, and finally he was very tired, so he dropped down on the sea the little round stone which his father had given to him. It became a large rock way out at sea. Giant rested on it and refreshed himself, and took off the raven skin.

At that time there was always darkness. There was no daylight then. Again Giant put on the raven skin and flew toward the east. Now, Giant reached the mainland and arrived at the mouth of Skeena River. There he stopped and scattered the salmon roe and trout roe. He said while he was scattering them, "Let every river and creek have all kinds of fish!" Then he took the dried sea-lion bladder and scattered the fruits all over the land, saying, "Let every mountain, hill, valley, plain, the whole land, be full of fruits!"

The whole world was still covered with darkness. When the sky was clear, the people would have a little light from the stars; and when clouds were in the sky, it was very dark all over the land. The people were distressed by this. Then Giant thought that it would be hard for him to obtain his food if it were always dark. He remembered that there was light in heaven, whence he had come. Then he made up his mind to bring down the light to our world. On the following day Giant put on his raven skin, which his father the chief had given to him, and flew upward. Finally he found the hole in the sky, and he flew through it. Giant reached the inside of the sky. He took off the raven skin and put it down near the hole in the sky. He went on, and came to a spring near the house of the chief of heaven. There he sat down and waited.

Then the chief's daughter came out, carrying a small bucket in which she was about to fetch water. She went down to the big spring in front of her father's house. When Giant saw her coming along, he transformed himself into the leaf of a cedar and floated on the water. The chief's daughter dipped it up in her bucket and drank it. Then she returned to her father's house and entered.

After a short time she was with child, and not long after she gave birth to a boy. Then the chief and the chieftainess were very glad. They washed the boy regularly. He began to grow up. Now he was beginning to creep about. They washed him often, and the chief smoothed and cleaned the floor of the house. Now the child was strong and crept about every day. He began to cry, "Hama, hama!" He was crying all the time, and the great chief was troubled, and called in some of his slaves to carry about the boy. The slaves did so, but he would not sleep for several nights. He kept on crying, "Hama, hama!" Therefore the chief invited all his wise men, and said to them that he did not know what the boy wanted and why he was crying. He wanted the box that was hanging in the chief's house.

This box, in which the daylight was kept, was hanging in one corner of the house. Its name was *Mā*. Giant had known it before he descended to our world. The child cried for it. The chief was annoyed, and the wise men listened to what the chief told them. When the wise men heard the child crying aloud, they did not know what he was saying. He was crying all the time, "Hama, hama, hama!"

One of the wise men, who understood him, said to the chief, "He is crying for the *mā*." Therefore the chief ordered it to be taken down. The man put it down. They put it down near the fire, and the boy sat down near it and ceased crying.

He stopped crying, for he was glad. Then he rolled the *mā* about inside the house. He did so for four days. Sometimes he would carry it to the door. Now the great chief did not think of it. He had quite forgotten it. Then the boy really took up the *mā*, put it on his shoulders, and ran out with it. While he was running, someone said, "Giant is running away with the *mā*!" He ran away, and the hosts of heaven pursued him. They shouted that Giant was running away with the *mā*. He came to the hole of the sky, put on the skin of the raven, and flew down, carrying the *mā*. Then the hosts of heaven returned to their houses, and he flew down with it to our world.

At that time the world was still dark. He arrived farther up the river, and went down river. Giant had come down near the mouth of Nass River. He went to the mouth of Nass River. It was always dark, and he carried the *mā* about with him. He went on, and went up the river in the dark. A little farther up he heard the noise of the people, who were catching *olachen* in bag nets in their canoes. There was much noise out on the river, because they were working hard. Giant, who was sitting on the shore, said, "Throw ashore one of the things that you are catching, my dear people!" After a while, Giant said again, "Throw ashore one of the things you are catching!" Then those on the water scolded him. "Where did you come from, great liar . . . ?" The [animal] people knew that it was Giant. Therefore they made fun of him. Then Giant said again, "Throw ashore one of the things that you are catching, or I shall break the *mā*!" and all those who were on the water answered, "Where did you get what you are talking about, you liar?" Giant said once more, "Throw ashore one of the things that you are catching, my dear people, or I shall break the *mā* for you!" One person replied, scolding him.

Giant had repeated his request four times, but those on the water refused what he had asked for. Therefore Giant broke the *mā*. It broke, and it was daylight. The north wind began to blow hard; and all the fisherman, the Frogs, were driven away by the north wind. All the Frogs who had made fun of Giant were driven away down river until they arrived at one of the large mountainous islands. Here the Frogs tried to climb up the rock; but they stuck to the rock, being frozen by the north wind, and became stone. They are still on the rock . . . and all the world had the daylight.

(Tsimshian, Northwest Coast)

15

The Bird Whose Wings
Made the Wind

An Indian family resided on the seashore. They had two sons, the oldest of whom was married and had a family of small children. They lived principally by fishing, and their favorite food was eels.

Now it came to pass at a certain time that the weather was so stormy they could not fish. The wind blew fiercely night and day, and they were greatly reduced by hunger. Finally the old father told his boys to walk along the shore, and perhaps they might find a fish that had floated ashore, as sometimes happened. So one of the young men started off to try his luck in this line; when he reached a point where the wind blew so fiercely that he could hardly stand against it, he saw the cause of all the trouble. At the end of the point there was a ledge of rocks, called Rocky Point, extending far out; at low water the rocks were separated from one another by the shallow water, but were nearly all covered when the tide was in. On the farthest rock a large bird, the storm-king, was standing, flapping his wings and causing all the trouble by the wind he raised. The Indian planned to outwit him. He called to the big bird, and addressing him as "my grandfather," said, "Are you cold?" He answered, "No." The man replied, "You are cold; let me carry you ashore on my back." "Do so," was the answer. So the man waded over to the rock on which the bird was sitting, took him on his back, and carefully carried him from rock to rock, wading over the intervening spaces of shoal water. In going down the last rock, he stumbled on purpose, but pretended that it was an accident; and the poor old bird fell and broke one of his wings. The man seemed very sorry, and immediately proceeded to set the bone and bind up the wing. He then directed the old fellow to keep quiet and not move his wings until the wounded one healed. He now inquired if it pained him much, and was told that it did not. "Remain there and I will visit you again soon, and bring you some food." He now returned home, and found that the wind had all died away; there was a dead calm, so that before long they were supplied with a great abundance of food, as the eels were plenty and easily taken. But there can be too much even of a good thing. Calm weather continued for a succession of days, causing the salt water to be covered with a sort of scum. The Indians say it is the result of sickness and vomiting among the larger fish; this scum prevents the fishermen from seeing into the water, and consequently is adverse to eel-spearing. This took place on the occasion referred to, and so they sought for a remedy. The big bird was visited and his wing examined. It was sufficiently recovered to admit of motion, and he was told to keep both his wings going, but that the motion must be steady and gentle. This produced the desired effect.

(Micmac, Northeast Woodland)

16
The Release of
the Wild Animals

Long ago two persons owned all the buffalo. They were an old woman and her young cousin. They kept them penned up in the mountains, so that they could not get out. Coyote came to these people. He summoned the Indians to a council. "That old woman will not give us anything. When we come over there, we will plan how to release the buffalo." They all moved near the buffalo enclosure. "After four nights," said Coyote, "we will again hold a council as to how we can release the buffalo. A very small animal shall go where the old woman draws her water. When the child gets water, it will take it home for a pet. The old woman will object; but the child will think so much of the animal that it will begin to cry and will be allowed to keep it. The animal will run off at daybreak, and the buffalo will burst out of their pen and run away." The first animal they sent failed. Then they sent the Kill-dee.

When the boy went for water, he found the Kill-dee and took it home. "Look here!" he said to his cousin, "this animal of mine is very good." The old woman replied, "Oh, it is good for nothing! There is nothing living on the earth that is not a rascal or schemer." The child paid no attention to her. "Take it back where you got it," said the woman. He obeyed. The Kill-dee returned.

The people had another council. "Well, she has got the better of these two. They have failed," said Coyote; "but that makes no difference. Perhaps we may release them, perhaps we shall fail. This is the third time now. We will send a small animal over there. If the old woman agrees to take it, it will liberate those buffalo; it is a great schemer." So they sent the third animal. Coyote said, "If she rejects this one, we shall surely be unable to liberate the game." The animal went to the spring and was picked up by the boy, who took a great liking to it. "Look here! What a nice pet I have!" The old woman replied, "Oh, how foolish you are! It is a good for nothing. All the animals in the world are schemers. I'll kill it with a club." The boy took it in his arms and ran away crying. He thought too much of his pet. "No! This animal is too small," he cried. When the animal had not returned by nightfall, Coyote went among the people, saying, "Well, this animal has not returned yet; I dare say the old woman has consented to keep it. Don't be uneasy, our buffalo will be freed." Then he bade all the people get ready just at daybreak. "Our buffalo will be released. Do all of you mount your horses." In the meantime the animal, following its instructions, slipped over to the pen, and began to howl. The buffalo heard it and were terrified. They ran toward the gate, broke it down, and escaped. The old woman, hearing the noise, woke up. The child asked, "Where is my pet?" He did not find it. The old woman said, "I told you so. Now you see the animal is bad, it has deprived us of our game." She vainly tried to hold the buffalo back. At daybreak all the Indians got on their horses, for they had confidence in Coyote. Thus the buffalo came to live on this earth. Coyote was a great schemer.

(Comanche, Plains)

17
The Empounded Water

Aglabem kept back all the water in the world, so that rivers stopped flowing, and lakes dried up, and the people everywhere began dying of thirst. As a last resort, they sent a messenger to him to ask him to give the people water; but he refused, and gave the messenger only a drink from the water in which he washed. But this was not enough to satisfy even the thirst of one. Then the people began complaining, some saying, "I'm as dry as a fish," "I'm as dry as a frog," "I'm as dry as a turtle," "I'm as dry as a beaver," and the like, as they were on the verge of dying of thirst.

At last a great man was sent to Aglabem to beg him to release the water for the people. Aglabem refused, saying that he needed it himself to lie in. Then the messenger felled a tree, so that it fell on top of the monster and killed him. The body of this tree became the main river [St. John's River], and the branches became the tributary branches of the river, while the leaves became the ponds at the heads of these streams. As the waters flowed down to the villages of the people again, they plunged in to drink, and became transformed into the animals to which they had likened themselves when formerly complaining of their thirst.

(Malecite, Northeast Woodland)

18
The Lizard-hand

It was Coyote who brought it about that people die. He made it thus because our hands are not closed like his. He wanted our hands to be like his, but a lizard said to him: "No, they must have my hand." He had five fingers and Coyote had only a fist. So now we have an open hand with five fingers. But then Coyote said: "Well, then they will have to die."

(Yokuts, California)

19

The Twins Alter
the Book of Life

They traveled all over the world and killed all the evil spirits they encountered. Then they went under the earth, under
the rivers, under the ocean and then above the earth, visiting
the Night spirits, the Sun, the Moon, the Stars, the Thunder-
birds—all of them. They visited the four worlds, too. Indeed
they did not miss anyplace.

In the course of their travels they came to the place where
the Earthmaker lives. They surprised him for never before had
anyone, of his own accord, ever visited him. Now there were
two very large lodges at that place, one belonging to
Earthmaker and the other to Herecgunina. Earthmaker and
Herecgunina lived there side by side. The boys went into the
lodge of Herecgunina first. "Well, my children, ever since I
have been here no one has ever come to me of his own accord. You are the first who have come in this way. Why have
you come and for what purpose?" Then the older of the twins
said, "We were just traveling all over the earth, for no purpose
in particular."

Herecgunina was sitting there writing in a book and marking off the number of years human beings were to live. He
was making them very short. "Say, why don't you make them
long?" asked the boys. "This is the way Earthmaker created
me. He put me in control of life. It is to be short because if all
people were to live long lives, the world would soon become
overcrowded. Then the people would be in a pitiable condi-

tion indeed. There would not be enough food to go around. This is the reason Earthmaker created me, that I might decrease the number of people." Then they asked him to let them have the book for a little while and do the marking. Finally they persuaded him to give it to them. When they had the book they marked all the lives long. "Don't do that," he said. But they refused to obey him. He tried to take the book back but they refused to give it up for, although Herecgunina was the equal of Earthmaker, these boys were more powerful still. He was afraid of them.

(Winnebago, Central Woodlands)

20
The Origin of the Pleiades

Once a party of Indians went through the woods toward a hunting ground which they had known for a long time. They traveled several days through very wild country, going slowly and camping on the way. At last they reached The Beautiful Lake of gray rocks and the great forest trees. Fish swarmed in the waters, and deer came down from the hills to drink. On the hills and in the valleys were huge beech and chestnut trees, where there were squirrels and bears.

The chief of the party was Tracks-in-the-Water, and he halted the group on the shore of the lake to give thanks to the Great Spirit for the safe arrival at the hunting grounds. "Here we will build our lodges for the winter and may the Great Spirit send us plenty of game and health and peace."

Autumn passed on. The lodges were built and hunting went well. The children began to dance to amuse themselves. They were getting lonesome, having nothing to do, so they went to a quiet spot by the lake to dance. They had done this a long time when one day a very old man came to them. They had never seen anyone like him before. He was dressed in white feathers and his white hair shone like silver. He spoke to them, telling them they must stop dancing or evil would happen to them. The children did not pay any attention to him. Day after day they danced. Again and again he appeared, repeating his warning.

One of the children suggested a feast the next time they met to dance. When they returned home, they all asked their parents for food. "You will waste and spoil good food," said one. "You can eat at home as you should," said another. So they got nothing. But they met again and danced anyway. They would have liked to have had something to eat after each dance. Their stomachs were empty.

One day, as they danced, they found themselves rising little by little into the air. Their heads were light from hunger. They didn't know how all this happened. One said, "Don't look back, for something strange is happening." A woman, who saw them, called them back, but with no effect, for they continued to rise slowly above the earth. She ran to the camp, and everyone rushed out with all kinds of food. But the children did not return, even though their parents cried after them.

One, who did look back, became a falling star. The others reached the sky. They are the Pleiades. Every falling star brings the story to mind, but the seven stars shine on—a band of dancing children.

(Onondaga, Iroquois)

21
How Old Age Came into the World

Five brothers and their sister lived alone on a mountain; the brothers had killed a great many people in the country around.

The sister gathered the wood and cooked the meat. When it was time for her maturity dance, she asked: "How can I dance when there is nobody to sing for me?"

"Walk around all the time," said her eldest brother; "pile stones, and don't sleep for five nights."

The girl kept awake four nights, then she was so tired that she fell asleep. She dreamed that her brothers were covered with sores and were starving. When she woke up, she cried and said: "I wish I had died long ago, then I shouldn't have brought trouble on my brothers. I have done this by not dancing and by going to sleep."

When she got home, she found that Sickness had been in the house. Sickness came every day for five days. Then each one of the five brothers had great sores on his body. There was nobody to hunt for deer, or rabbits, and soon the brothers were starving. The sister brought wood and kept the fire, but she couldn't find anything to eat. Everybody was glad that the brothers were sick and hoped they would die.

One of the brothers saw two swans on a pond near the house, and when the sister came with a load of wood on her back, he said: "I wish we could kill one of those swans."

"Maybe I can kill one," said the sister. She got her brothers' bows and tried the strings to see which string was the strongest. She put down one bow after another, saying: "That isn't strong." The strings had been strong enough for her brothers, but for her they were weak. She took the bow that belonged to her youngest brother, pulled the string, and said: "This will do."

When she started for the pond, one of the brothers watched her; he said: "Now she is near the pond; now she is sitting down on the bank!" She drew the bow, and when he thought she had missed the swan, he nearly fell, he was so sorry. He didn't look out again. The arrow went through both swans.

The sister brought the swans home and left them outside; she took the bow and arrow in and put them away. Her brothers felt bad; they were disappointed. When she asked: "Shall I cook them in the house?" they were glad. They tried to get up, but they couldn't stand on their feet, they were so weak.

The girl cooked the swans and gave her brothers some of the meat. She said: "Eat a little at a time, so it will last longer." She saved the fat and rubbed her brothers with it, to heal their sores.

"Now I am stronger," said the eldest brother. "Give me my bow; I feel as if I could shoot something." Each brother said the same.

When the people at the foot of the mountain heard that the five brothers were sick, they were glad and sent a young man to find if it were true. He came back, and said: "They are sick and are going to die."

When the sister had gone for wood, the eldest brother said: "I know that somebody is coming; I want to be strong." They all had the same feeling, and each one tried his bow-string. When the sister came back, the eldest brother said: "You must roll us up in our blankets, and tie them around us as though we were dead. Put our bows and arrows and beads near us."

When she had done that, she went off to the mountains, for she felt bad and didn't want to stay with her brothers; she didn't want to live any longer.

The brothers waited for her, and when it was dark and she didn't come, one said: "Our sister is always talking about dying; maybe she is dead."

Now the people at the foot of the mountain sent a little boy to see if the five brothers were alive. He crossed the pond in a canoe; he rowed the canoe by saying: *"Peldack! Peldack!"* [Go fast]. When the boy saw the men tied up in their blankets, he went back, and said: "They are dead. In their house there are bows and arrows and nice beads. You must go and get them."

The chief said: "Get ready; we will go and scalp those men, and take their things."

When the brothers saw the men coming, they said: "We will lie here as if we were dead, and when they pack up our things and start away, we will spring up and fight them with knives."

The men came into the house. They unrolled the brothers and kicked them around; they took their blankets, bows, arrows and beads, took everything they could find, and started off.

Then the five brothers jumped up and ran at them with knives. They killed every man, threw the bodies into the pond, and started off to hunt for their sister. They hunted a long time. At last they found her body and burned it; then the eldest brother said: "Let us leave this country and kill every man we can find."

They started and traveled toward the west. They killed every man or woman they met. When people saw them coming they ran and hid, they were so afraid of them. The brothers traveled a long time, and killed a great many people. At last they came to a big lake. They made a canoe and started to cross it, but before they got to land, the canoe sank. It went under the water and under a mountain and out into another lake. There they met Storm.

He was a man then and could kill anybody he could catch and draw into the water. He tried to kill the five brothers, but the youngest brother fought with him, cut him to pieces with his knife, and said: "You will be a person no longer; you will only be something to scare people," and he drove him away. All the people under the water hid, for they were afraid of the brothers.

When the brothers couldn't find anyone to kill, they turned toward the east and traveled till they came to a country where they found a very old man and a very old woman. They said: "We have come to fight you."

"I don't want to fight," said the old man. "We have always lived here, this is our place; nobody ever came here before to trouble us. We don't bother anyone. Go away and leave us."

"You must fight," said the brothers. "If you don't, we will kill you; we kill every one we meet."

"You can't kill us or harm us, no matter what you do," said the old man. "We are *Komúchass* [Old Age]. We shall live always."

The five brothers were mad; they didn't listen to the old man, but shot at him with arrows, and pounded him with clubs; then they built a fire and tried to burn him. When they couldn't kill him in any way, they got scared and ran off.

The old man called to them to stop, but they didn't listen; then he said: "We shall follow you; you cannot get away; wherever you go we shall go. You will never get home."

The old man and old woman followed the brothers for a long time, and at last they caught up with the eldest brother. Right away he was old and weak. He stumbled along for a little way, then fell to the ground and died.

They overtook the second brother; he also grew old and weak, fell to the ground and died. The third brother reached the lake; he was running on the ice when *Komúchass* overtook him; he grew weak and fell; the ice broke and he was drowned. The fourth brother died in the same manner. The youngest brother thought he was going to get away from the old man; he was only a few steps from home when *Komúchass* overtook him. Right off he was an old man; he stumbled along a step or two, then fell to the ground and died.

This is how old age came into our world. If the five brothers had let the old man and his wife alone, they would have stayed in their own country, and there would have been no such thing as old age.

Komúchass turned the bodies of the five brothers into five rocks, and those rocks are still to be seen in the Klamath country.

(Modoc, California)

II
Trickster

22

From the Winnebago
Trickster Cycle

As he, Trickster, walked along, suddenly he came in sight of a knoll. As he approached it, he saw, to his surprise, an old buffalo near it. . . . Thereupon he took a knife, cut down the hay and fashioned it into figures of men. These he placed in a circle, leaving an opening at one end. The place was very muddy. Having constructed this enclosure, he went back to where he had seen the buffalo and shouted, "Oho! My younger brother, here he is! Here he is indeed eating without having anything to worry about. Indeed let nothing prey on his mind! I will keep watch for him against intruders." Thus he spoke to the buffalo who was feeding to his heart's content. Then he continued, "Listen, younger brother, this place is completely surrounded by people! Over there, however, is an opening through which you might escape." Just then the buffalo raised his head unsuspiciously and, to his surprise, he seemed really to be completely surrounded by people. Only at the place Trickster had designated did an opening appear. In that direction, therefore, the buffalo ran. Soon he sank in the mire and Trickster was immediately upon him with his knife and killed him. Then he dragged him over to a cluster of wood and skinned him. Throughout all these operations he used his right arm only.

In the midst of these operations suddenly his left arm grabbed the buffalo. "Give that back to me, it is mine! Stop that or I will use my knife on you!" So spoke the right arm. "I

will cut you to pieces, that is what I will do to you," continued
the right arm. Thereupon the left arm released its hold. But,
shortly after, the left arm again grabbed hold of the right arm.
This time it grabbed hold of his wrist just at the moment that
the right arm had commenced to skin the buffalo. Again and
again this was repeated. In this manner did Trickster make
both his arms quarrel. That quarrel soon turned into a vicious
fight and the left arm was badly cut up. "Oh, oh! Why did I do
this? Why have I done this? I have made myself suffer!" The
left arm was indeed bleeding profusely.

Then he dressed the buffalo. When he was finished he
started off again. As he walked along the birds would exclaim,
"Look, look! There is Trickster!" Thus they would cry and fly
away. "Ah, you naughty little birds! I wonder what they are
saying?" This continued right along. Every bird he met would
call out, "Look, look! There is Trickster! There he is walking
about!"

As he walked along, he came unexpectedly to a place
where he saw a man with a club. "Hoho!" said Trickster, "my
younger brother, he, too, is walking about! Younger brother,
what are you doing?" But he received no answer. Suddenly
this man spoke, "Oh, my poor children! They must be very
hungry." Trickster plied him with many questions. Indeed he
made quite a nuisance of himself with his questions. Yet not
once did he receive an answer. Trickster now saw the man do
as follows. It so happened that he was near a knoll. He took
his club, struck the knoll and, to Trickster's surprise, killed a
large, old bear. After this he built a fire and singed the hair off
the bear's body. Then he took a pail which he was carrying
along with him and boiled the bear in it. As soon as it was
cooked he served the meat and spoke again, "Hurry, children,
hurry for you must indeed be very hungry!" Thereupon he

took a wooden bowl, put some soup in it and cooled it. Finally he untied a bladder which he had attached to his belt. In it there were four tiny little children. To these it was that he had been speaking so lovingly.

Then Trickster said, "My, my, younger brother, what fine little children you have!" Thus spoke Trickster. The father of the children let them eat but he was careful not to let them eat very much. When they finished, he put them back again into the bladder and attached it to his belt. After this he broke off some branches, dished out the remaining contents of the kettle and, sitting down, began to eat himself. He ate all in the bowl. Then he drank all the soup that he had cooled in the pail.

Finally, when he was all through, and only then, did he speak to Trickster, "I was busy before, that is why I did not speak to you." Thereupon Trickster replied, "Truly, you have beautiful children, younger brother. Would you not care to entrust two of them to me?" "No, indeed, you would certainly kill them." "No, indeed, younger brother, that is not so," said Trickster, "you exaggerate. I wish merely to have the children as companions. That is why I am asking you to let me have them. I will take care of them in the same manner you have been doing." Thus he continued and finally persuaded the man to let him have two of the children. The father gave him a club, a pail, a bowl, and the bear he had killed. Then he took the bladder that was suspended from his belt and put two of the little children in it. "Now, Trickster, remember, if you kill any of these children you will die. Remember if you kill these little children, no matter where you may be, I will pursue and kill you. Keep what I am giving you and feed these children once a month. Do not change this rule. If you change it in any respect, you will kill them. You have seen what I have done and do you do the same." Thus he spoke and Trickster replied, "My younger brother, you have spoken and I have heard. Just as you have ordered so I will do." Then they separated, each one having a bladder suspended from his belt.

Not long after they had separated, as Trickster was walking along, he suddenly exclaimed to himself, "My, my! My dear little children must be hungry by now. But why waste time talking about it? I will let them have something to eat immediately." He was quite near a knoll, so he took his club, struck it and in this manner killed a large old bear. Then he hurriedly built a fire and singed the hair off the bear. The body he cut up and boiled. As soon as it had begun to boil a little, he dished the meat out, cooled it and when it was cool opened the bladder and said, "My dear little children, I miss them a great deal!" Then he uncovered them and fed them. He filled the wooden bowl high and gave it to them. In spite of all that the man had told him he did many things strictly forbidden to him. After he had done all these prohibited things, he put the children back in the bladder and attached it dangling to his belt.

He had been gathering together pieces of broken wood as he walked along and now he was ready to sit down for his meal. He ate up everything that remained and drank all the soup that was in the pail. Then he proceeded on his journey. All the animals in the world mocked him and called out, "Trickster!"

After a little while he himself got hungry. "The little children were to eat once a month I was told," he thought to himself. But now he himself was hungry. So again he said, "My, my! It is about time for my dear little children to be hungry again. I must get something for them to eat." He immediately searched for a knoll, struck it and killed a bear of enormous size. He then built a fire, singed the hairs off the bear; cut it up and put it on to boil. As soon as it was boiled he dished it out and cooled it quickly. When it was cooled off he took the bladder attached to his belt and opened it. To his surprise the children were dead. "The dear little children! How unfortunate that they have died!"

Just as he said this the father of the children appeared and said, "Well, Trickster, you will die for this! I will kill you, as I said I would if you killed my children." As he approached him, Trickster exclaimed appealingly, "O my younger brother!" However, the man rushed at him so menacingly that Trickster drew back at once and fled from him. He ran with all his speed with the other behind him throwing objects at him which barely missed him. There seemed to be no escape. Only by making sudden and unexpected turns did Trickster escape being struck.

Thus did the man pursue Trickster. In desperation he thought of seeking refuge up in the sky or under the ground, yet he felt that there, too, he would be followed. "Trickster, nowhere, no matter where you flee, will you be able to save your life," shouted the man. "No matter where you go, I will pursue and kill you. So you might as well give up now and be done with it. You are exhausted already as you see. You have nowhere to go. Indeed, you will not be able to find a refuge-place anywhere." Thus spoke the man.

He pursued Trickster everywhere. It was only by adroit dodging that he escaped being hit by objects thrown at him. Then, suddenly, Trickster got frightened. By this time he had run over the whole earth and he was now approaching the place where the sun rises, the end of the world. Toward a pointed piece of land that projected, in the form of a steep wall of rock, into the ocean, toward this he ran. It was the edge of the ocean. He pressed up against it and finally jumped into the water. Right into the middle of the ocean he fell. "Ah, Trickster, you have saved yourself! You were indeed destined to die!" Then the man gave up the pursuit. Trickster uttered an exclamation of heartfelt relief and said to himself, "That such a thing should happen to Trickster, the warrior, I never imagined! Why, I almost came to grief!"

————

There in the water he remained. As he did not however know where to find the shore, he swam along aimlessly. As he was thus moving about aimlessly, he suddenly saw a fish swimming. Him Trickster addressed, "My younger brother, you have always had the reputation of being very clever, would you not tell me where the shore is?" "I do not know, brother, for I have never seen the shore," answered the fish. So Trickster went on again. Soon he came across a catfish and, addressing him, said, "Brother, you have always had the reputation of being clever, do please tell me where the shore is." "I do not know," answered the catfish, "for I have never been anywhere near it, brother." So again Trickster went on. Then he saw another fish, the *nasidjaga*, and Trickster spoke to him, "Brother, you have always been here in these waters; perhaps you would tell me where the shore is, for I cannot find it." "Alas, my brother, never, no, never, do I get anywhere near the shore," the fish answered. And so the situation remained.

Trickster was forced to remain in the water swimming about aimlessly. As he was thus engaged, suddenly he came across a spoonbill catfish and to him he spoke, "Brother, O brother, you have always had the reputation of being clever; perhaps you can tell me where the shore is? I, myself, do not know." "Alas, brother, never indeed do I get anywhere near the shore," answered the spoonbill catfish. So again Trickster had to go on. Soon, unexpectedly, he came upon a yellow catfish. "Brother, O brother, I have been told that you know everything; perhaps you know where the shore is? If you do, please tell me." "Alas, my brother, never indeed, have I been anywhere near the shore," answered the yellow catfish. Again he had to go on. As he swam along, suddenly he came across another fish and said "Brother, O brother, you have always had the reputation of being clever; perhaps you know where the shore is? I am lost, so please tell it to me." "Alas, brother, never, indeed, do I get anywhere near the shore," answered the fish. And thus it continued as he encountered fish upon fish. Of all he made inquiries. There was the *witcugera*, the *hogagira*, the buffalo fish, the red-finned fish, the *hocdjagera*, the *howiregera*, the *homingera*, the *citcgagera*, the *hopagura*, the *wirara*, the *tcatutcgera*, the eel, the bullhead. Every fish imaginable he encountered.

Finally, quite unexpectedly, he came upon the white fish, a whole school of them, and them he addressed, "My younger brothers, I know that nothing is unknown to you; perhaps you know where the shore is? If you do, please tell me, for I myself, do not know." "Why, older brother, the shore is right there, just exactly where you are," answered the fish. And indeed he could see the shore from where he was swimming! It did not take him long to emerge from the water. "Thank you, thank you, younger brothers!" Thus he spoke to the fish. He had actually been swimming along the edge of the ocean right along.

He was very hungry so when he got out of the water he hurriedly made a pail for himself, a clay pail. Then he went back to the edge of the ocean, for he coveted fish, the wonderful man that he was! He wanted to kill one very much. As soon as he saw one come running, he started after it. But it always got away from him. One ran very near him and he hurriedly started after it and dipped the pail in the water. "Ha, ha! From this one I will positively prepare soup for myself," he said. So he built himself a fire, and boiled the water and drank it. "My, my, what fine soup that was! The meat, I imagine, must be just delicious!"

Then he started off and all the way he managed to get fish by dipping his pail into the water and preparing a soup from it. In this manner he filled himself to his utmost capacity. Indeed he made his stomach shine from being distended. Suddenly, he saw a red-finned fish drifting toward the bank. "Well, well, my younger brother, your breathing must be entirely gone! Dead you probably are." Thus he spoke. "Now I will put you aside and you will taste good to me after a while!" So he took it and went inland. There he dug a hole and buried it.

Again he wandered aimlessly about the world. On one occasion he came in sight of the shore of a lake. To his surprise, he noticed that right near the edge of the lake a person was standing. So he walked rapidly in that direction to see who it was. It was someone with a black shirt on. When Trickster came nearer to the lake, he saw that this individual was on the other side of the lake and that he was pointing at him. He called to him, "Say, my younger brother, what are you pointing at?" But he received no answer. Then, for the second time, he called, "Say, my younger brother, what is it you are pointing at?" Again he received no answer. Then, for the third time, he addressed him, again receiving no answer. There across the lake the man still stood, pointing. "Well, if that's the way it's going to be, I, too, shall do that. I, too, can stand pointing just as long as he does. I, too, can put a black shirt on." Thus Trickster spoke.

Then he put on his black shirt and stepped quickly in the direction of this individual and pointed his finger at him just as the other one was doing. A long time he stood there. After a while Trickster's arm got tired so he addressed the other person and said, "My younger brother, let us stop this." Still there was no answer. Then, for the second time, when he was hardly able to endure it any longer, he spoke, "Younger brother, let us stop this. My arm is very tired." Again he received no answer. Then, again he spoke, "Younger brother, I am hungry! Let us eat now and then we can begin again afterward. I will kill a fine animal for you, the very kind you like best, that kind I will kill for you. So let us stop." But still he received no answer. "Well, why am I saying all this? That man has no heart at all. I am just doing what he is doing." Then he walked away and when he looked around, to his astonishment, he saw a tree stump from which a branch was protruding. This is what he had taken for a man pointing at him. "Indeed, it is on this account that the people call me the Foolish One. They are right." Then he walked away.

Again Trickster started out walking along aimlessly. After a while, as he went along, he heard something shrieking in the air. He listened and there to his great amazement was a very large bird flying above him. It was coming straight toward him. Then the thought suddenly struck him that it would be nice to be like this bird. So, when the bird, a turkey-buzzard, came close, Trickster spoke to it, "My, my, my, younger brother! You certainly are a lucky one to have such a fine time! I wish I could be able to do what you are doing." Thus he addressed it. Then, again, he spoke, "Younger brother, you can carry me on your back if you want to, for I like your ways very much." "All right," said the bird. So he got on the bird's back. The bird exerted himself to fly and, after a while, succeeded. They were now high in the air and Trickster chattered contentedly, "My younger brother, it is very pleasant. This is indeed a pleasant time we are having." Then the turkey-buzzard began to fly sideways and Trickster, uneasy, appealed to him in a loud tone of voice, saying, "Be very careful, younger brother, be very careful, for you might drop me." So the bird continued to carry Trickster around properly, and the latter was enjoying himself hugely. The turkey-buzzard, however, was busily looking for a hollow tree. He wanted to play a trick on Trickster. After searching for a while he saw a hollow tree, one entirely without branches. He flew rather close to it and then dropped Trickster right down into it. That is exactly what happened. "Alas! That horrible thing! He is indeed a very wicked being. He has turned the tables on me." Thus Trickster spoke.

———

After a while, he heard echoes sounding like the noise of trees being cut down. "Oh! oh! I wonder whether these are people that I hear. But even if they are I don't suppose that they will come here," he said to himself. Gradually the people came nearer and nearer and soon he could hear them talking. They were women conversing. Thereupon he sang:

"A bob-tailed racoon am I here!"

One of the women heard it and said, "Listen, there is someone here talking." Then again he sang the same thing. Finally, when they came very close, the women said, "Come let us cut it out." So they began to cut him out of the tree. He held his racoon-skin blanket next to the hole and this it was the women saw. Finally the women said, "Ah, it is going to be a fine, large racoon." Hearing this, the so-called racoon spoke to them and said, "As soon as my hiding place has been plugged up by women's clothing, then leave me here and come back after me shortly. I assure you, I am very fat." "Yes, we'll do just that," they answered. So they took off their clothing, plugged up the hole and went home.

Then he came out and went on. When the women returned they found nothing.

As he was running along, he came to a valley. There he heard someone beating a drum, the drumming followed by many war whoops. Somebody there was making a great noise. So loud was this noise that it seemed to reach the skies. "Well, I wonder what these people are up to? I guess I will go over and see for I have not had any fun for a long time. Whatever they are doing, I will join them. If they are going to dance, why I will dance too. I used to be a fine dancer." Thus Trickster spoke. Then, as he walked across the valley, again and again he heard that noise. Everyone was shouting with joy. It was wonderful! "Ah! There must be many people over there," he was thinking to himself. Again he heard them shout and, once again, when the drum was beaten, it seemed as if the heavens would burst asunder. Then again the people gave a tremendous shout. Now he became so anxious to join them that he began to run. The shouting was now quite close to him. Yet he could see no one anywhere. Again he heard the shouting. It was very loud. It sounded as if the sky would burst asunder.

To him it seemed as if, even at that moment, he was walking in the midst of people shouting. Yet he did not see anything. Not far away, however, he saw, lying around, the bones of an animal and, farther still, he saw an object that turned out, on closer inspection, to be an elk's skull. It had many horns branching in every direction. He watched this head quite carefully and then he saw where the noise had come from and where the celebration was taking place. It was in the elk's skull. The head was filled with many flies. They would go inside and then, when they rushed out, they made the noise that he had heard and which he had taken to be shouting. He looked at the flies and he saw that they were enjoying themselves greatly and he envied them.

"Well, I said that I would join in whatever they were doing and I am going to. I wonder what I would have to do in order to join them?" Thus pondered Trickster. Then he said, "Younger brothers, you are certainly having a lot of fun. You surely are doing an important thing. I would very much like to be like one of you. How can I do it? Do show me how I can do it so that I, too, can join you." Thus he spoke. Then they answered him, "Well, there is no difficulty involved. We enter through the neck as you must have seen by this time." Thus they spoke. Then Trickster tried to enter but failed. He wanted very much to enter but he was unable. "How do you manage to get in, my younger brothers?" he asked. Great man that he was, he could not accomplish it, much as he wished to! Then they said to him, "If you wish to come in just say, 'Neck, become large!' and it will become large. In that way you can enter. That is the way we do it." Thus they told him.

So he sat down and said, "Neck, become large!" and the hole in the neck became large. Then he put his head in and entered. He put his head in up to his neck. All the flies ran away and the opening into which he had thrust his head became small again. Thus he was held fast. He tried to free himself exerting all his power but it was of no avail. He could do absolutely nothing. He was unable to free his head from the skull of the elk. When he realized that nothing could be done, he went down to the stream wearing the skull. He had long branching antlers, for he was wearing an elk's skull. When he came to the river he walked along the edge, and as he went along he came to a place inhabited by human beings. There he waited until night. The next morning he did the following. As soon as the people came to get water from the river, he stretched himself out and lay there with his racoon-skin blanket, quite a fear-inspiring object to look upon. His whole body was covered with the racoon-skin blanket and he had long branching horns on his head.

Early in the morning a woman came for water and saw him. She started to run back but he said to her, "Turn back; I will bless you!" So she turned back and when she got there, he said to her, "Now, go home. Get an axe and bring it over here. Then use all the offerings that are customary, of which your relations will tell you. If you strike the top of my head with the axe, you will be able to use what you find therein as medicine and obtain anything that you wish. I am an elk-spirit. I am blessing this village." Thus he spoke to her. Then he continued, "I am one of the great spirits living in these waters."

So the woman went home and when she got there she told all the people what had happened. "There is a water-spirit at the place where we dip for water who blessed me. He told me that he had a 'medicine-chest' in the box that he carried and that if we brought an axe and suitable offerings, placed them there and then split his head open, what we found within his skull we could use for making various medicines." Thus she spoke.

Thereupon the people went to the river with their various offerings and, sure enough, there they found him, quite fear-inspiring to look upon. The offerings—red feathers, white deer skin, and red-yarn belts—they brought in great quantities. After they had placed all these things before him, they selected a man who was to take the axe. He struck the skull and split it open and behold! there they found Trickster laughing at them. He arose and said, "A nice headdress I have been wearing but now you have spoiled it!" Then he laughed uproariously. When he got up the people said, "It is Trickster!" However he spoke to them and said, "Inasmuch as you have made these offerings to me they will not be lost. For whatsoever be the purpose for which you use this head, that purpose will be accomplished." So then they made themselves various medicinal instruments and afterwards found that they were efficacious. Then Trickster left and continued wandering.

In the village in which they were staying the people owned two horses. The coyote had married into the village. Trickster was very desirous of revenging himself on him and coyote, on his side, had the desire of playing a trick on Trickster. However, Trickster discovered what coyote intended to do and did not like it. "Many times he has done me wrong and I let it pass, but this time I am not going to overlook it. This time I intend to play a trick on him," said Trickster.

Then he went into the wilderness, to the place where the

horses belonging to the village generally stayed. He found one of them and put it to sleep. When he was quite certain that the horse was asleep he went after mouse and said, "Say, there is an animal dead here. Go to coyote and tell him, 'My grandson, there is an animal dead over there and I was unable to move him. It is over there near the village. Pull it to one side and then we will be able to have it to ourselves.' " Mouse was quite willing and ran over to coyote and said, "Grandson, I know you are very strong and therefore I wish to tell you that there is an animal over there near the village, lying dead. If you will push it aside, it will be good. I wanted to do it myself but I was unable to pull it and that is why I have come over here to tell you, for I have compassion upon you." Coyote was very much delighted and went to the place. Trickster, at the same moment ran back to the village and waited for them. The mouse and the coyote soon arrived and the mouse tied the horse's tail to the coyote. Tightly she tied the two together. Then the coyote said, "I am very strong and I know that I can pull this animal. The animal that I am about to pull is called an elk or a deer." "Well, everything is ready, you may pull it now," said the mouse. "All right," said the coyote and tried to pull it. He woke the horse up and it got scared. Up it jumped and finding an animal tied to its tail it got even more frightened and began racing at full speed. Coyote was pulled along looking as though he were a branch being dragged. The horse ran to the village and Trickster shouted at the top of his voice, "Just look at him, our son-in-law, coyote! He is doing something very disgraceful. Look at him!" Then all the people ran out and there, unexpectedly, they saw coyote tied to the horse's tail bouncing up and down. The horse finally went to its master and there it was caught. They untied the coyote and his mouth just twitched as he sat up. He was very much ashamed. He did not even go back to his lodge. He left the village and was no more seen. He had a wife and many children but those too he left. From that time on he has not lived among people. If a person sees him anywhere he is ashamed of himself and when one gets very close to him his mouth twitches. He is still ashamed of what happened to him long ago.

Trickster stayed at that village for a long time and raised many children. One day he said, "Well, this is about as long as I will stay here. I have been here a long time. Now I am going to go around the earth again and visit different people, for my children are all grown up. I was not created for what I am doing here."

Then he went around the earth. He started at the end of the Mississippi River and went down to the stream. The Mississippi is a spirit-village and the river is its main road. He knew that the river was going to be inhabited by Indians and that is why he traveled down it. Whatever he thought might be a hindrance to the Indians he changed. He suddenly recollected the purpose for which he had been sent to the earth by Earthmaker. That is why he removed all those obstacles along the river.

As he went along he killed and ate all those beings that were molesting the people. The waterspirits had their roads only at a short distance below the surface of the earth so he pushed these farther in. These waterspirit roads are holes in the rivers. Many rivers have eddies which it would be impossible for a boat to pass through and these he pushed farther down into the ground.

He went all over the earth, and one day he came to a place where he found a large waterfall. It was very high. Then he said to the waterfall, "Remove yourself to some other location for the people are going to inhabit this place and you will annoy them." Then the waterfall said, "I will not go away. I chose this place and I am going to stay here." "I tell you, you are going to some other place," said Trickster. The waterfall, however, refused to do it. "I am telling you that the earth was made for man to live on and you will annoy him if you stay here. I came to this earth to rearrange it. If you don't do what I tell you, I will not use you very gently." Then the waterfall said, "I told you when I first spoke to you that I would not move and I am not going to." Then Trickster cut a stick for himself and shot it into the falls and pushed the falls onto the land. . . . Then he left and went first into the ocean and then up to the heavens.

Under the world where Earthmaker lives, there is another world just like it and of this world, he, Trickster, is in charge. Turtle is in charge of the third world and Hare is in charge of the world in which we live.

(Winnebago, Central Woodland)

23
Hare's Adventures

One day, the child, Hare, went farther than usual and suddenly came upon a being walking on two legs. It seemed so
weak that he expected it to fall over at any moment. Hare ran
ahead of it and waited. When it came near he blew at it,
thinking he could thus blow it over but he did not succeed.
Again and again he blew at it, in each case without avail. The
fourth time he did it, the being walking on two legs became
aware of something white (namely the hare) and shot at it
with an arrow. Hare cried out in pain as he was hit and ran
home to his grandmother. She pulled the arrow out of him
and said, "It must have been one of your uncles and you must
have been annoying him for otherwise he would not have
shot at you." "What great people my uncles must be," said
Hare, "for he shot me when I was quite some distance away
from him." "Grandson, that is the weapon these people use
for killing game," she said. Hare then seized the arrow and
took great care of it.

The next morning he took the arrow and went out to the
woods. There he came upon an elk. He put the arrow in the
fork of a tree in line with the elk and said, "Arrow, go!" Then
he pushed it but it would not go. He flattered it and tried
again to direct it but it would not go. So he went home and
spoke thus to his grandmother: "Grandmother, the arrow
would not obey me and so I could not kill an elk. I pleaded
with it repeatedly but still it would not go." Then, his grandmother said, "My grandson, that is not the way hunters act.

They send the arrow off by means of an object they call a bow." "Make me one, grandmother," said Hare. Thereupon the old woman answered, "Grandson, the human beings make bows out of a substance called the hickory tree. The hickory tree is a tree with smooth bark. If you will go and get some of it for me, I will make a bow for you." "There are many such trees right around here, grandmother," said Hare, and ran out to fetch some. He came back soon with some poplar twigs. "This is not the right kind; this is what we call poplar," said the old woman. Then he went out again and brought some hickory twigs and with these she made a bow. Then she told him the kind of wood to use for arrows. In order to get these he had to go out four times before he brought the right ones.

After she had made some arrows for him she sent him out to get some turkey feathers, telling him what they were like. He went out and caught a turkey alive and when he brought it home he asked her what he was to use with which to kill it. She answered, "a frog tree." Then he went in search of a frog tree. But he only succeeded in obtaining one after four attempts. The old woman then told him that she would have to have some glue and that he could get some from the vertebrae of a long fish, the sturgeon. After four attempts he got some. Then the old woman completed making the arrows for him. He immediately took them and began shooting holes into the lodge.

The next morning he went out hunting and, on the way, came across an animal, a straight-horned elk. He shot it and told it to fall down dead on the outskirts of Sharp-elbow's village. Then Hare came home. When he got home he told his grandmother that he had shot an elk in the belly and that he would go and trail it in the morning.

The next morning he took up the trail and finally came to the place where he had ordered it to fall dead. To his surprise it had been dressed and nothing remained of it except the entrails. So he continued on to the village. There, on the outskirts, lived an old woman. Her lodge he entered. "Grandmother," he said, "yesterday I wounded an elk and my coming here is for the purpose of finding it." "Grandson, this is what happened. A great number of warriors were gathered here. In fact they have just left. When they were here a wounded elk with an arrow in it came by and fell dead just outside the lodge. All of them tried to pull it out. I, too, went over, but you might know that a person like myself would hardly get permission from those people to try to pull it out. So all I could obtain was a little blood. From that blood I am now making some soup." Thus she spoke.

"Grandmother, who pulled out my arrow?" inquired Hare. "Grandson, the chief, Sharp-elbow, pulled it out." "That arrow is mine. It is a fear-inspiring thing. I don't suppose you have any such arrows around here?" "Indeed it was fearful. However, let me see one of your arrows," said the old woman. So he took one out. As he did so the entire lodge became filled with lightning. "Oh, grandson, put your arrow back in its quiver," she said. "Now I know," she added, "that the arrow which was pulled out was yours." "Grandson," so she continued, "I have made some broth from the blood of the elk and here is a little for you." After she had handed him a bowl of soup, she said, "You can warm your arrow-quiver with it." "Very well," said Hare, and was about to pour it into his arrow-quiver when the old woman stopped him and said, "Grandson, I did not mean that. I meant that you can warm up your ribs with it." So he took it up again and was about to draw up his clothes and pour it upon his ribs. But, again she stopped him, and it was only at the fourth time that he finally did what she meant and drank it.

"Now, grandmother, let my friend go after my arrow."
"Oh, grandson, he will be killed," she answered. "I thought
you said he was a chief? How, therefore, can he fight and be
killed?" Then turning to the young man in question he said,
"Young man, go after my arrow." Now the young man was a
grandson of the old woman and yet there he was calling him
friend!

The friend started out and when he came to the village of
Sharp-elbow, he said, "My friend wants his arrow." But the
chief did not so much as answer him and so he went back
without it. "Go again," said Hare. Three times he went back.
At the fourth time Sharp-elbow said, "There it is, take it!" The
friend went forward and tried to reach it but the chief, Sharp-
elbow, using his elbows, thereupon tore him open and said to
his attendants, "Hang him up to dry. I will soon make a nice
meal of him."

Someone ran over to the old woman and told her that her
grandson had been killed by Sharp-elbow. Then Hare, who
was present, turned to the old woman and said, "I thought
you told me your grandson was a chief and yet this man says
he has been killed. However, I will now go over and see this
chief Sharp-elbow myself. Have you a whetstone, grandmother?" "Here is one," she said. Taking it, he went over to
Sharp-elbow's village, and when he got there he found the
chief in a long lodge full of the best-looking women, all of
them his wives. "Say," said Hare, "I understand my arrow is
here. I sent for it before but I hear that you are killing people
on account of it, killing them because they ask for it. So,
therefore, I thought I would come for it myself."

The arrow was stuck between the lodge wall and the poles,
just above where Sharp-elbow was lying. "There it is," said
the latter. "You can get it." Then Hare put the whetstone
between himself and the chief and bent forward to reach it. As
he did so Sharp-elbow jabbed him with his elbow but he
struck the whetstone and broke his elbow. "Well," said Hare,

"if you have any more jabs just come on with them." "All right," said Sharp-elbow and jabbed him with his other elbow. But he broke that too so then he used his knees and broke those. "Well!" said Hare, "now I will show you how to kill people." So he shot him, the arrow going clear through him. Then Hare took his friend down from where he had been hung and, throwing the body aside, said, "What makes you go to sleep here? I sent you for my arrow, not for you to go to sleep." Immediately his friend came to life again and went home. Hare then took his arrow down and told the people to burn up all of Sharp-elbow's children and all of his wives who were pregnant. This they did. Then the people said to Hare, "We would like to go over to the place where you live and take care of the village for you." But Hare answered, "No. You can have your old chief back again and live as you used to for I have killed the one who was abusing you." So the people thanked him and Hare returned home.

When he got home he said to his grandmother, "Listen, grandmother, I went to trail my elk, but Sharp-elbow's people had already taken it when I reached his lodge. What a great man Sharp-elbow is!" "Yes," said his grandmother, "Sharp-elbow is one of the great spirits." "Oh," said Hare, "I think you make too much of him, for I took grandmother's whetstone and let him break his elbows on it and then I killed him and had him burnt up." "Oh, you big-eyed, big-eared, big-footed creature, you have killed my brother," she exclaimed. "Oh, you evil old woman, I will shoot you and burn you up also," he answered. "Ah, grandson, I only said that in fun. I am really glad, for my brother had been abusing your uncles and aunts and you did a good thing in killing him."

One day, shortly after this, Hare said, "Grandmother I am going over to my grandfather, the bear, to pay him a visit." "It is good, my dear grandson," said the old woman, "you may go and he will be glad to see you." "Grandmother, I will take a sack of acorns for him." "All right, you may do so." So Hare went off. When he got there he placed the sack of acorns outside of the lodge and went in. "Oh, my dear grandson," exclaimed the bear, "so you have come at last!" "Yes, I have come," said Hare, "and I have brought you a sack of acorns which I have left outside." After a while, Bear walked out and came back and asked, "Grandson, where is the sack?" "Why, I left it right outside," said Hare. After the bear had come back for the fourth time Hare went out to show him but it was nowhere to be found. So he said, "Grandfather, you have eaten it up already." "Grandson, I found a half of an acorn out here and I took it up with my left hand and ate it. Is that what you meant? You said that you had brought a sack full of acorns and it is for that I have been looking," said the bear. "Yes, that is what I meant," said Hare, "and it was a sack full."

The Bear spoke to Hare saying, "Grandson, I don't suppose you have had your meal yet." So he put a kettle full of fat to boil and soon Hare had a big meal.

After the meal Hare suddenly said, "Grandfather, you have been living here a long time, have you not?" "Yes, grandson, I have been living here for a long time." "Don't you ever get frightened?" "No, grandson, I am not afraid of anything."[1] Then, after a pause, Hare said again, "Grandfather, do you know that the country is full of wars?" "Yes, indeed, grandson, but I am not afraid of it." "Well, grandfather," said Hare, "I feel rather uneasy about it and that is why I am talking in this way." Then Hare went out and scattered dung all around the lodge, stuck feathers in the dung and told the piles of dung to give the war-whoop early in the morning. Thereupon he went back and said, "Grandfather, aren't you

---

[1] Bear is supposed to be fearless and, as we shall see later on, originally unwilling to permit himself to be used by man for food.

really afraid of this?'' and he took out one of his arrows and showed it to him. "No," said he. Then he took out another, but it was only when he took out the fourth one that the old man said, "Grandson, put that away quickly for of that one I am afraid."

As soon as night came they went to bed. During the night the old man had a nightmare and yelled in his sleep, so Hare called to him, "Grandfather, wake up, you are having a nightmare!" The old man woke up immediately and said, "Grandson, I had a nightmare. I dreamt that I was shot under the arm with an arrow like the one that you showed me." "Now, there you are, grandfather. I told you that I have been feeling uneasy ever since I came here this evening."

Early in the morning the war-whoop was given outside. It was so loud that it seemed as if the enemy were right upon them. "Oh!" said Hare and rushed outside and waited at the door for the old man to come out. When finally he did come Hare took aim and shot him under the arm, the arrow going clear through him.

Then Hare went home and said, "Grandmother, what a great man my grandfather is!" "Yes," she said, "he is one of the great spirits." "Oh, I wouldn't praise him too much. This is what I did to him." And he went through the motions of shooting. "Oh, you big-eyed, big-eared, big-footed creature, you must have killed my brother," she exclaimed. "Well, you evil old woman, I will wait for you outside and shoot you under the arm just as I did him," said Hare. "Oh, I only said that in fun. Actually I am glad, for now we shall have plenty of fat to eat," she said.

They went over to pack the bear home. They skinned him and cut him into pieces. After this was done Hare said, "Grandmother, will you carry the head?" "No," said the old woman, "I am not a man that I should be carrying heads. He who does the killing is the one to carry the head." "Well, grandmother, will you carry the hind end then?" "How could

I carry a bear's hind end with such a back as I have?"[2] "Well, grandmother, will you carry the ribs then?" "If I were to do that I am sure my ribs would grow long." Thereupon she began to sing:

"*Grandson, that I will pack;*
Grandson, that I will pack."

Then she began to dance. However, he let her pack the hind end[3] and she started off right away. He followed her but after a short time she turned off the road. Then he began to think and wonder what grandmother was up to by turning off the road.

Now the old woman had a deer skin with her which she took up to the top of a hill and upon which she slid down, pack and all. When at last she got home she told her grandson that she had lost her way and had finally turned up in a village where they had used her pack for a ball. That is why it was dirty she explained. Continuing, she said that one of Hare's friends, who happened to be there, finally got the pack back for her, whereupon she came home. Then Hare asked, "Grandmother, was it my friend *Gicoknuxgiga*?" "Yes, yes, grandson, he is the one I mean." Now there really was no such person. Hare had merely invented the name to see what she would say and to find out what she had been doing all the time. Suddenly Hare said, "Grandmother, you must cook for yourself and I will do the same."[4] So they each cooked for themselves and each had plenty of fat to eat.

---

[2] Here for the first time Earth is referring to herself as the earth proper and not as an anthropomorphic being.

[3] This incident has been greatly foreshortened in this version. To understand it, it should be remembered that Bear is really Earth's husband. Hare gives her the hind end, which she really wishes but which she is afraid to ask for because it contains Bear's penis.

[4] The reason for this is not clear. Winnebago women and men always eat together. It is best to take Hare's statement as a stylistic device for

"Grandmother," said Hare one day, "I am going over to visit my uncles." "You may go," said she. So he left. On the way he came to a large river and he shouted, "Crabs, come here!" Immediately a large number of crabs came over to him. He caught a large one and said, "Lend me your boat!" Then he skinned the crab and, turning up its tail for a sail, exclaimed, "Blow me across!" Then the wind changed and blew him across the river. So he sailed across in the shell of a crab, singing as he proceeded.

Finally he got to the other side and, pulling his boat to one side, went on. Soon he came to a lodge and this he entered. Those within said, "Haho! Our grandson has come." Those within were people without bodies; they consisted only of heads. All in turn stopped to greet him and said, "Our grandson must indeed be hungry." So they boiled something for him to eat. They boiled bear ribs with corn. This he ate and he thought it delicious, and he ate a great deal of it. In eating he used a knife that they handed him. He would first bite a piece of meat and then cut it off. Suddenly, accidently, he cut a slit in his nose. Blowing his nose, he yelled with pain. "Our grandson has cut himself. Give him another knife." He was very much pleased with the new knife they gave him and did not seem to mind the fact that he had cut himself.

Soon Hare went home. When he got home his grandmother said, "Oh, my grandson has disfigured himself while visiting." Ever since that time, even to the present day, whenever anyone goes visiting his uncles, they say he is going somewhere to slit his nose.

---

indicating that he is beginning to realize that she is a woman who has not yet reached her climacteric and that he, now grown up, should not be living with her anymore. In fact there is still a saying among Winnebago—"Stay home with your grandmother!"—which implies that a man is still not grown up.

———————

One day Hare went to visit his uncles, or, as they say, to slit his nose. He came to another long lodge full of the same kind of people as before, that is, people without bodies. He went in and again they said, "Oh, our grandson must be hungry. Let us boil something for him." This they did and he ate large quantities of food again.

When he was finished, the heads said, "Let us eat our grandson. He looks so good to eat." So they closed the doors and blocked all other possible places of exit. However, he spied a little opening somewhere and ran out there. One of the heads said, "He has gone. Run after him!" So they all pursued him. One in particular followed behind the rest, shouting, "Catch him! Catch him!" Finally Hare got tired so he ran up a tree. But the head behind came up and said, "Gnaw the tree down!" So all encircled the tree and began to gnaw it down. But Hare got away again. "Oh, he has got away again!" So they spurred one another on again and shouted, "Chase him!" They chased him and he ran up a tree again. Again they gnawed it down and again he ran away. Now, for the fourth time, he went up a tree and again they began to gnaw at it. Suddenly one of them said, "Ah, it is bitter! It is bitter!" and began to spit. But another one spurring the others on to continue, said, "Wait till he comes down." So they stopped and waited till he would have to come down. Finally Hare got tired of staying there and pondered to himself, "What shall I do now?" Then he began to sing:

"Bodiless heads, I want to go by,
  Go to sleep! Go to sleep!"

And so they said to one another, "Our grandson says sleep, so let us sleep." Thus they spoke, but they only feigned sleep. Finally, however, after he had sung the song four times, they actually went to sleep. Then he came down very quietly. However, when he reached the ground he made a noise. Immediately he rushed away. The heads woke up and shouted, "Our grandson has gone!" and gave pursuit. Hare kept running until he came to a creek over which he jumped. Then the pursuers yelled, "He has jumped across!" and the last one exclaimed, "Jump across too!" So all tried. But they failed and fell into the creek and were drowned. Hare thereupon chased the dead heads down the stream, built a fire and threw them in. Then he took some stones, ground their remains very finely and threw them back into the creek saying, "You tried to abuse people. From now on the people will call you fast-fish and when they step into the water you will nibble at their ankles."

Then he went home to his grandmother. She scolded him again, as on former occasions and said that the heads were her brothers. But he told her that he would make fast-fish of her and, thereupon, as always, she said that she was really glad that he killed them because they were abusing his uncles and aunts and that he had done a good thing.

One day as Hare was wandering about in his usual fashion he heard something moving, so he went to see what it was. It turned out to be a tall man with a big cane and very small about the waist. Hare thought to himself, "How is it he does not break in two?" So he blew upon him and tried to break him in two. After each attempt—he tried three times and failed—he would run ahead and wait for him and blow upon him again. The fourth time the tall being noticed a small white object sitting on the ground, so he placed his cane upon it and smashed it flat.

As Hare did not come home for some time, his grandmother began to worry and went to look for him, saying to herself, "That grandson of mine must be up to one of his foolish tricks again." Finally she came to where the tall being was living and said, "Brother, my little grandson is missing and I am looking for him. He is full of mischief so I thought you might, without intending it, have harmed him in some way. That is why I have come to see you." Then she went over to the place where he had placed his cane and she found him. "Oh, you big-eyed, big-eared, big-footed, slit-nosed, evil creature, get up and come away from here," and she took him by the arm and lifted him up. "Grandmother," replied Hare, "I was sitting far away from this being yet he could do this to me. What a great man grandfather must be!"

The next morning Hare started for the home of his grandfather but this time he made himself very tall, even taller than the tall being itself. He also took a cane with him. Then he went looking around for him. The cane that he took along was a big cedar tree which he had pulled up by the roots. Finally, as he came near the tall being, that one was singing:

"Who is the equal of me? Who is the equal of me?"

Then Hare likewise began to sing the same song. The big being saw him and exclaimed, "Well, well! In all my life I have never met anyone equal to me.[5] Where did you come from?" he asked. Then Hare asked the same question. "Well," said the other, "come, we will walk together." So they walked on together and as they were going, Hare placed his cane on the tall being and smashed him to pieces. And the tall being turned out to be a large ant. Then Hare spoke, "You were trying to abuse human beings and, for that reason, you will henceforth remain down there close to the earth and the people will tramp on you."

---

[5] Boasting is always used as a literary device to imply weakness. Every Winnebago would know immediately that the tall being is going to be killed because he has boasted of his powers.

Then Hare proceeded on until he came to a nice road. "Now, what kind of a being constructed this road?" he mused. "Whoever it was I am going to catch him," he thought to himself. So he took some nettle-weeds and made a trap. The next morning he went to inspect it but whoever it was who was walking along this road had broken the trap. So he made another trap, this time of sinew strings and, in the morning, he went over to inspect it, but again the trap was broken. So, again, he made some rope, this time out of basswood bark, and set up another trap. But that which he was trying to trap broke away again. Finally, he went to his grandmother and said, "Grandmother, will you make me a very strong rope?" She agreed and took some of her hair and braided it. With this he made another trap. The next morning he heard someone singing:

> "Hare, come and untie me; Hare, come untie me!
> Hare, what will the people do?
> Hare, come and untie me! Hare, come and untie me!"

"So you are up to your tricks again, you big-eyed, big-eared, big-footed, slit-nosed, evil object," exclaimed his grandmother and, taking a wooden poker, she hit him with it. Hare cried out in pain, "Ouch! Ouch!" and ran away in the direction of the singing. When he got near he saw something shining. He tried in vain to untie it, so he went home, borrowed a knife from his grandmother, and ran over to the object he had captured. When he got there he closed his eyes and, running up as far as he could, cut it loose. However, his buttocks got thoroughly scorched and sore for what he had trapped was the sun. And thus he was scorched by the sun.[6]

---

[6] This gives Hare his final physical trait, his "burnt buttocks."

———

One night something came outside of Hare's lodge and sang:

"You who live with your grandmother, wherever you go I will trail you with dogs and crush you in my mouth."

"Oh, grandmother, we are in a bad fix! Now we shall surely die," said Hare. "Only if we hide between the reed mattings will we be able to save ourselves."

"You who live with your grandmother, if you hide between the reed matting I shall find your scent with dogs," it sang.

"Oh, grandmother, we are in bad straits! The only place we can hide is under the floor mattings."

But the being sang:

"You who live with your grandmother, if you hide under the floor mattings, I will find your scent with dogs."

"Grandmother, we are in bad straits! Let us change ourselves into charcoal and sit under the embers," said Hare.

"If you change yourselves into charcoal and sit under the embers, I will find your scent with dogs."

"Oh, grandmother, the only thing we can do now is to go up to the sky."

But the being said:

"If you go up to the sky, I will find your scent with dogs."

Then Hare got angry and went outside and looked around the lodge but could see nothing. So finally he asked his grandmother whether she knew where the being was who was speaking and she answered, "Over in that direction." He looked in the direction she mentioned and there he saw a little frog. "So it is you? How come you to speak in such a fashion?" he said and smashed it with his club. Yet he wondered how it had been possible for such an object to speak in this way, so he opened its mouth and he saw that it had long teeth. Then he knocked out the frog's teeth, burned the frog up and exclaimed, "You talk too

much and you scare people. Henceforth you will never be
able to harm anyone."

In the morning Hare departed taking with him a hoe and
an axe. He came to the place where beaver lived with his wife
and his children. "Oh, my grandson has come!" said beaver.
"Well, I am sure you did not come without some reason. You
certainly must have something on your mind." "Yes, grandfather, I have. I wish to stay here overnight with you and I want
you to take me across the lake in the morning. That is why I
have come. For your troubles let me present you with a hoe."
"Oh, grandson, this is good. I have been carrying people
across for nothing and was glad to do it. This is indeed great.
In the morning I will take you across." Then said the female
beaver to her husband, "Old man, I think I had better take
our grandson across. He has treated us well and you are so
slow that I think it would suit him better if I carried him."
"All right," said the male beaver.

Then the old couple said to their children, "Which one of
you shall our grandson eat?" "Me," they all shouted in
chorus. Thus the young beavers shouted. There were some
very large ones and some very small ones so they selected one
of medium size and boiled it for Hare. When it was cooked
they put it on a plate and gave it to him. Then the old man
said, "Grandson, do not separate the bones but pick the meat
off very carefully and leave all the sinews attached." Hare,
however, was very hungry and was therefore not very careful
and broke some of the sinews of the forepaw. When he had
finished, the bones were taken and put into the water. Soon
after, a beaver came in crying, and when his parents looked
him over they noticed that the sinews in his forepaw were
broken and that he was crying for that reason. And this is why
beavers' paws to this day are drawn together. "I am very
sorry," said Hare, "I really tried to be careful."

Then Hare began to think of the work he had been appointed to do and he said to himself, "By this time I must have trampled upon all the evil beings that were abusing my uncles and aunts. That is what Earthmaker sent me here for." Thus he mused. "My uncles and my aunts will now live on earth as peacefully as myself since the evil beings that had been abusing them are now all dead." Then all the birds that had been abusing the human beings he pushed higher up into the sky and he trampled upon and pushed under the earth the evil spirits who had inhabited the earth so that the people might live in peace here.

Then he thought to himself, "Those that I have destroyed were all bad animals. Now I must prepare some for the human beings to eat." So he decided to ask the animals themselves. All the animals gathered together, not only the large, but also the small ones such as the racoon, the skunk, the muskrat, etc. Then Hare got some oil ready. With this he intended to fatten those animals that were going to be used as food by human beings.

He asked the elk first, "How do you wish to live?" and the elk answered, "I wish to live by eating human beings." So Hare asked him to show his teeth. The elk's teeth were long and fearful to look at. "Well," said Hare, "if that is your wish, take this and eat it. It is blood from the human beings." He then gave him some kind of fruit which was so sour that it knocked the elk's teeth out so that only a few of his front teeth remained. The elk wept and said, "Hare, I take back what I said for I was wrong. Your uncles may kill me and eat me at all times." Then Hare thanked him and said, "It is good."

Then the bear was asked. He said that the people could eat him, but that they would have to fast before they could find him and that if anyone tried to find him without having fasted, he would not be successful for he would hold his paw in front of the opening of his cave. "Bear, you ought not to have said that," said Hare, "because my uncles have medicine that is hard to overcome and they have dogs that can find anything."

Then the horse was asked, and he answered, "Hare, with your uncles and aunts will I ever live and I will work for them. Whenever they have anything heavy I will carry it for them." Hare thanked him, saying, "It is good. You have proved yourself a chief and you will be a great help to the people throughout their life. I knew that you would do something good because you are good-natured. For that reason I dreaded to ask you for fear you would say that you wanted to eat human beings. It is good."

Then Hare said to the other animals, "All of you who said you were willing to be eaten by the people may take a bath in this oil. You will be fattened thereby." So the bear went in first and rolled himself in the oil, and that is why he is so fat. Then the mink jumped in. But they said he was not fit to be eaten so they fished him out and wrung him dry and that is why he is so thin and lean. Then the skunk jumped in without being asked and they said that he was not fit to be eaten because he smelled so badly. But the skunk said that if anyone ate him when he was ill he would drive away his illness. So Hare told the people to let him alone if he kept his promise to prolong their life. They all agreed to let him go. Then all the rest who were to be eaten took their baths of fat and went to their homes.

After they were gone Hare took two dogs and prepared some medicine for he was going to show how bears were to be hunted. Then he heated some stones and prepared a vapor-bath lodge. When it was ready he entered it and "concentrated his mind."[7] He had also boiled a kettle of dried corn. In

---

[7] This was necessary for all ceremonies but vital in this particular one. In the preparations for the bear hunt it was customary for the prospec-

the vapor-bath he communed with all the trees and with all the grasses and weeds, with all the stones and even with the earth.[8] Then he poured tobacco as an offering and began the ceremony. He started to sing and asked his grandmother to sing along with him to which she consented. He began with blackroot songs.[9] As he proceeded the bear was seized with a great desire to look toward him. Finally the bear did look in his direction. Then Hare cried out, "Grandmother, someone's mind came to me just then!" But she only said, "Try harder!" The bear in his cave could hear all that was said and regretted what he had said on the previous day.

Then Hare started to sing again. This time he sang his dancing songs. Again the bear was seized with a strong desire to dance. Finally he was seized with the desire to come over to where Hare was singing for the savor of the food was so enticing that he wished to have some of it.[10] Thus he could not keep his mind off Hare and the things Hare was doing.

Now Hare knew when the bear's mind[11] had come to him. At that very point he stopped and retired. The next morning he took his dogs and started for the bear. "In this direction there came a mind to me last night," he said to his dogs, urging them on. Finally one of the dogs started toward the bear's cave. The bear put his paw in front of the opening in order to close it but the dog found it anyhow.

tive hunter to gaze steadily at the burning firelogs until he thought an ember had flown toward him. This ember flying toward him was interpreted as the bear's mind turning in his direction. *Cf.* the end of this paragraph.
[8] He means the objects on the earth.
[9] These songs were generally connected with the curing of disease. Some, however, had magical efficacy.
[10] One of the theories of why animals are killed is that they, more particularly their spirit-prototypes, cannot resist the odor of the food sacrificed to them. The same theory holds for the granting of power from the spirits. Only there it is the tobacco whose fumes the spirits cannot resist.
[11] *Cf.* note 7.

Finally the bear said to the dog, "Don't tell on me and I will give you a piece of fat." But the dog began to bark at him and the other dog came up. They both tried to pull him out of the cave. Just then Hare came up. "Oh, it is good," he said. "Now come out of this cave," and poked the bear until he came out. Thereupon Hare pointed an arrow toward his side. The bear looked askance, expecting to be shot at any minute. But Hare instead ran around ahead of him and waited for him while the dogs chased him. Indeed Hare stood there and waited. Finally the bear came right up to where Hare was standing. Again Hare pointed his arrow at him, right at his heart. The bear now stopped running and simply walked. But Hare did not shoot him. The fourth time Hare pointed the arrow at the bear he began to cry. Then Hare began to make fun of him saying, "So you are not as strong-minded as you thought? Why do you cry? This is what human beings could do to you even if you did put your paw in front of the opening of your cave. If I had been one of your uncles you would have been killed by this time." "Hare," said the bear, "you were right. From now on the people will be able to find me whenever they hunt for me." Then the bear gave himself up, and the people to this day do as Hare did when they want to hunt bears.

Then Hare thought to himself, "Now the people will live peacefully and forever." But the old woman, his grandmother, said, "Grandson, your talk makes me sad. How can your uncles and aunts live as you do? Earthmaker did not make them thus. All things have to have an end. You yourself in your travels around the country must have seen trees fallen to the ground. That is their end; that is their death. And when you see grass lying flat on the ground, it is dead. Everything will have an end. I also will have an end as I am created that way." Then Hare looked in her direction and some of her back caved in just as the earth does sometimes. That was what he saw. And he saw people cave in with the earth. "Grandson, thus it is," said the old woman, "I have been created small and if all the people live forever they would soon fill up the earth. There would then be more suffering than there is now, for some people would always be in want of food if they multiplied greatly. That is why everything has an end." Then Hare thought for a long time. "A good thing I had obtained for my uncles and my aunts but my grandmother has spoiled it." So he felt sad, took his blanket, covered himself with it, lay down in the corner and wept.

He wept for the people. It was at that time that he thought of creating the Medicine Rite.

Now this is the story of the origin of the Medicine Rite. All the birds of the air that were evil or abusive of man Hare killed. That is why it is said that he pushed them farther up into the air. All the evil spirits that lived on this earth he also killed so that they could not roam over it any longer. This is what is meant when they say that he tramped down deeper those whose backs protruded through the earth.

Hare was sent by Earthmaker to teach the people on earth a better life. That is why he roamed over its whole extent. As soon as he grew up he did away with all the things that were hindrances to the people.[12]

The reason why he called the people his uncles and aunts is because his mother was a human being. He was born of an earthly and human mother and that is why he called the men uncles. As his mother was a virgin he could have no other relatives except these uncles and aunts. All the hares are sons of all the women and the nephews of the men.

(Winnebago, Central Woodland)

---

[12] This and what follows is the comment of the narrator.

24
The Deceived Blind Men

There was a large settlement on the shore of a lake, and among its people were two very old blind men. It was decided to remove these men to the opposite side of the lake, where they might live in safety, as the settlement was exposed to the attack of enemies, when they might easily be captured and killed. So the relations of the old men got a canoe, some food, a kettle, and a bowl, and started across the lake, where they built for them a wigwam in a grove some distance from the water. A line was stretched from the door of the wigwam to a post in the water, so that they would have no difficulty in helping themselves. The food and vessels were put into the wigwam, and after the relations of the old men promised them that they would call often and keep them provided with everything that was needful, they returned to their settlement.

The two old blind men now began to take care of themselves. On one day one of them would do the cooking while the other went for water, and on the next day they would change about in their work, so that their labors were evenly divided. As they knew just how much food they required for each meal, the quantity prepared was equally divided, but was eaten out of the one bowl which they had.

Here they lived in contentment for several years; but one day a Racoon, which was following the water's edge looking for crawfish, came to the line which had been stretched from the lake to the wigwam. The Racoon thought it rather curious to find a cord where he had not before observed one, and wondered to himself, "What is this? I think I shall follow this cord to see where it leads." So he followed the path along which the cord was stretched until he came to the wigwam. Approaching very cautiously, he went up to the entrance, where he saw the two old men asleep on the ground, their heads at the door and their feet directed toward the heap of hot coals within. The Racoon sniffed about and soon found there was something good to eat within the wigwam; but he decided not to enter at once for fear of waking the old men; so he retired a short distance to hide himself and to see what they would do.

Presently the old men awoke, and one said to the other, "My friend, I am getting hungry; let us prepare some food." "Very well," replied his companion, "you go down to the lake and fetch some water while I get the fire started."

The Racoon heard this conversation, and, wishing to deceive the old man, immediately ran to the water, untied the cord from the post, and carried it to a clump of bushes, where he tied it. When the old man came along with his kettle to get water, he stumbled around the brush until he found the end of the cord; then he began to dip his kettle down upon the ground for water. Not finding any, he slowly returned and said to his companion, "We shall surely die, because the lake is dried up and the brush is grown where we used to get water. What shall we do?"

"That cannot be," responded his companion, "for we have not been asleep long enough for the brush to grow upon the lake bed. Let me go out to try if I cannot get some water." So taking the kettle from his friend he started off.

So soon as the first old man had returned to the wigwam, the Racoon took the cord back and tied it where he had found it, then waited to see the result.

The second old man now came along, entered the lake, and getting his kettle full of water returned to the wigwam, saying as he entered, "My friend, you told me what was not true. There is water enough; for here, you see, I have our kettle full." The other could not understand this at all and wondered what had caused the deception.

The Racoon approached the wigwam and entered to await the cooking of the food. When it was ready, the pieces of meat, for there were eight of them, were put into the bowl and the old men sat down on the ground facing each other, with the bowl between them. Each took a piece of meat, and they began to talk of various things and were enjoying themselves.

The Racoon now quietly removed four pieces of meat from the bowl and began to eat them, enjoying the feast even more than the old blind men. Presently one of them reached into the bowl to get another piece of meat, and finding that only two pieces remained, said, "My friend, you must be very hungry to eat so rapidly; I have had but one piece, and there are but two pieces left."

The other replied, "I have not taken them, but suspect you have eaten them yourself"; whereupon the other replied more angrily than before. Thus they argued, and the Racoon, desiring to have more sport, tapped each of them on the face. The old men, each believing the other had struck him, began to fight, rolling over the floor of the wigwam, upsetting the bowl and the kettle, and causing the fire to be scattered. The Racoon then took the two remaining pieces of meat and made his exit from the wigwam, laughing ha, ha, ha, ha; whereupon the old men instantly ceased their strife, for they now knew they had been deceived. The Racoon then remarked to them, "I have played a nice trick on you; you should not find fault with each other so easily." Then the Racoon continued his crawfish-hunting along the lake shore.

(Menominee, Central Woodland)

25
The Theft from the Sun

Once Old Man was traveling around, when he came to the Sun's lodge, and the Sun asked him to stay awhile. Old Man was very glad to do so.

One day the meat was all gone, and the Sun said, "Kyi! Old Man, what say you if we go and kill some deer?

"You speak well," replied Old Man. "I like deer meat."

The Sun took down a bag and pulled out a beautiful pair of leggings. They were embroidered with porcupine quills and bright feathers. "These," said the Sun, "are my hunting leggings. They are great medicine. All I have to do is to put them on and walk around a patch of brush, when the leggings set it on fire and drive the deer out so that I can shoot them."

"Hai-yah!" exclaimed Old Man. "How wonderful!" He made up his mind he would have those leggings, if he had to steal them.

They went out to hunt, and the first patch of brush they came to, the Sun set on fire with his hunting leggings. A lot of white-tail deer ran out, and they each shot one.

That night, when they went to bed, the Sun pulled off his leggings and placed them to one side. Old Man saw where he put them, and in the middle of the night, when everyone was asleep, he stole them and went off. He traveled a long time, until he had gone far and was very tired, and then, making a pillow of the leggings, lay down and slept. In the morning, he heard someone talking. The Sun was saying, "Old Man, why are my leggings under your head?" He looked around, and saw he was in the Sun's lodge, and thought he must have wandered around and got lost, and returned there. Again the Sun spoke, and said, "What are you doing with my leggings?" "Oh," replied Old Man, "I couldn't find anything for a pillow, so I just put these under my head."

Night came again, and again Old Man stole the leggings and ran off. This time he did not walk at all; he just kept running until pretty near morning, and then lay down and slept. You see what a fool he was. He did not know that the whole world is the Sun's lodge. He did not know that, no matter how far he ran, he could not get out of the Sun's sight. When morning came, he found himself still in the Sun's lodge. But this time the Sun said: "Old Man, since you like my leggings so much, I will give them to you. Keep them." Then Old Man was very glad and went away.

One day his food was all gone, so he put on the medicine leggings and set fire to a piece of brush. He was just going to kill some deer that were running out when he saw that the fire was getting close to him. He ran away as fast as he could, but the fire gained on him and began to burn his legs. His leggings were all on fire. He came to a river and jumped in, and pulled off the leggings as soon as he could. They were burned to pieces.

Perhaps the Sun did this to him because he tried to steal the leggings.

(Blackfoot, Plains)

26
The Eye Juggler

There was a man who could send his eyes out of his head, on the limb of a tree, and call them back again by saying "Eyes, hang upon a branch." White-man saw him doing this, and came to him crying; he wanted to learn this too. The man taught him, but warned him not to do it more than four times in one day. White-man went off along the river. When he came to the highest tree he could see, he sent his eyes to the top. Then he called them back. He thought he could do this as often as he wished, disregarding the warning.

The fifth time his eyes remained fastened to the limb. All day he called, but the eyes began to swell and spoil, and flies gathered on them. White-man grew tired and lay down, facing his eyes, still calling for them, though they never came; and he cried. At night he was half asleep, when a mouse ran over him. He closed his lids that the mice would not see he was blind, and lay still, in order to catch one.

At last one sat on his breast. He kept quiet to let it become used to him, and the mouse went on his face, trying to cut his hair for its nest. Then it licked his tears, but let its tail hang in his mouth. He closed it and caught the mouse. He seized it tightly, and made it guide him, telling it of his misfortune. The mouse said it could see the eyes, and they had swelled to an enormous size. It offered to climb the tree and get them for him, but White-man would not let it go. It tried to wriggle free, but he held it fast. Then the mouse asked on what condition he would release it, and White-man said, only if it gave him one of its eyes. So it gave him one, and he could see again, and let the mouse go. But the small eye was far back in his socket, and he could not see very well with it.

A buffalo was grazing nearby, and as White-man stood near him crying, he looked on and wondered. White-man said: "Here is a buffalo, who has the power to help me in my trouble." So the buffalo asked him what he wanted. White-man told him he had lost his eye and needed one. The buffalo took out one of his and put it in White-man's head. Now White-man could see far again. But the eye did not fit the socket; most of it was outside. The other was far inside. Thus he remained.

(Cheyenne, Southeast)

27
The Big Turtle's War Party

A turtle went on the warpath, and as he went along, he met Coyote, who said: "And where are you going, Grandson?" The turtle said: "I am on the warpath." Coyote said: "Where are you going?" "I am going to a camp where there are many people," said the turtle. "Let me see you run," the turtle said. Coyote ran. The turtle said: "You cannot run fast; I do not want you."

The turtle went on, and he met a fox. "Well, brother," said the fox, "where are you going?" "I am going on the warpath," said the turtle. "Where are you going?" said the fox. "I am going where there are many people," said the turtle. "Can I go with you?" said the fox. The turtle said: "Let me see you run." The fox ran, and he went so fast that the turtle could hardly see him. The turtle said: "You cannot run fast; I do not want you."

The turtle then went on, and a hawk flew by him, and the hawk heard the turtle say: "I am on the warpath; I am looking for people to join me." The hawk said: "Brother, what did you say?" "I am on the warpath," said the turtle. "Can I join you?" said the hawk. "Let me see you fly your best," said the turtle. The hawk flew so fast that the turtle could not see him for a while. When the hawk came back, the turtle said: "You cannot fly fast; I do not want you."

Again the turtle went on, and kept on saying: "I am on the warpath; I am looking for people to join me." A rabbit jumped up and said: "Can I go along?" "Let me see you run," said the

turtle. The rabbit ran, and ran fast. The turtle said: "You cannot run fast; I do not want you."

The turtle went on, saying: "I am looking for people to join
me." Up jumped a flint knife and said: "Brother, can I join
you?" "You may if you can run fast," said the turtle; "let me
see you run." The knife tried to run, and could not. "You will
do," said the turtle; "come with me."

They went on, and the turtle was saying: "I am looking for
people to go on the warpath with me." Up jumped a hair-
brush. "What did you say?" said the brush. "I am on the
warpath," said the turtle. "Can I go along?" said the brush.
The turtle said: "Let me see you run." The brush tried to run,
but could not. The turtle said: "You will do; come with us."

They went on, and the turtle was saying: "I am on the
warpath; I am looking for people to join me." Up jumped an
awl, and it said: "Can I join you?" The turtle said: "Let me see
you run." The awl tried to run, but could not. "You will do,"
said the turtle; "come with us."

So the four went on, and they came to a big camp, and the
turtle sent the knife into camp. The knife went into camp, and
one man found it, took it home, and while trying to cut meat
the man cut his fingers, and threw the knife at the doorway.
The knife went back to the turtle and said: "I was picked up,
and while the man was trying to cut meat, I cut his hand and
he threw me at the doorway, so I came back."

The turtle said: "Very well. Now, Brush, you go and see
what you can do." So the brush went into camp, and a young
girl picked it up and commenced to brush her hair. The brush
pulled the girl's hair out, so that the girl threw the brush at
the doorway, and it came back. It said: "Brother Turtle, there
is a young girl who has lovely hair. She used me on her head,
and I pulled on her hair, so that she threw me away. See I
have her hair here." "Well done," said the turtle.

"Now, Awl, go and be brave," said the turtle. The awl

went into camp, and an old woman picked it up. She began to sew her moccasins, and all at once she stuck the awl in one of her fingers. The woman threw it away, and it came back and said: "Brother Turtle, I hurt a woman badly. She was using me while she was sewing her moccasins, and I stuck one of her fingers; she threw me away." "Well done, brothers, now it is my turn," said the turtle.

The turtle went into camp, and people saw him and said, "What does this mean? Look at Turtle; he is on the warpath. Let us kill him." So they took him, and people said: "Let us spread hot coals and put him in there." "All right," said the turtle, "that will suit me for I will spread out my legs and burn some of you." People said: "True, let us then put a kettle over the fire, and when the water boils let us put him in." The turtle said: "Good! Put me in, and I will scald some of you." People said: "True! Let us throw him into the stream." The turtle said: "No, do not do that. I am afraid, I am afraid!" People said: "He is afraid of water; let us throw him in there." But the turtle hallooed the more: "I am afraid! Do not throw me in the water!" So the people threw the turtle in the water. The turtle came up to the surface and said: "I am a cheat. Heyru! Heyru!" poking his tongue out.

The people picked up the knife, awl, and brush and used them. The turtle stayed in the water, and every time the people went to the water, Turtle would say: "I cheated you; water is my home." People would throw stones at it, and it would dive.

(Pawnee, Plains)

28
The Sky Has Fallen

One time Coyote met a turkey, and he ran and said, "Oh, the sky is falling." The turkey said, "How do you know?" "A piece of the sky has fallen on my tail. I am looking for a hole to save myself." "May I go with you?" "Come along." As they went they met a rooster, and Coyote said, "Oh, the sky is falling." The rooster said, "How do you know?" "A piece of the sky has fallen on my tail. I am looking for a hole to save myself." "May I go with you?" "Come along." As they went they met a lamb, and Coyote said, "Oh, the sky is falling." The lamb said, "How do you know?" "A piece of the sky has fallen on my tail. I am looking for a hole to save myself." "May I go with you?" "Come along." As they went they met a goose, and Coyote said, "Oh, the sky is falling." The goose said, "How do you know?" "A piece of the sky has fallen on my tail. I am looking for a hole to save myself." "May I go with you?" "Come along." At last they came to a hole and, when they were in, Coyote turned and ate the goose. When he had eaten the goose he ate the lamb. When he had eaten the lamb he ate the rooster. When he had eaten the rooster he ate the turkey. He ate them all up and these animals never came out any more.

⊞

(Zuni, Southwest)

III
Tales of Heroes, Supernatural Journeys, and Other Folktales

29
The Sun Tests
His Son-in-law

In a place on Bellacoola River, there used to be a salmon weir. A chief and his wife lived at this place. One day the wife was cutting salmon on the bank of the river. When she opened the last salmon, she found a small boy in it. She took him out and washed him in the river. She placed him nearby, entered the house, and said to the people, "Come and see what I have found in my salmon!" She had a child in her house, which was still in the cradle. The little boy whom she had found was half as long as her forearm. She carried him into the house, and the people advised her to take good care of him. She nursed him with her own baby. When the people were talking in the house, the baby looked around as though he understood what they were saying. On the following day the people were surprised to see how much he had grown, and in a few days he was as tall as any ordinary child. Her own baby also grew up with marvelous rapidity. She gave each of them one breast. After a few days they were able to walk and to talk.

➤ *When they mature, the boys go on adventures.*

The two young men were passing by the houses, and looked into the doorways. There was a house in the center of this town; there they saw a beautiful girl sitting in the middle of the house. Her hair was red and reached down to the floor.

She was very white. Her eyes were large and as clear as rock crystal. The boy fell in love with the girl. They went on, but his thoughts were with her. The Salmon boy said, "I am going to enter this house. You must watch closely what I do, and imitate me. The Door of this house tries to bite everyone who enters." The Door opened, and the Salmon jumped into the house. Then the Door snapped, but missed him. When it opened again, the boy jumped into the house. They found a number of people inside, who invited them to sit down. They spread food before them, but the boy did not like their food. It had a very strong smell and looked rather curious. It consisted of algae that grow on logs that lie in the river.

When the boy did not touch it, one of the men said to him, "Maybe you want to eat those two children. Take them down to the river and throw them into the water, but do not look." The two children arose, and he took them down to the river. Then he threw them into the water without looking at them. At the place where he had thrown them down, he found a male and a female salmon. He took them up to the house and roasted them. The people told him to preserve the intestines and the bones carefully. After he had eaten, one of the men told him to carry the intestines and the bones to the same place where he had thrown the children into the water. He carried them in his hands, and threw them into the river without looking. When he entered the house, he heard the children following him. The girl was covering one of her eyes with her hands. The boy was limping, because he had lost one of his bones. Then the people looked at the place where the boy had been sitting, and they found the eye, and a bone from the head of the male salmon. They ordered the boy to throw these into the water. He took the children and the eye and the bone, and threw them into the river. Then the children were hale and well.

After a while the youth said to his Salmon brother, "I wish to go to the other house where I saw the beautiful girl." They went there, and he said to his Salmon brother, "Let us enter. I should like to see her face well." They went in. Then the man arose, and spread a caribou blanket for them to sit on, and the people gave them food. Then he whispered to his brother, "Tell the girl I want to marry her." The Salmon boy told the girl, who smiled, and said, "He must not marry me. Whoever marries me must die. I like him, and I do not wish to kill him; but if he wishes to die, let him marry me."[1]

The woman was the Salmonberry Bird. After one day she gave birth to a boy, and on the following day she gave birth to a girl. She was the daughter of the Spring Salmon.

After a while the girl's father said, "Let us launch our canoe, and let us carry the young man back to his own people." He sent a messenger to call all the people of the village; and they all made themselves ready, and early the next morning they started in their canoes. The young man went in the canoe of the Spring Salmon, which was the fastest. The canoe of the Sockeye Salmon came next. The people in the canoe of the Calico Salmon were laughing all the time. They went up the river; and a short distance below the village of the young man's father they landed, and made fast their canoes. Then they sent two messengers up the river to see if the people had finished their salmon weir. Soon they returned with information that the weir had been finished. Then they sent the young man and his wife, and they gave them a great many presents for the young man's father.

The watchman who was stationed at the salmon weir saw two beautiful salmon entering the trap. They were actually the canoes of the salmon; but they looked to him like two

---

[1] At this point of the tale comes the adventure with the dangerous woman who killed all her husbands by means of her toothed vagina. The hero grinds off her teeth by means of a stone. *Cf.* tale 3.

salmon. Then the watchman put the traps down over the
weir, and he saw a great many fish entering them. He raised
the trap when it was full, and took the fish out. The young
man thought, "I wish he would treat me and my wife carefully"; and his wish came true. The man broke the heads of
the other salmon, but he saved the young man and his wife.
Then he carried the fish up to the house and hung them over
a pole.

During the night the young man and his wife resumed
their human shape. The youth entered his father's house. His
head was covered with eagle down. He said to his father, "I
am the fish whom you caught yesterday. Do you remember
the time when you lost me? I have lived in the country of the
Salmon. The Salmon accompanied me here. They are staying
a little farther down the river. It pleases the Salmon to see the
people eating fish." And, turning to his mother, he continued,
"You must be careful when cutting Salmon. Never break any
of their bones, but preserve them, and throw them into the
water." The two children of the young man had also entered
into the salmon trap. He put some leaves on the ground,
placed red and white cedar bark over them, and covered them
with eagle down, and he told his mother to place the Salmon
upon these.

As soon as he had given these instructions, the Salmon
began to come up the river. They crossed the weir and entered
the traps. They went up the river as far as Stuick, and the
people dried the Salmon according to his instructions. They
threw the bones into the water, and the Salmon returned to
life, and went back to their own country, leaving their meat
behind. The Cohoes Salmon had the slowest canoe, and
therefore he was the last to reach the villages. He gave many
presents to the Indians. He gave them many-colored leaves,
and thus caused the leaves of the trees to change color in the
autumn.

Now all the Salmon had returned. The Salmonberry Bird

and her children had returned with them. Then the young man made up his mind to build a small hut, from which he intended to catch eagles. He used a long pole, to which a noose was attached. The eagles were baited by means of Salmon. He spread a mat in his little house, and when he had caught an eagle he pulled out its down. He accumulated a vast amount of down. Then he went back to his house and asked his younger brother to accompany him. When they came to the hut which he had used for catching eagles, he gave the boy a small staff. Then he said to him, "Do not be sorry when I leave you. I am going to visit the Sun. I am not going to stay away a long time. I stayed long in the country of the Salmon, but I shall not stay long in heaven. I am going to lie down on this mat. Cover me with this down, and then begin to beat time with your staff. You will see a large feather flying upward, then stop." The boy obeyed, and everything happened as he had said. The boy saw the feather flying in wide circles. When it reached a great height, it began to soar in large circles, and finally disappeared in the sky. Then the boy cried and went back to his mother.

The young man who had ascended to heaven found there a large house. It was the House of Myths. There he resumed his human shape and peeped in at the door. Inside he saw a number of people who were turning their faces toward the wall. They were sitting on a low platform in the rear of the house. In the right-hand corner of the house he saw a large fire and women sitting around it. He leaned forward and looked into the house. An old woman discovered him, and beckoned him to come to her. He stepped up to her, and she warned him by signs not to go to the rear of the house. She said, "Be careful! The men in the rear of the house intend to harm you." She opened a small box and gave him the bladder of a mountain goat, which contained the cold wind. She told him to open the bladder if they should attempt to harm him. She said that if he opened it, no fire could burn him. She told him that the men were going to place him near the fire, in order to burn him; that one of them would wipe his face, then fire would come forth from the floor, scorching everything. The old woman told him everything that the people were going to do. Now the man in the rear of the house turned round. He was the Sun himself. He was going to try the strength of the visitor. When he saw the young man, he said to the old woman, "Did anybody come to visit you? Let the young man come up to me. I wish him to sit down near me." The young man stepped up to the Sun, and as soon as he had sat down, the Sun wiped his face and looked at the young man (he had turned his face while he was wiping it). Then the young man felt very hot. He tied his blanket tightly round his body and opened the bladder which the woman had given him. Then the cold wind that blows down the mountains in the winter was liberated, and he felt cool and comfortable. The Sun had not been able to do him any harm. The old man did not say anything, but looked at his visitor.

After a while he said, "I wish to show you a little underground house that stands behind this house." They both rose and went outside. The small house had no door. Access was had to it by an opening in the center of the roof, through which a ladder led down to the floor. Not a breath of air entered this house. It was made of stone. When they had entered, the Sun made a small fire in the middle of the house; then he climbed up the ladder and closed the door, leaving his visitor inside. The Sun pulled up the ladder, in order to make escape impossible. Then the house began to grow very hot. When the boy felt that he could not stand the heat any longer, he opened the bladder, and the cold wind came out; snow began to fall on the fire, which was extinguished; icicles began to form on the roof, and it was cool and comfortable inside. After a while the Sun said to his four daughters, "Go to the little underground house that stands behind our house, and sweep it," meaning that they were to remove the remains of the young man whom he believed to be burned. They obeyed at once, each being eager to be the first to enter. When they opened the house, they were much surprised to find icicles hanging down from the roof.

When they were climbing down the ladder, the youth arose and scratched them. The youngest girl was the last to step down. The girls cried when the youth touched them, and ran away. The Sun heard their screams, and asked the reason. He was much surprised and annoyed to hear that the young man was still alive. Then he devised another way of killing his visitor. He told his daughters to call him into his house. They went, and the young man reentered the House of Myths. In the evening he lay down to sleep. Then the Sun said to his daughters, "Early tomorrow morning climb the mountain behind our house. I shall tell the boy to follow you." The girls started while the visitor was still asleep. The girls climbed up to a small meadow which was near a precipice. They had taken the form of mountain goats. When the Sun saw his daughters on the meadow, he called to his visitor, saying, "See those mountain goats!" The young man arose when he saw the mountain goats. He wished to kill them. The Sun advised him to walk up the right-hand side of the mountain, saying that the left-hand side was dangerous. The young man carried his bow and arrow. The Sun said, "Do not use your own arrows! Mine are much better." Then they exchanged arrows, The Sun giving him four arrows of his own. The points of these arrows were made of coal.

Now the young man began to climb the mountain. When he came up to the goats, he took one of the arrows, aimed it, and shot. It struck the animals, but fell down without killing it. The same happened with the other arrows. When he had spent all his arrows, they rushed up to him from the four sides, intending to kill him. His only way of escape was in the direction of the precipice. They rushed up to him, and pushed him down the steep mountain. He fell headlong, but when he was halfway down he transformed himself into a ball of bird's down. He alighted gently on a place covered with many stones. There he resumed the shape of a man, arose, and ran into the house of the Sun to get his own arrows. He took them, climbed the mountain again, and found the mountain goats on the same meadow. He shot them and killed them, and threw them down the precipice; then he returned. He found the goats at the foot of the precipice and cut off their feet. He took them home. He found the Sun sitting in front of the house. He offered him the feet, saying, "Count them and see how many I have killed." The Sun counted them, and now he knew that all his children were dead. Then he cried, "You killed my children!" Then the youth took the bodies of the goats, fitted the feet on, and threw the bodies into the little river that was running past the place where they had fallen down. Thus they were restored to life. He had learned this art in the country of the Salmon. Then he said to the girls, "Now run to see your father! He is wailing for you." They gave him a new name, saying, "He has restored us to life." The boy followed them. Then the Sun said, when he entered, "You shall marry my two eldest daughters."

On the next morning the people arose. Then the Sun said to them, "What shall I do to my son-in-law?" He called him and said, "Let us raise the trap of my salmon weir." They went up to the river in the Sun's canoe. The water of the river was boiling. The youth was in the bow of the canoe, while the Sun was steering. He caused the canoe to rock, intending to throw the young man into the water. The water formed a small cascade, running down over the weir. He told the young man to walk over the top of the weir in order to reach the trap. He did so, walking over the top beam of the weir. When he reached the baskets, the beam fell over, and he himself fell into the water. The Sun saw him rise twice in the whirlpool just below the weir. When he did not see him rise again, he turned his canoe, and thought, "Now the boy has certainly gone to Nuskyakek." The Sun returned to his house, and said to his daughters, "I lost my son-in-law in the river. I was not able to find him." Then his daughters were very sad.

When the boy disappeared in the water, he was carried to Nuskyakek; and he resumed the shape of a salmon while in the water, and as soon as he landed he resumed human shape and returned to his wife. The Sun saw him coming and was much surprised. In the evening they went to sleep. On the following morning the Sun thought, "How can I kill my son-in-law?" After a while he said to him, "Arise! We will go and split wood for fuel." He took his tools. They launched their canoe and went down the river to the sea. When they reached there, it was perfectly calm. There were many snags embedded in the mud in the mouth of the river, some of which were only half-submerged. They selected one of these snags a long distance from the shore and began to split it. Then the Sun intentionally dropped his hammer into the water, and thought at the same time, "Do not fall straight down, but fall sideways, so that he will have much difficulty in finding you." Then he sat down in his canoe and said, "Oh! I lost my old hammer. I had it at the time when the Sun was created." He looked down into the water and did not say word. After a while he said to the young man, "Do you know how to dive? Can you get my hammer? The water is not very deep here." The young man did not reply. Then the Sun continued, "I will not go back without my hammer." Then the boy said, "I know how to dive. If you so wish, I will try to get it." The Sun promised to give him supernatural power if he was able to bring the hammer back. The youth jumped into the water, and then the Sun ordered the sea to rise, and he called the cold wind to make the water freeze. It grew so cold that a sheet of ice a fathom thick was formed at once on top of the sea. "Now," he thought, "I certainly have killed you!" He left his canoe frozen up in the ice and went home. He said to his daughters, "I have lost my son-in-law. He drifted away when the cold winds began to blow down the mountains. I have also lost my little hammer." But when he mentioned his hammer, his daughters knew at once what had happened. The young man found the hammer, and after he had obtained it, he was going to return to the canoe, but he struck his head against the ice and was unable to get out. He tried everywhere to find a crack. Finally he found a very narrow one. He transformed himself into a fish, and came out of the crack. He jumped about on the ice in the form of a fish, and finally resumed his own shape.

He went back to the Sun's house, carrying the hammer. The Sun was sitting in front of the fire, his knees drawn up, and his legs apart. His eyes were closed, and he was warming himself. The young man took his hammer and threw it right against his stomach, saying, "Now take better care of your treasures." The young man scolded the Sun, saying, "Now stop trying to kill me. If you try again, I shall kill you. Do you think I am an ordinary man? You cannot conquer me." The Sun did not reply.

In the evening he said to his son-in-law, "I hear a bird singing which I should like very much to have." The young man asked, "What bird is it?" The Sun replied, "I do not know it. Watch it early tomorrow morning." The young man resolved to catch the bird. Very early in the morning he arose; then he heard the bird singing outside. He knew at once that it was the ptarmigan. He left the house and thought, "I wish you would come down!" Then the bird came down, and when it was quite nearby he shot it. He hit one of its wings, intending to catch it alive. He waited for the Sun to arise. The bird understood what the young man said, who thus spoke: "The chief here wishes to see you. Do not be afraid; I am not going to kill you. The chief has often tried to kill me, but he has been unable to do so. You do not need to be afraid." The young man continued, "When it is dark I shall tell the Sun to ask you to sit near him, and when he is asleep I want you to peck out his eyes." When the Sun arose, the youth went into the house carrying the bird, saying, "I have caught the bird; now I hope you will treat it kindly. It will awaken us when it is time to arise. When you lie down, let it sit down near you; then it will call you in the morning."

In the evening the Sun asked the bird to sit down next to his face. When he was asleep, the bird pecked out his eyes without his knowing it. Early in the morning he heard the bird singing. He was going to open his eyes, but he was not able to do so. Then he called his son, saying, "The bird has blinded me." The young man jumped up and went to his father-in-law and said, "Why did you wish for the bird? Do you think it is good? It is a bad bird. It has pecked out your eyes." He took the bird and carried it outside and thanked it for having done as it was bidden. Then the bird flew away.

When it was time for the Sun to start on his daily course, he said, "I am afraid I might fall, because I cannot see my way." For four days he stayed in his house. He did not eat, he was very sad. Then his son-in-law made up his mind to cure him. He did not do so before, because he wanted to punish him for his badness. He took some water and said to his father-in-law, "I will try to restore your eyesight." He threw the water upon his eyes, and at once his eyes were healed and well. He said, "Now you can see what power I have. While I was in the country of the Salmon, I bathed in the water in which the old Salmon bathed, in order to regain youth; therefore the water in which I wash makes everything young and well." From this time on, the Sun did not try to do any harm to the young man.

Finally he wished to return to his father's village. He left the house, and jumped down through the hole in heaven. His wife saw him being transformed into a ball of eagle down, which floated down gently. Then her father told her to climb as quickly as she could down his eyelashes. She did so, and reached the ground at the same time as her husband. He met his younger brother, who did not recognize him. He had been in heaven for one year.

⊞

(Bellacoola, Northwest Coast)

30
Lodge-boy and Thrown-away

Once upon a time there lived a couple, the woman being pregnant. The man went hunting one day, and in his absence a certain wicked woman named Red-Woman came to the tepee and killed his wife and cut her open and found boy twins. She threw one behind the tepee curtain, and the other she threw into a spring. She then put a stick inside the woman and stuck one end in the ground, to give her the appearance of a live person, and burned her upper lip, giving her the appearance as though laughing.

When her husband came home, tired from carrying the deer he had killed, the saw his wife standing near the door of the tepee, looking as though she were laughing at him, and he said: "I am tired and hungry. Why do you laugh at me?" and pushed her. As she fell backwards, her stomach opened, and he caught hold of her and discovered she was dead. He knew at once that Red-Woman had killed his wife.

While the man was eating supper alone one night a voice said, "Father, give me some of your supper." As no one was in sight, he resumed eating, and again the voice asked for supper. The man said, "Whoever you are, you may come and eat with me, for I am poor and alone." A young boy came from behind the curtain, and said his name was Thrown-behind-the-Curtain. During the day, while the man went hunting, the boy stayed home. One day the boy said, "Father, make me two bows and the arrows for them." His father asked him why he wanted two bows. The boy said, "I want them to change about." His father made them for him, but surmised the boy had other reasons, and concluded he would watch the boy, and on one day, earlier than usual, he left his tepee and hid upon a hill overlooking his tepee, and while there, he saw two boys of about the same age shooting arrows.

That evening when he returned home, he asked his son, "Is there not another little boy of your age about here?" His son said, "Yes, and he lives in the spring." His father said, "You should bring him out and make him live with us." The son said, "I cannot make him, because he has sharp teeth like an otter, but if you will make me a suit of rawhide, I will try and catch him."

One day, arrangements were made to catch the boy. The father said, "I will stay here in the tepee and you tell him I have gone out." So Thrown-behind-the-Curtain said to Thrown-in-Spring. "Come out and play arrows." Thrown-in-Spring came out just a little, and said, "I smell something." Thrown-behind-the-Curtain said, "No, you don't; my father is not home," and after insisting, Thrown-in-Spring came out, and both boys began to play. While they were playing, Thrown-behind-the-Curtain disputed a point of their game, and as Thrown-in-Spring stooped over to see how close his arrow came, Thrown-behind-the-Curtain grabbed him from behind and held his arms close to his sides, and Thrown-in-Spring turned and attempted to bite him, but his teeth could not penetrate the rawhide suit. The father came to the assistance of Thrown-behind-the-Curtain, and the water of the spring rushed out to help Thrown-in-Spring; but Thrown-in-Spring was dragged to a high hill where the water could not reach him, and there they burned incense under his nose, and he became human. The three of them lived together.

One day one of the boys said, "Let us go and wake up Mother." They went to the mother's grave and one said, "Mother, your stone pot is dropping," and she moved. The other boy said, "Mother, your hide dresser is falling," and she sat up. Then one of them said, "Mother, your bone crusher is falling," and she began to arrange her hair, which had begun to fall off. The mother said, "I have been asleep a long time." She accompanied the boys home.

The boys were forbidden by their father to go to the river bend above their tepee; for an old woman lived there who had a boiling pot, and every time she saw any living object, she tilted the kettle towards it, and the object was drawn into the pot and boiled for her to eat. The boys went one day to see the old woman, and they found her asleep, and they stole up and got her pot and awakened the old woman and said to her, "Grandmother, why have you this here?" at the same time tilting the pot towards her, by which she was drowned and boiled to death. They took the pot home and gave it to their mother for her own protection.

The father told them not to disobey him again and said, "There is something over the hill I do not want you to go near." They were very anxious to find out what this thing was, and they went over to the hill, and as they poked their heads over the hilltop, the thing began to draw in air, and the boys were drawn in also; and as they went in, they saw people and animals, some dead and others dying. The thing proved to be an immense alligator-like serpent. One of the boys touched the kidneys of the thing and asked what they were. The alligator said, "That is my medicine; do not touch it." And the boy reached up and touched its heart and asked what it was, and the serpent grunted and said, "This is where I make my plans." One of the boys said, "You do make plans, do you?" and he cut the heart off and it died. They made their escape by cutting between the ribs and liberated the living ones and took a piece of the heart home to their father.

After the father had administered another scolding, he told the boys not to go near the three trees standing in a triangular shaped piece of ground; for if anything went under them, they would bend to the ground suddenly, killing everything in their way. One day the boys went towards these trees, running swiftly and then stopping suddenly near the trees, which bent violently and struck the ground without hitting them. They jumped over the trees, breaking the branches, and they could not rise after the branches were broken.

Once more the boys were scolded and told not to go near a tepee over the hill; for it was inhabited by snakes, and they would approach anyone asleep and enter his body through the rectum. Again the boys did as they were told not to do and went to the tepee, and the snakes invited them in. They went in and carried flat pieces of stone with them, and as they sat down, they placed the flat pieces of stones under their rectums.

After they had been in the tepee a short while, the snakes began putting their heads over the poles around the fireplace and the snakes began to relate stories, and one of them said, "When there is a drizzling rain, and when we are under cover, it is nice to sleep." One of the boys said, "When we are lying down under the pine trees and the wind blows softly through them and has a weird sound, it is nice to sleep." All but one of the snakes went to sleep, and that one tried to enter the rectum of each of the boys and failed, on account of the flat stone. The boys killed all of the other snakes but that one, and they took that one and rubbed its head against the side of a cliff, and that is the reason why snakes have flattened heads.

Again the boys were scolded by their father, who said "There is a man living on the steep-cut bank, with deep water under it, and if you go near it, he will push you over the bank into the water for his father in the water to eat." The boys went to the place, but before going, they fixed their headdresses with dried grass. Upon their arrival at the edge of the bank, one said to the other, "Just as he is about to push you over, lie down quickly." The man from his hiding place suddenly rushed out to push the boys over, and just as he was about to do it, the boys threw themselves quickly upon the ground, and the man went over their heads, pulling their headdress with him, and his father in the water ate him.

Upon the boys' return, and after telling what they had done, their father scolded them and told them, "There is a man who wears moccasins of fire, and when he wants anything, he goes around it and it is burned up." The boys ascertained where this man lived and stole upon him one day when he was sleeping under a tree, and each one of the boys took off a moccasin and put it on, and they awoke him and ran about him, and he was burned and went up in smoke. They took the moccasins home.

Their father told them that something would yet happen to them; for they had killed so many bad things. One day while walking the valley, they were lifted from the earth and, after traveling in midair for some time, they were placed on top of a peak in a rough high mountain with a big lake surrounding it and the Thunder-Bird said to them, "I want you to kill a long otter that lives in the lake; he eats all the young ones that I produce and I cannot make him stop." So the boys began to make arrows, and they gathered dry pine sticks and began to heat rocks, and the long otter came towards them. As it opened its mouth the boys shot arrows into it; and as that did not stop it from drawing nearer, they threw the hot rocks down its throat, and it curled up and died afterwards. They were taken up and carried through the air and gently placed upon the ground near their homes, where they lived for many years.

(Crow, Plains)

31
Dirty-boy

The people of a certain region were living together in a very large camp. Their chief had two beautiful daughters of marriageable age. Many young men had proposed to them, but all had been refused. The chief said, "Whom do my daughters wish to marry? They have refused all the men." Sun and Star, who were brother and sister, lived in the sky and had seen all that had happened. Sun said to his sister, "The chief's daughters have rejected the suits of all our friends. Let us go down and arrange this matter! Let us try these girls!" They made clothes, and at night they descended to earth.

During the darkness they erected a lodge on the outskirts of the camp. It had the appearance of being very old, and of belonging to poor people. The poles were old and badly selected. The covering was tattered and patched, and made of tule mats. The floor was strewn with old dried brush and grass, and the beds were of the same material. Their blankets consisted of old mats and pieces of old robes; and their kettles and cups were of bark, poorly made. Star had assumed the form of a decrepit old woman dressed in rags; and Sun, that of a dirty boy with sore eyes.

On the following morning the women of the camp saw the lodge and peered in. When they returned, they reported, "Some very poor people arrived during the night and are camped in an old mat lodge. We saw two persons inside—a dirty, sore-eyed boy; and his grandmother, a very old woman in ragged clothes."

Now, the chief resolved to find husbands for his daughters. He sent out his speaker to announce that in four days there would be a shooting contest open to all the men, and the best marksman would get his daughters for wives. The young men could not sleep for eagerness. On the third day the chief's speaker announced, "Tomorrow morning everyone shall shoot. Each one will have two shots. An eagle will perch on the tall tree yonder, and whoever kills it shall have the chief's daughters." Coyote was there and felt happy. He thought he would win the prize. On the following morning an eagle was seen soaring in the air, and there was much excitement as it began to descend. It alighted on a tree which grew near one end of the camp. Then the young men tried to shoot it. Each man had two arrows. The previous evening Sun had said to Star, "Grandmother, make a bow and arrows for me." She said, "What is the use? You cannot shoot. You never used bow and arrows." He replied, "I am going to try. I shall take part in the contest tomorrow. I heard what the chief said." She took pity on him, and went to a red willow bush, cut a branch for a bow and some twigs for arrows. She strung the bow with a poor string and did not feather the arrows.

Coyote, who was afraid someone else might hit the bird, shouted, "I will shoot first. Watch me hit the eagle." His arrow struck the lowest branch of the tree and fell down, and the people laughed. He said, "I made a mistake. That was a bad arrow. This one will kill the eagle." He shot, and the arrow fell short of the first one. He became angry and pulled other arrows from his quiver. He wanted to shoot them all. The people seized him and took away his arrows, saying, "You are allowed to shoot twice only." All the people shot and missed. When the last one had shot, Sun said, "Grandmother, lift the door of the lodge a little, so that I can shoot." She said, "First get out of bed." She pulled the lodge mat aside a little, and he shot. The arrow hit the tail of the eagle. The people saw and heard the arrow coming from Dirty-boy's lodge, but saw no one shooting it. They wondered. He shot the second arrow, which pierced the eagle's heart.

Now, Wolf and others were standing near Dirty-boy's lodge, and Wolf desired much to claim the prize. He shouted, "I shot the bird from the lodge door!" and ran to pick it up; but the old woman Star ran faster than he, picked up the bird, and carried it to the chief. She claimed his daughters for her grandson. All the people gathered around and made fun of Dirty-boy. They said, "He is bedridden. He is lousy, sore-eyed, and scabby-faced." The chief was loath to give his daughters to such a person. He knew that Dirty-boy could not walk. Therefore he said, "Tomorrow there shall be another contest. This will be the last one; I cannot break my word. Whoever wins this time shall have my daughters."

He announced that on the morrow each man should set two traps for fishers, an animal very scarce at the place where the camp was located. If anyone should catch a fisher one night, then he was to stay in the mountains another day to catch a second one. After that he had to come back. Those who caught nothing the first night had to come home at once. Only two traps were allowed to each man; and two fishers had to be caught—one a light one, and one a dark one—and both prime skins. When all the men had gone to the mountains, Sun said to his sister, "Grandmother, make two traps for me." She answered, "First get out of bed!" However, she had pity on him and made two deadfalls of willow sticks. She asked him where she should set them; and he said, "One on each side of the lodge door."

On the following morning all the men returned by noon; not one of them had caught a fisher. When Star went out, she found two fine fishers in the traps. Now the chief assembled the men to see if anyone had caught the fishers. He was glad, because he knew that Dirty-boy could not walk; and unless he went to the mountains, he had no chance to kill fishers. Just then the old grandmother appeared, dragging the fishers. She said, "I hear you asked for two fishers; here are two that my grandson caught." She handed them over to him and then left.

Coyote had boasted that he would certainly catch the fishers. When he went up the mountain, he carried ten traps instead of two. He said, "Whoever heard of setting only two traps? I shall set ten." He set them all, remained out two nights, but got nothing.

The chief said to his daughters, "You must become the wives of Dirty-boy. I tried to save you by having two contests; but since I am a great chief, I cannot break my word. Go now, and take up your abode with your husband." They put on their best clothes and went. On the way they had to pass Raven's house, and heard the Ravens laughing inside, because the girls had to marry Dirty-boy. The elder sister said, "Let us go in and see what they are laughing about!" The younger one said, "No, our father told us to go straight to our husband." The elder one went in, and sat down beside Raven's eldest son. She became his wife. Like all the other Ravens he was ugly and had a big head; but she thought it better to marry him than to become the wife of a dirty, sickly boy.

The younger one went on, entered Dirty-boy's lodge, and sat down by his side. The old woman asked her who she was, and why she had come. When the old woman had been told, she said, "Your husband is sick, and soon he will die. He stinks too much. You must not sleep with him. Go back to your father's lodge every evening; but come here in the daytime, and watch him and attend him."

Now, the Raven family that lived close by laughed much at the younger daughter of the chief. They were angry because she had not entered their house and married there, as her elder sister had done. To hurt her feelings, they dressed their new daughter-in-law in the finest clothes they had. Her dress was covered with beads, shells, elk's teeth, and quill work. They gave her necklaces, and her mother-in-law gave her a finely polished celt of green stone [jade] to hang at her belt. The younger sister paid no attention to this, but returned every morning to help her grandmother-in-law to gather fire wood, and to attend to her sick husband.

For three days matters remained this way. In the evening of the third day Sun said to his sister, "We will resume our true forms tonight, so that people may see us tomorrow." That night they transformed themselves. The old mat lodge became a fine new skin lodge, surpassing those of the Blackfeet and other tribes, richly decorated with ornaments, and with streamers tied to the top and painted. The old bark kettle became a bright copper kettle; and new, pretty woven baskets and embroidered and painted bags were in the house. The old woman became a fine-looking person of tall figure, with clothes covered with shining stars. Dirty-boy became a young, handsome man of light complexion. His clothes were covered with shining copper. His hair reached to the ground and shone like the rays of the sun. In the morning the people saw the new lodge and said, "Some rich chief has arrived and has camped where the poor people were. He has thrown them out."

When the girl arrived, she was much surprised to see the transformation. She saw a woman in the door, wearing a long skin dress covered with star pendants, with bright stars in her hair. She addressed her in a familiar voice, saying, "Come in and sit with your husband!" The girl then knew who she was. When she entered, she saw a handsome man reclining, with his head on a beautiful parfleche. His garments and hair were decorated with bright suns. The girl did not recognize him, and looked around. The woman said, "That is your husband; go and sit beside him." Then she was glad.

Sun took his wife to the copper kettle which stood at the door. It contained a shining liquid. He pushed her head into it, and when the liquid ran down over her hair and body, lines of sparkling small stars formed on her. He told her to empty the kettle. When she did so, the liquid ran to the chief's lodge, forming a path, as of gold-dust. He said, "This will be your trail when you go to see your father."

(Okanagon, Plateau)

32
The Jealous Uncle

In a village lived a man known to his neighbors as Unnatural Uncle. When his nephews became a few years old, he would kill them. Two had already suffered death at his hands. After the second had disappeared, his wife went to the mother of the boys and said: "Should another boy be born to you, let us conceal the fact from my husband, and make him believe the child a girl. In that case he will not harm him, and we may succeed in bringing him up."

Not long after the above conversation another nephew was born. Unnatural Uncle, hearing that a child was born, sent his wife to ascertain the sex of the child. She, as had been agreed upon, reported the child a girl. "Let her live," he said.

The two women tended and dressed the boy as if he were a girl. When he grew older, they told him to play with the girls and impressed upon him that he should at all times imitate the ways, attitudes, and postures of the girls, especially when attending to the calls of nature. Unnatural Uncle watched the boy as he was growing up and often wondered at his boyish looks. One day the boy, not knowing that his uncle was about and observing him, raised up his parka, and so exposed his body. "Ah," said Unnatural Uncle to his wife, on reaching home, "this is the way you have fooled me. But I know everything now. Go and tell my nephew I wish to see him." With tears in her eyes the poor woman delivered the message to the nephew, told him of the disappearance of his brothers and of his probable fate. The father and mother of the boy wept bitterly, for they were certain he would never return. The boy himself, although frightened, assured his parents to the contrary and begged them not to worry, for he would come back safe and sound.

"Did my brothers have any playthings?" he asked before going.

He was shown to a box where their things were kept. In it he found a piece of a knife, some eagle down, and a sour cranberry. These he hid about his person, and went to meet his uncle. The latter greeted him and said: "Nephew, let us go and fetch some wood."

When they came to a large forest, the boy remarked: "Here is good wood; let us take some of it and go back."

"Oh, no! There is better wood farther on," said the uncle.

From the forest they stepped into a bare plain. "Let us go back. There is no wood here," called the boy. But the uncle motioned to him to come on, telling him that they would soon find better wood. A little later they came to a big log. "Here is what I want," exclaimed the uncle, and began splitting it. "Here, Nephew, jump in, and get that wedge out," called the uncle to the boy as one of the wedges fell in. When the boy did so, the man knocked out the other wedges; the log closed in on the boy and held him fast. "Stay there!" said Unnatural Uncle, and walked off.

For some time the boy remained in this helpless condition, planning a means of escape. At last he thought of his sour cranberry, and, taking it in his hand, he rubbed with it the interior of the log from edge to edge. The sourness of the berry caused the log to open its mouth, thus freeing him.

On his way back to the village, he gathered a bundle of wood, which he left at his uncle's door, announcing the fact to him: "Here, Uncle, I have brought you the wood." The latter was both surprised and vexed at his failure, and determined more than ever to kill the boy. His wife, however, warned him: "You had better not harm the boy; you have killed his brothers, and if you hurt him, you will come to grief."

"I will kill him, too," he savagely replied.

When the boy reached his father's home, he found them weeping and mourning. "Don't weep!" he pleaded. "He cannot hurt me; no matter where he takes me, I will always come back." In the morning he was again summoned to appear at his uncle's. Before going, he entreated his parents not to feel uneasy, assuring them that no harm would befall him and that he would be back. The uncle called the boy to go with him after some ducks and eggs. They passed several places abounding in ducks and eggs, and each time that the boy suggested, "Let us take these and go back," the uncle replied: "Oh, no! There are better ducks and eggs farther on." At last they came to a steep bluff, and, looking down, saw a great many ducks and eggs. "Go down carefully, Nephew, and gather those ducks and eggs. Be quick, and come back as soon as you can."

The boy saw the trap at a glance and prepared for it by taking the eagle down in each hand, between thumb and finger. As the boy took a step or two downward, the uncle gave him a push, causing him to lose his footing. "He will never come back alive from here," smiled the uncle to himself as he walked back. If he had remained awhile longer and looked down before going, he would have seen the boy descending gently instead of falling. The eagle down had kept him up in the air, and he lighted at his own pleasure safe and sound. After gathering all the ducks and eggs he wanted, he ascended by holding up the down, as before, and blowing under it. Up, up he went, and in a short time stood on the summit. It was night before he sighted his uncle's home. At the door he deposited the birds and eggs, and shouted: "Here, Uncle, are the ducks and eggs."

"What! Back again!" exclaimed the man very much mortified. His wife again pleaded with him to leave the boy in peace. "You will come to grief if you don't," she said. "No; he cannot hurt me," he replied angrily, and spent the remainder of the night thinking and planning.

Although he assured them that he would return, the boy's parents did not have much faith in it; for he found them on his return weeping for him. This grieved him. "Why do you weep?" said he. "Didn't I say I would come back? He can take me to no place from which I cannot come back."

In the evening of the third day the aunt appeared and said that her husband wished the boy. He told his parents not to be disturbed and promised to come back soon. This time the uncle invited him to go with him after clams. The clams were very large, large enough to enclose a man. It was ebb tide, and they found plenty of clams not far from the beach. The boy suggested that they take these and go back, but the uncle put him off with, "There are better clams farther out." They waded into the water, and then the man noticed an extraordinarily large clam. "Take him," he said, but when the boy bent over, the clam took him in. So confident was Unnatural Uncle of his success this time that he uttered not a word, but with a triumphant grin on his face and a wave of his hand he walked away. The boy tried to force the valves apart, but not succeeding, he cut the ligament with his piece of a knife, compelling the clam to open up little by little until he was able to hop out. He gathered some clams and left them at his uncle's door as if nothing had happened. The man, on hearing the boy's voice outside, was almost beside himself with rage. His wife did not attempt to pacify him. "I will say nothing more," she said. "I have warned you, and if you persist in your ways, you will suffer."

The next day Unnatural Uncle was busy making a box.

"What is it for?" asked his wife.

"A plaything for our nephew," he replied.

In the evening the boy was sent for. On leaving his parents

he said: "Do not feel uneasy about my absence. This time I may be away a long time, but I will come back nevertheless."

"Nephew, here is something to amuse you," said his uncle. "Get inside of it, so that I may see whether it fits you." It fitted him; so did the lid, the box; and the rope, the lid. He felt himself borne along, and from the noise of the waves he knew it was to the sea. The box was lowered, and with a shove it was set adrift. It was stormy, the waves beat over the box, and several times he gave himself up as lost. How long he drifted he had no idea; but at last he heard the waves dashing against the beach, and his heart rejoiced. Louder and louder did the joyful peal sound. He gathered himself together for the sudden stop which soon came, only to feel himself afloat again the next moment. This experience he went through several times before the box finally stopped and he realized he was on land once more.

As he lay there, many thoughts passed through his mind: where was he? was any one living there? would he be saved? or would the flood tide set him adrift again? what were his people at home doing? These and many other thoughts passed through his brain, when he was startled by hearing voices, which he recognized a little later as women's. This is what he heard: "I saw the box first," said one. "No, I saw it first," said the other.

"I am sure I saw it before you," said the first speaker again, "and, therefore, it is mine."

"Well, you may have the box, but its contents shall belong to me," replied the other.

They picked up the box and began to carry it, but finding it somewhat heavy and being anxious to know what it contained, they stopped to untie it.

"If there are many things in there, I shall have some of them," said the first speaker, who rued her bargain. The other one said nothing. Great was their surprise on beholding him. He was in turn surprised to see two such beautiful girls, the

large village, the numerous people, and their peculiar appearance, for he was among the Eagle people in Eagle land. The
full-grown people, like the full-grown eagles, had white faces
and heads, while those of the young people, like those of
young eagles, were dark. Eagle skins were hanging about all
over the village; and it amused him to watch some of the
people put on their eagle skins and change to eagles and, after
flying around, take them off and become human beings again.

The girls, being the daughters of the village chief, led the
boy to their father, each claiming him. When he had heard
them both, the chief gave the boy to the older girl [the second
speaker]. With her he lived happily, but his thoughts would
very often wander back to his former home, the people there,
his parents; and the thought of his uncle's cruelty to them
would make his heart ache. His wife noted these spells of
depression and questioned him about them until he told her
of his parents and uncle. She, like a good wife, bade him cheer
up, and then went to have a talk with her father. He sent for
his son-in-law and advised him to put on his [chief's] eagle
skin, soar up high until he could see his village, fly over there,
visit his parents, and bring them back with him. He did as he
was told, and in a short time found himself in the village.
Although he could see all other people, his parents were not
in sight.

This was in the evening. During the night he went out to
sea, brought back a large whale, and placed it on the beach,
knowing that all the villagers would come out for the meat.
The first person to come to the village beach in the morning
was Unnatural Uncle; and when he saw the whale, he
aroused the village, and a little later all, except the boy's father and mother, were there, cutting and storing up the
whale. His parents were not permitted to come near the
whale, and when some of the neighbors left some meat at
their house, Unnatural Uncle scolded, and forbade it being
done again. "I can forgive him the killing of my brothers, the

attempts on my life, but I will avenge his treatment of my parents." With these thoughts in his mind, the eagle left his perch and flew over to the crowd. He circled over its head a little while, and then made a swoop at his uncle. "Ah, he knows that I am chief, and the whale is mine, and he asks me for a piece of meat." Saying this, he threw a piece of meat at the eagle. The second time the eagle descended it was still nearer the man's head, but he tried to laugh it off and turn it to his glory. The people, however, did not see it that way and warned him to keep out of the eagle's clutches, for the eagle meant mischief. When the eagle dropped the third time, it was so near his head that he fell on his face. The fourth time the eagle swooped him and flew off with him.

Not far from the shore was a high and steep rock, and on its summit the eagle put down the man, placing himself opposite. When he had taken off the skin and disclosed himself, he said to his trembling uncle: "I could have forgiven you the death of my brothers, the four attempts on my life, but for the cruel treatment of my parents you shall pay. The whale I brought was for my parents and others, and not for you alone; but you took entire possession of it and would not allow them even to approach it. I will not kill you without giving you a chance for your life. Swim back to the shore, and you shall be spared." As he could not swim, Unnatural Uncle supplicated his nephew to take him back, but the latter, putting on the eagle skin and hardening his eagle heart, clutched him, and from a dizzy height in the air dropped him into the sea.

From the beach the crowd watched the fatal act, understood and appreciated it, and, till it was dark, continued observing from the distance, the eagle. When all had retired, he pulled off the skin, and set out for his father's barrabora.[1] He related to his parents his adventures and invited them to ac-

---

[1] An Eskimo earth lodge, set below the surface of the ground and with a sod or earth dome-shaped roof.

company him to his adopted land, to which they gladly consented. Early in the morning he put on again his skin, and, taking a parent in each claw, flew with them to Eagle land, and there they are living now.

(Kodiak, Eskimo)

33
The Man Who
Acted as the Sun

Once upon a time there lived a woman some distance up Bellacoola River. She refused the offer of marriage from the young men of the tribe, because she desired to marry the Sun. She left her village and went to seek the Sun. Finally she reached his house and married the Sun. After she had been there one day, she had a child. He grew very quickly, and on the second day of his life he was able to walk and to talk. After a short time he said to his mother, "I should like to see your mother and your father"; and he began to cry, making his mother feel homesick. When the Sun saw that his wife felt downcast and that his son was longing to see his grandparents, he said, "You may return to the earth to see your parents. Descend along my eyelashes." His eyelashes were the rays of the Sun, which he extended down to his wife's home, where they lived with the woman's parents.

The boy was playing with the children of the village, who were teasing him, saying that he had no father. He began to cry and went to his mother, whom he asked for bow and arrows. His mother gave him what he requested. He went outside and began to shoot his arrows toward the sky. The first arrow struck the sky and stuck in it; the second arrow hit the notch of the first one; and thus he continued until a chain was formed, extending from the sky down to the place where he was standing. Then he ascended the chain. He found the house of the Sun, which he entered. He told his father that the boys had been teasing him, and he asked him to let him carry the sun. But his father said, "You cannot do it. I carry many torches. Early in the morning and late in the evening I burn small torches, but at noon I burn the large ones." The boy insisted on his request. Then his father gave him the torches, warning him at the same time to observe carefully the instructions that he was giving him in regard to their use.

Early the next morning, the young man started on the course of the sun, carrying the torches. Soon he grew impatient and lighted all the torches at once. Then it grew very hot. The trees began to burn, and many animals jumped into the water to save themselves, but the water began to boil. Then his mother covered the people with her blanket and thus saved them. The animals hid under stones. The ermine crept into a hole, which, however, was not quite large enough, so that the tip of its tail protruded from the entrance. It was scorched, and since that time the tip of the ermine's tail has been black. The mountain goat hid in a cave, hence its skin is perfectly white. All the animals that did not hide were scorched and therefore have black skins, but the skin on their lower side remained lighter. When the Sun saw what was happening, he said to his son, "Why do you do so? Do you think it is good that there are no people on the earth?"

The Sun took him and cast him down from the heavens, saying, "You shall be the mink, and future generations of man shall hunt you."

(Bellacoola, Northwest Coast)

34
Orpheus

The Sun lived on the other side of the sky vault, but her daughter lived in the middle of the sky, directly above the earth, and every day as the Sun was climbing along the sky arch to the west she used to stop at her daughter's house for dinner.

Now, the Sun hated the people on the earth, because they could never look straight at her without screwing up their faces. She said to her brother, the Moon, "My grandchildren are ugly; they grin all over their faces when they look at me." But the Moon said, "I like my younger brothers; I think they are very handsome"—because they always smiled pleasantly when they saw him in the sky at night, for his rays were milder.

The Sun was jealous and planned to kill all the people; so every day when she got near her daughter's house she sent down such sultry rays that there was a great fever and the people died by hundreds, until everyone had lost some friend and there was fear that no one would be left. They went for help to the Little Men, who said the only way to save themselves was to kill the Sun.

The Little Men made medicine and changed two men to snakes, the Spreading-adder and the Copperhead, and sent them to watch near the door of the daughter of the Sun to bite the old Sun when she came next day. They went together and hid near the house until the Sun came, but when the Spreading-adder was about to spring, the bright light blinded him and he could only spit out yellow slime, as he does to this day when he tries to bite. She called him a nasty thing and went by into the house, and the Copperhead crawled off without trying to do anything.

So the people still died from the heat, and they went to the Little Men a second time for help. The Little Men made medicine again and changed one man into a great Uktena and another into the Rattlesnake and sent them to watch near the house and kill the old Sun when she came for dinner. They made the Uktena very large, with horns on his head, and everyone thought he would be sure to do the work, but the Rattlesnake was so quick and eager that he got ahead and coiled up just outside the house, and when the Sun's daughter opened the door to look out for her mother, he sprang up and bit her and she fell dead in the doorway. He forgot to wait for the old Sun, but went back to the people, and the Uktena was so very angry that he went back, too. Since then we pray to the rattlesnake and do not kill him, because he is kind and never tries to bite if we do not disturb him. The Uktena grew angrier all the time and very dangerous, so that if he even looked at a man, that man's family would die. After a long time the people held a council and decided that he was too dangerous to be with them, so they sent him up to Galunlati, and he is there now. The Spreading-adder, the Copperhead, the Rattlesnake, and the Uktena were all men.

When the Sun found her daughter dead, she went into the house and grieved, and the people did not die any more, but now the world was dark all the time, because the Sun would not come out. They went again to the Little Men, and these told them that if they wanted the Sun to come out again they must bring back her daughter from Tsusginai, the Ghost Country, in Usunhiyi, the Darkening Land in the west. They chose seven men to go, and gave each a sourwood rod a hand-breadth long. The Little Men told them they must take a box with them, and when they got to Tsusginai they would find all the ghosts at a dance. They must stand outside the circle, and when the young woman passed in the dance they must strike her with the rods and she would fall to the ground. Then they must put her into the box and bring her back to her mother, but they must be very sure not to open the box, even a little way, until they were home again.

They took the rods and a box and traveled seven days to the west until they came to the Darkening Land. There were a great many people there, and they were having a dance just as if they were at home in the settlements. The young woman was in the outside circle, and as she swung around to where the seven men were standing, one struck her with his rod and she turned her head and saw him. As she came around the second time another touched her with his rod, and then another and another, until at the seventh rod she fell out of the ring, and they put her into the box and closed the lid fast. The other ghosts seemed never to notice what had happened.

They took up the box and started home toward the east. In a little while the girl came to life again and begged to be let out of the box, but they made no answer and went on. Soon she called again and she said she was hungry, but still they made no answer and went on. After another while she spoke again and called for a drink and pleaded so that it was very hard to listen to her, but the men who carried the box said nothing and still went on. When at last they were very near home, she called again and begged them to raise the lid just a little, because she was smothering. They were afraid she was really dying now, so they lifted the lid a little to give her air, but as they did so there was a fluttering sound inside and something flew past them into the thicket and they heard a redbird cry, "Kwish! Kwish! Kwish!" in the bushes. They shut down the lid and went on again to the settlements, but when they got there and opened the box it was empty.

So we know the Redbird is the daughter of the Sun, and if the men had kept the box closed, as the Little Men told them to do, they would have brought her home safely, and we could bring back our other friends also from the Ghost Country, but now when they die we can never bring them back.

The Sun had been glad when they started to the Ghost Country, but when they came back without her daughter she grieved and cried, "My daughter, my daughter," and wept until tears made a flood upon the earth, and the people were afraid the world would be drowned. They held another council, and sent their handsomest young men and women to amuse her so that she would stop crying. They danced before the Sun and sang their best songs, but for a long time she kept her face covered and paid no attention, until at last the drummer suddenly changed the song, when she lifted up her face, and was so pleased at the sight that she forgot her grief and smiled.

(Cherokee, Southeast)

35

The Man Who Brought His Wife Back from Spiritland

There once was a village in which lived a young man. He was married to a woman who was very beautiful and whom he loved intensely. Whatever kind and loving act he could do for his beloved one, he did.

In the course of time his beloved fell sick. All the doctors he could get ahold of he bade come, but it seemed of little avail. Finally he had an extremely holy medicine man come but he, too, could accomplish nothing and his wife died.

Then, at night, they held the ghost-lighting rites[1] [the Four Nights' Wake]. Very many people came for he was a good and kind person and so they came to honor his dead wife. He had always associated in the most hospitable fashion with everyone and that is why they came. They came for the second night of the wake too. Four times everyone attended. On the fourth night, games were played in honor of the ghost. When these were finished all the people went home.

Then the man made preparations to follow his dead wife, proceeding toward the west, for it is said that the souls of those who have become ghosts travel to the west.

In such fashion did the man pursue the ghost of his wife, thus in her direction did he go, he thought. Finally he became exhausted and made use of a cane. After a while even with

---

[1] The funeral rites that will help the ghost of the deceased to find the road that leads to spiritland.

this help he could make it no longer and could just barely crawl along. Then his knees, too, were worn out from crawling. Thereupon he peeled off some basswood bark and tied them around his knees. Finally, however, he became completely exhausted and barely succeeded in reaching a little knoll. Here, all around this little knoll, the country was beautiful. "In yonder very beautiful spot I would like to die," he thought to himself. So he rolled over the best he could and, moving and crawling, finally attained his wish and got there. Arrived there he awaited his death.

He lay there with his eyes closed when, to his surprise, he heard a man speaking. "Let us go home. I live here," the voice said. Then he opened his eyes and, to his surprise, there stood a man. He was fear-inspiring in appearance, his body covered with a hairy-like covering. However, the young man was unable to get up.

"Come on!" this man said, so he immediately jumped up. Then he followed him, walked around a lodge that stood there and finally entered it. There this man spoke to him, "Grandson, your plight is indeed pitiable and there is little in which I can help you. But if I can help I will certainly do it"; thus he spoke.

Then he gave him something to eat and said, "Now continue what you are doing. Ahead of me you will come to my friend and there, on this side, you will find a stream. It will be a wide stream. Across that stream you are to jump. Now, remember, what I say you are to do. If you fail to do this, you will not succeed. So, remember, jump across!"

Thereupon he proceeded on and as he walked along there, much to his surprise, he came to a very wide stream. It was flowing at great speed, indeed it was flowing as fast as a stream could flow. The water actually whirled in turbulent fashion and he was afraid to jump across. The land across this stream looked like a little speck. Like an infinitesimal speck of green it appeared, seemingly like a man's eyebrow it appeared. It did not seem possible for anyone to jump across it. Then, however, he remembered that he had been told to jump across and so he decided to jump no matter what would happen. He, accordingly, took death in his hands for he thought to himself, "I died a long time ago." Thereupon he closed his eyes, came with a running start and jumped across. He landed on the other side and then looked back across at the water, that is, he meant to look across, but when he turned he saw nothing [no water]. Thereupon he scrutinized everything very carefully and after a while, to his amazement, noticed a very small little creek; this it was which he had jumped across from where he was standing. This small little creek had been the swift-whirling, wide body of water which he had seen. It had been an illusion [it was not so].

Then he thought to himself, "Perhaps everything that is [looks] difficult will be as easy as this has been." This being so he took courage. What he was attempting, he felt, might now be attained.

On he went. After a while he came to a round lodge. This he was told to enter and this, accordingly, he entered. There he saw, to his surprise, the man he had first encountered but with him was another man; there were two of them.

Once again a kettle had been put on and he was given something to eat; food was dished out to him. They [the two] spoke to him, "Grandson, we will concentrate our minds on what you are doing. It is difficult and you will have to exert all your powers to accomplish it. So go on! Ahead of you you will find our friend and he might be able to tell you something and to help you." Thus they spoke to him.

Again he pursued his way. After a while, as he was walking along, he came to a round lodge which, as before, he was told to enter and where, after he had entered, he saw, to his surprise, three men. Two of them he had seen before but, in addition, there was now a third one. That one gave him something to eat and then talked to him. "Grandson, what you are attempting to do is very difficult but we are going to help you. Exert your utmost powers! That is what we wish to tell and urge on you, if you wish to accomplish your purpose. If you fail, you will indeed find yourself in a pitiable condition," so he spoke to him. Then when he was through eating, the young man continued on his way.

As he walked along a knoll came in sight. To his surprise a large cluster of lodges appeared there; it was a village. It was so large that the end was lost to view. He soon reached this village. However, no people were to be found there, not a single person did he see. The lodges were all made of bark. He peeped into one of the lodges but it was empty.

Finally he entered one of them and found four men there. Three of them he had seen before but, in addition, there was a fourth one. This fourth person now spoke to him. "Grandson, this is the place that you have come in search of. Your wife, however, you will not be able to see. Remember, you must do what I am going to tell you now for unless you obey me [do it] you will see your wife. Tonight there is going to be a dance. Never look around you anywhere. We will be watching out for you, I and my friends. If you look in any direction, all for which you came you will fail to secure." Thus he spoke to him.

In the evening, without warning, a drum was struck and the sound spread immediately. At different places, shortly after, shouts resounded. Then, after a while, the drum was again beaten and the shouting became louder and more frequent. Now, for the third time, the drum was struck. Then it happened the fourth time and, finally, someone said, "It is about time to begin. It is going to be crowded in front of the lodge," this person said and so they went inside.

In the center of this village there was a long lodge; this was the one that they [the husband and his aides] had gone to. It was the dance-lodge and as soon as they entered they were placed in the middle of the lodge. Immediately, from some-

where behind him, the husband heard whispering. "Wagisga
has come here. He is in pursuit of his wife. But his task is a
fruitless one. What he is attempting to accomplish, in that he
will fail," [doubtful the-what he is attempting to accomplish]
they said. These words he heard. Then they began teasing
him. "His wife has married again," they were saying. "Listen,
it is I who, in fact, am married to her," they were saying.

Then the singing started and it was tremendous. Wagisga's
relations had come and they sang specifically about him. They
sang just about him, "Wagisga's wife has come. Many more
will come," thus they sang. Thus they teased him all night.
Then as the sun appeared in the morning they all disappeared.
His wife, in spite of what was said, knew nothing about it.

Then they returned to the lodge where they were staying.
When they arrived there, the occupants thanked him. "This
one night you have passed through well, grandson, but the
next one is going to be far worse. There you must exert all
your power"; thus they spoke to him.

Evening had again arrived and the drum, once more, was
struck; they struck it the second time and people responded
with shouts. Then, for the third time, it was struck. "Let us go
now," someone said, "for it is going to be crowded."

Once more they started out and then when they got there,
immediately he was teased. In whatever way they could they
tried, by their talking, to get him to say something. Then the
singing started up. If, on the previous night, [before] he had
thought that the singing was tremendous, that was not com-
parable to this, so much more wonderful was it. On this occasion, during the night, the ghosts began to put their hands on
his head and press him down and annoy him even more.
Finally morning came upon them.

Once more they went to their homes. There he, the husband, was thanked, "Grandson, you have done well, but this
that is coming will demand much more of your powers. Exert
all your powers therefore."

Now evening had come and, immediately, the drum was struck. Shouting was the response. At first, this was not marked but, then, it increased greatly. A second time the drum was struck and then they [husband and attendants] started to leave. "Indeed, we must go now," the attendants said, "for it is going to be crowded." Soon they arrived there. At once, after their arrival, they [the ghosts] began to tease him. This time there were six attendants but they could do nothing for him. Once more the singing was started. This time he was hardly able to resist. The earth shook, as it were, from the impact of the drumming. The ghosts grabbed hold of the blanket and tried to pull him along with them; they would throw-themselves-and-fall beside him. At last slowly, with great effort, the sun appeared; morning came upon them and, suddenly, the ghosts disappeared.

Once more they returned to their homes. "Well, grandson, this is going to be the last night. Exert all your powers! We will not be able to help you at all. This time there will be eight of us as attendants but that will not amount to anything unless you exert your utmost powers"; thus they spoke to him.

It was already evening and the drum was being struck. The noise was tremendous and the shouting that followed simply soared up to the sky. "Let us go now," they said, "for it is going to be crowded."

As soon as they got there, they noticed that the village had grown rapidly. Every day many ghosts step into the trail. Every day deaths take place on this earth and thus it results that the ghosts increase [that is why it is thus].

When they got to the dancing-lodge, they found very many people, indeed they almost stepped on one another. Immediately, upon his arrival, to his bewilderment, his wife spoke to him, "If you are going to be indifferent to me, why did you come here? If, indeed, you are going to be indifferent," thus she said, "why did you come?" He almost looked in her direction. Then the singing started. It was wonderful. The earth trembled. On this occasion they were able to pull him along and throw him down. His wife was the most active in all this. At all times her voice was audible. He sat within his blanket but it was almost jerked off of him. At times they all piled upon him and the eight attendants he had were treated as though they did not exist. At length, toward morning, he grew tired and began to weaken and the ghosts grabbed ahold of his knees and ran along pulling him at will. At length, with extremely great difficulty, the sun appeared and morning came upon them.

"Well done! Now let us go on!" they said. "Well done, grandson, you have attained your purpose!"

When they reached the lodge where they were staying, then one of the men spoke, saying, "Grandson, never from now on will this be permitted to happen. Earthmaker has not ordained it thus. But I have blessed you and my friends have blessed you and that is why you have been able to do this. Now you are to get your wife and take her home with you." Then he spoke to someone, "Go and get her for him!"

Then they went after her and brought her to him. Finally he spoke thus to Wagisga, "I have blessed you and you can return to your home. With this we bless you. It is something that can be heard over the whole world." Saying this, he gave them a drum. It was painted blue, with blue clay. "If anyone is about to die," they continued, "the soul shall be brought to you. Indeed the soul that is wavering near death, that shall be brought to you," thus he spoke to them. "All the tobacco you pour out for me, of that I shall take cognizance for you," they said.

"You are now to go home. The ghosts will pursue you for they are wicked. Eight attendants will accompany you on your way home." Then he gave the man and his wife some ashes. "Now when the ghosts have caught up with you," he told them, "throw the ashes behind you. As soon as you get home, ask immediately that a lodge be built; this lodge you are to use," thus he continued.

After a while, the ghosts pursued them. "Alas, alas! Wagisga has taken our wife with him. Let us take her away from him!" they exclaimed. As soon as they came close to the two, the husband threw some ashes in back of him. "Oh my, our clothes are going to be ruined!" they shouted and ran back. Then the two continued on their way. Once again, the ghosts overtook them but as the man repeated what he had done [threw ashes at them], they soon gave up. Thereupon the attendants also went back.

The two were now reaching the village.[2] To their surprise they heard the sound of someone chopping wood, the echo being distinctly audible. So, in that direction, they pursued their way. To their amazement the person chopping wood was crying. To their further amazement, this person turned out to be the man's mother. Beyond expectation her son had returned, she saw. However, fear seized upon her when she noticed that he was in the company of one-who-was-dead. Nevertheless, they talked to each other and the son said, "Mother, go home and get ten young men for me, ten who have not as yet known intercourse with women and ten young women, virgins. Have them come here. Have them bring some incense along with them," thus he spoke to her.

She thereupon returned home and told this to the people.

Then those designated, and others as well, went over to where the two were and the man had them build a lodge. He had them build one with ten fireplaces and sprinkle the place with incense. After that the two entered. That very night a dance was given—the drums had already been placed inside—and the man sang the songs he had been taught. . . .

Since then they have been continuing to do the same

---

[2] The section from here to the end is not part of the origin myth, but represents what was added to adapt it as an origin myth.

thing. Indeed they are still performing this ceremony, beating the drums and deriving great pleasure from the dance. Indeed they are still performing it. The one who originated this rite was named Wagisga and because of what he did they call the rite the Ghost Dance. It is a very exciting-and-noisy rite. And it is also a sacred feast-rite.

This is the end of the Ghost Dance.

(Winnebago, West Coast, California)

36
Coyote and Eagle Visit the Land of the Dead

In the days of the animal people, Coyote was sad because people died and went away to the land of the spirits. All around him was the sound of mourning. He wondered and wondered how he could bring the dead back to the land of the living.

Coyote's sister had died. Some of his friends had died. Eagle's wife had died and Eagle was mourning for her. To comfort him Coyote said, "The dead shall not remain forever in the land of the dead. They are like the leaves that fall, brown and dead, in the autumn. They shall come back again. When the grass grows and the birds sing, when the leaf buds open and the flowers bloom, the dead shall come back again."

But Eagle did not want to wait until spring. He thought that the dead should be brought back without any delay. So Coyote and Eagle started out together to the land of the dead, Eagle flying along over Coyote's head. After several days they came to a big body of water, on the other side of which were a great many houses.

"Bring a boat and take us across the water!" shouted Coyote.

But there was no answer—no sound and no movement.

"There is no one there," said Eagle. "We have come all the way for nothing."

"They are asleep," explained Coyote. "The dead sleep during the day and come out at night. We will wait here until dark.''

After sunset, Coyote began to sing. In a short time, four spirit men came out of the houses, got into a boat, and started toward Coyote and Eagle. Coyote kept on singing, and soon the spirits joined him, keeping time with their paddles. But the boat moved without them. It skimmed over the water by itself.

When the spirits reached the shore, Eagle and Coyote stepped into the boat and started back with them. As they drew near the island of the dead, the sound of drums and of dancing met them across the water.

"Do not go into the house," warned the spirits as they were landing. "Do not look at the things around you. Keep your eyes closed, for this is a sacred place."

"But we are hungry and cold. Do let us go in," begged Eagle and Coyote.

So they were allowed to go into a large lodge made of tule mats, where the spirits were dancing and singing to the beating of the drums. An old woman brought to them some seal oil in a basket bottle. Dipping a feather into it, she fed them from the oil until their hunger was gone.

Then Eagle and Coyote looked around. Inside the lodge everything was beautiful, and there were many spirits. They were dressed in ceremonial robes, beautifully decorated with shells and with elks' teeth. Their faces were painted, and they wore feathers in their hair. The moon, hanging from above, filled the big lodge with light. Near the moon stood Frog, who has watched over it ever since he jumped into it long ago. He saw to it that the moon shone brightly on the crowd of dancers and singers.

Eagle and Coyote knew some of the spirits as their former friends, but no one paid any attention to the two strangers. No one saw the basket which Coyote had brought with him. In this basket he planned to carry the spirits back to the land of the living.

Early in the morning, the spirits left the lodge for their day of sleep. Then Coyote killed Frog, took his clothes, and put them on himself. At twilight the spirits returned and began again a night of singing and dancing. They did not know that Coyote, in Frog's clothing, stood beside the moon.

When the dancing and singing were at their gayest, Coyote swallowed the moon. In the darkness, Eagle caught the spirit people, put them into Coyote's basket, and closed the lid tight. Then the two started back to the land of the living, Coyote carrying the basket.

After traveling a great distance, they heard noises in the basket and stopped to listen.

"The people are coming to life," said Coyote.

After they had gone a little farther, they heard voices talking in the basket. The spirits were complaining.

"We are being bumped and banged around," groaned some.

"My leg is being hurt," groaned one spirit.

"My legs and arms are cramped," groaned another.

"Open the lid and let us out!" called several spirits together.

Coyote was tired, for the basket was getting heavier and heavier. The spirits were turning back into people.

"Let's let them out," said Coyote.

"No, no," answered Eagle quickly.

A little later, Coyote set the basket down. It was too heavy for him.

"Let's let them out," repeated Coyote. "We are so far from the spirit land now that they won't return."

So he opened the basket. The people took their spirit forms and, moving like the wind, went back to the island of the dead.

Eagle scolded at first, but soon he remembered Coyote's earlier thought. "It is now autumn. The leaves are falling, just as people die. Let us wait until spring. When the buds open and the flowers bloom, let us return to the land of the dead and try again."

"No," replied Coyote. "I am tired. Let the dead stay in the land of the dead forever and forever."

So Coyote made the law that, after people have died, they shall never come to life again. If he had not opened the basket and let the spirits out, the dead would have come to life every spring as the grass and flowers and trees do.

(Wishram, Plateau)

37
The Arrow Chain

Two very high-caste boys were chums. The father of one was town chief and had his house in the middle of the village, but the house of the other boy's father stood at one end. These boys would go alternately to each other's house and make great quantities of arrows which they would play with until all were broken up.

One time both of the boys made a great quantity of arrows to see which could have the more. Just back of their village was a hill on the top of which was a smooth grassy place claimed by the boys as their playground, and on a certain fine, moonlight night they started thither. As they were going along, the lesser chief's son, who was ahead, said, "Look here, friend. Look at that moon. Don't you think that the shape of that moon is the same as that of my mother's labret and that the size is the same, too?" The other answered, "Don't: You must not talk that way of the moon."

Then suddenly it became very dark about them, and presently the head chief's son saw a ring about them just like a rainbow. When it disappeared his companion was gone. He called and called to him but did not get any answer and did not see him. He thought, "He must have run up the hill to get away from that rainbow." He looked up and saw the moon in the sky. Then he climbed the hill, and looked about, but his friend was not there. Now he thought, "Well! The moon must have gone up with him. That circular rainbow must have been the moon."

The boy thus left alone sat down and cried, after which he

began to try the bows. He put strings on them one after the other and tried them, but every one broke. He broke all of his own bows and all of his chum's, except one that was made of very hard wood. He thought, "Now I am going to shoot that star next to the moon." In that spot was a large and very bright one. He shot an arrow at this star and sat down to watch, when, sure enough, the star darkened. Now he began shooting at that star from the big piles of arrows he and his chum had made, and he was encouraged by seeing that the arrows did not come back. After he had shot for some time he saw something hanging down very near him and, when he shot up another arrow, it stuck to this. The next did likewise, and at last the chain of arrows reached him. He put a last one on to complete it.

Now the youth felt bad for the loss of his friend and, lying down under the arrow chain, he went to sleep. After a while he awoke, found himself sleeping on that hill, remembered the arrows he had shot away, and looked up. Instead of the arrows there was a long ladder reaching right down to him. He arose and looked so as to make sure. Then he determined to ascend. First, however, he took various kinds of bushes and stuck them into the knot of hair he wore on his head. He climbed up his ladder all day and camped at nightfall upon it, resuming his journey the following morning. When he awoke early on the second morning his head felt very heavy. Then he seized the salmonberry bush that was in his hair, pulled it out, and found it was loaded with berries. After he had eaten the berries off, he stuck the branch back into his hair and felt very much strengthened. About noon of the same day he again felt hungry, and again his head was heavy, so he pulled out a bush from the other side of his head and it was loaded with blue huckleberries. It was already summer there in the sky. That was why he was getting berries. When he resumed his journey next morning his head did not feel heavy until noon. At that time he pulled out the bush at the back of his head and found it loaded with red huckleberries.

By the time he had reached the top the boy was very tired. He looked around and saw a large lake. Then he gathered some soft brush and some moss and lay down to sleep. But, while he slept, some person came to him and shook him saying, "Get up. I am after you." He awoke and looked around but saw no one. Then he rolled over and pretended to go to sleep again but looked out through his eyelashes. By and by he saw a very small but handsome girl coming along. Her skin clothes were very clean and neat, and her leggings were ornamented with porcupine quills. Just as she reached out to shake him he said, "I have seen you already."

Now the girl stood still and said, "I have come after you. My grandmother has sent me to bring you to her house." So he went with her, and they came to a very small house in which was an old woman. The old woman said, "What is it you came way up here after, my grandson?" and the boy answered, "On account of my playmate who was taken up hither." "Oh!" answered the old woman. "He is next door, only a short distance away. I can hear him crying every day. He is in the moon's house."

Then the old woman began to give him food. She would put her hand up to her mouth, and a salmon or whatever she was going to give would make its appearance. After the salmon she gave him berries and then meat, for she knew that he was hungry from his long journey. After that she gave him a spruce cone, a rosebush, a piece of devil's club, and a small piece of whetstone to take along.

As the boy was going toward the moon's house with all of these things he heard his playmate screaming with pain. He had been put up on a high place near the smoke hole, so, when his rescuer came to it, he climbed on top and, reaching down through the smoke hole, pulled him out. He said, "My friend, come. I am here to help you." Putting the spruce cone down where the boy had been, he told it to imitate his cries, and he and his chum ran away.

After a while, however, the cone dropped from the place where it has been put, and the people discovered that their captive had escaped. Then the moon started in pursuit. When the head chief's son discovered this, he threw behind them the devil's club he had received from the old woman, and a patch of devil's club arose which the moon had so much trouble in getting through that they gained rapidly on him. When the moon again approached, the head chief's son threw back the rosebushes, and such a thicket of roses grew there that the moon was again delayed. When he approached them once more, they threw back the grindstone, and it became a high cliff from which the moon kept rolling back. It is on account of this cliff that people can say things about the moon nowadays with impunity. When the boys reached the old woman's house they were very glad to see each other, for before this they had not had time to speak.

The old woman gave them something to eat, and, when they were through, she said to the rescuer, "Go and lie down at the place where you lay when you first came up. Don't think of anything but the playground you used to have." They went there and lay down, but after some time the boy who had first been captured thought of the old woman's house and immediately they found themselves there. Then the old woman said, "Go back and do not think of me any more. Lie there and think of nothing but the place where you used to play." They did so, and, when they awoke, they were lying on their playground at the foot of the ladder.

As the boys lay in that place they heard a drum beating in the head chief's house, where a death feast was being held for them, and the head chief's son said, "Let us go," but the other answered, "No, let us wait here until that feast is over. Afterward the boys went down and watched the people come out with their faces all blackened. They stood at a corner, but, as this dance is always given in the evening, they were not seen.

Then the head chief's son thought, "I wish my younger brother would come out," and sure enough, after all of the other people had gone, his younger brother came out. He called to his brother saying, "Come here. It is I," but the child was afraid and ran into the house instead. Then the child said to his mother, "My brother and his friend are out here." "Why do you talk like that?" asked his mother. "Don't you know that your brother died some time ago?" And she became very angry. The child, however, persisted, saying, "I know his voice, and I know him." His mother was now very much disturbed, so the boy said, "I am going to go out and bring in a piece of his shirt." "Go and do so," said his mother. "Then I will believe you."

When the boy at last brought in a piece of his brother's shirt his mother was convinced, and they sent word into all of the houses, first of all into that of the second boy's parents, but they kept both with them so that his parents could come there and rejoice over him. All of the other people in that village also came to see them.

(Tlingit, Northwest Coast)

38
The Girls Who Wished
To Marry Stars

At the time of which my story speaks people were camping just as we are here. In the wintertime they used birchbark wigwams. All the animals could then talk together. Two girls, who were very foolish, talked foolishly and were in no respect like the other girls of their tribe, made their bed out-of-doors and slept right out under the stars. The very fact that they slept outside during the winter proves how foolish they were.

One of these girls asked the other, "With what star would you like to sleep, the white one or the red one?" The other girl answered, "I'd like to sleep with the red star." "Oh, that's all right," said the first one, "I would like to sleep with the white star. He's the younger; the red is the older." Then the two girls fell asleep. When they awoke, they found themselves in another world, the star world. There were four of them there, the two girls and the two stars who had become men. The white star was very, very old and was grey-headed, while the younger was redheaded. He was the red star. The girls stayed a long time in this star world, and the one who had chosen the white star was very sorry, for he was so old.

There was an old woman up in this world who sat over a hole in the sky, and, whenever she moved, she showed them the hole and said, "That's where you came from." They looked down through and saw their people playing down below, and then the girls grew very sorry and very homesick.

One evening, near sunset, the old woman moved a little away from the hole.

The younger girl heard the noise of the *mitewin* down below. When it was almost daylight, the old woman sat over the hole again and the noise of *mitewin* stopped; it was her spirit that made the noise. She was the guardian of the *mitewin*.

One morning the old woman told the girls, "If you want to go down where you came from, we will let you down, but get to work and gather roots to make a string-made rope, twisted. The two of you make coils of rope as high as your heads when you are sitting. Two coils will be enough." The girls worked for days until they had accomplished this. They made plenty of rope and tied it to a big basket. They then got into the basket and the people of the star world lowered them down. They descended right into an Eagle's nest, but the people above thought the girls were on the ground and stopped lowering them. They were obliged to stay in the nest, because they could do nothing to help themselves.

Said one, "We'll have to stay here until someone comes to get us." Bear passed by. The girls cried out, "Bear, come and get us. You are going to get married sometime. Now is your chance!" Bear thought, "They are not very good-looking women." He pretended to climb up and then said, "I can't climb up any farther." And he went away, for the girls didn't suit him. Next came Lynx. The girls cried out again, "Lynx, come up and get us. You will go after women someday!" Lynx answered, "I can't, for I have no claws," and he went away. Then an ugly-looking man, Wolverine, passed and the girls spoke to him. "Hey, Wolverine, come and get us." Wolverine started to climb up, for he thought it a very fortunate thing to have these women and was very glad. When he reached them, they placed their hair ribbons in the nest. Then Wolverine agreed to take one girl at a time, so he took the first one down and went back for the next. Then Wolverine went away with his two wives and enjoyed himself greatly, as he was ugly and nobody else would have him. They went far into the woods, and then they sat down and began to talk. "Oh!" cried one of the girls, "I forgot my hair ribbon." Then Wolverine said, "I will run back for it." And he started off to get the hair ribbons. Then the girls hid and told the trees, whenever Wolverine should come back and whistle for them, to answer him by whistling. Wolverine soon returned and began to whistle for his wives, and the trees all around him whistled in answer. Wolverine, realizing that he had been tricked, gave up the search and departed very angry.

(Ojibwa, North Pacific Coast)

39
The Girl Enticed
to the Sky

There was a camp circle. A party of women went out after some wood for the fire. One of them saw a porcupine near a cottonwood tree and informed her companions of the fact. The porcupine ran around the tree, finally climbing it, whereupon the woman tried to hit the animal, but he dodged from one side of the trunk of the tree to the other, for protection. At length one of the women started to climb the tree to catch the porcupine, but it ever stopped just beyond her reach. She even tried to reach it with a stick, but with each effort it went a little higher. "Well!" said she, "I am climbing to catch the porcupine, for I want those quills, and if necessary I will go to the top."

When porcupine had reached the top of the tree the woman was still climbing, although the cottonwood was dangerous and the branches were waving to and fro; but as she approached the top and was about to lay hands upon the porcupine, the tree suddenly lengthened, when the porcupine resumed his climbing. Looking down, she saw her friends looking up at her, and beckoning her to come down; but having passed under the influence of the porcupine and fearful for the great distance between herself and the ground, she continued to climb, until she became the merest speck to those looking up from below, and with the porcupine she finally reached the sky.

The porcupine took the woman into the camp circle where

his father and mother lived. The folks welcomed her arrival and furnished her with the very best kind of accommodation. The lodge was then put up for them to live in. The porcupine was very industrious and, of course, the old folks were well supplied with hides and food.

One day she decided to save all the sinew from the buffalo, at the same time doing work on buffalo robes and other things with it, in order to avoid all suspicion on the part of her husband and the old folks as to why she was saving the sinew. Thus she continued to save a portion of the sinew from each beef brought in by her husband, until she had a supply suitable for her purpose. One day her husband cautioned her that, while in search of roots, wild turnips and other herbs, she should not dig and that, should she use the digging stick, she should not dig too deep, and that she should go home early when out for a walk. The husband was constantly bringing in the beef and hide, in order that he might keep his wife at work at home all the time. But she was a good worker and soon finished what was required for them.

Seeing that she had done considerable work, one day she started out in search of hog potatoes, and carried with her the digging stick. She ran to a thick patch and kept digging away to fill her bag. She accidentally struck a hole, which surprised her very much, and so she stooped down and looked in and through the hole, seeing below, a green earth with a camp circle on it. After questioning herself and recognizing the camp circle below, she carefully covered the spot and marked it. She took the bag and went to her own tepee, giving the folks some of the hog potatoes. The old folks were pleased and ate the hog potatoes to satisfy their daughter-in-law. The husband returned home too, bringing in beef and hides.

Early one morning the husband started off for more beef and hides, telling his wife to be careful about herself. After he was gone, she took the digging stick and the sinew she had to the place where she struck the hole. When she got to the hole, she sat down and began tying string, so as to make the sinew long enough to reach the bottom. She then opened the hole and laid the digging stick across the hole which she had dug, and tied one of the sinew strings in the center of this stick, and then also fastened herself to the end of the lariat. She gradually loosened the sinew lariat as she let herself down, finally finding herself suspended above the top of the tree which she had climbed, but not near enough so that she could possibly reach it.

When the husband missed her, he scolded the old people for not watching their daughter-in-law. He began to look for her in the direction in which she usually started off, but found no fresh tracks, though he kept traveling until he tracked her to the digging stick which was lying across the hole. The husband stooped down and looked into this hole and saw his wife suspended from this stick by means of a sinew lariat or string. "Well, the only way to do is to see her touch the bottom," said he. So he looked around and found a circular stone two or three inches thick, and brought it to the place. Again he continued, "I want this stone to light right on top of her head," and he dropped the stone carefully along the sinew string, and it struck the top of her head and broke her off and landed her safe on the ground. She took up the stone and went to the camp circle. This is the way the woman returned.

(Arapaho, Plains)

40
The Stretching Tree

Once an old man and a young man and two women lived together. The two women were the young man's wives. Now, the young man needed some feathers for his arrows; and one day, seeing a hawk's nest in a high tree, he started to climb to it to get the hawk feathers. Now, the old man was jealous of the young man, and had followed him. And when he saw him climbing the tree, he used his magic and made the tree grow higher and higher, and at the same time peeled off all the bark so that the trunk was slippery; and as the young man was naked, he could not come down, but had to remain in the top of the tree. When the young man failed to appear that night, the old man said he wished to move camp and that the women were to come with him. And the next morning they started. Now, one of the women liked the old man; but the other one, who had a baby, disliked him, and when they camped for the night, she would take her baby and make a fire for herself outside the camp and away from the old man. So they went on for several days.

All this time the young man stayed up in the tree; and as it was cold and he had no clothes, he took his hair, which was very long, and wove feathers in it, and so made a blanket to protect himself. The little birds who built their nests in the sticks of the hawk's nest tried their best to carry him down to the ground, but could not lift him, and so he stayed on.

Finally one day he saw coming, a long way off, an old woman bent over, and with a stick in each hand. She came to the bottom of the tree where the young man was, and began to climb, and climbed until she reached the young man, and then she turned out to be Spider. Then Spider spun a web for him, and of the web the young man made a rope and so reached the ground.

When he came back to his camp, he found it deserted, but discovered the trail of the fugitives, and started to follow. He trailed them a long time, and finally saw them in the distance. Now, the woman who did not like the old man was following behind with her little boy; and the child, looking back, saw his father and cried out, "Why, there is my father!" But the mother replied, "What do you mean? Your father has been dead a long time." But looking back herself, she saw her husband and waited for him to come up, and they stopped together.

Then she told her husband all that had happened, how the old man had wished to take both his wives, and how she would not have him, but how the other one took him. Now, the woman was carrying a large basket, and she put her husband into it and covered him up. When they reached the old man's camp she put the basket down close to the fire; but the old man took it and placed it some distance away. The woman brought it back and as she did so the young man sprang out and struck the old man and killed him. Then he killed his faithless wife; and taking the other woman, who was true, and the little boy, they went back to their old home together.

(Chilcotin, North Pacific Coast)

41
The Piqued Buffalo-wife

Once a young man went out and came to a buffalo-cow fast in the mire. He took advantage of her situation. After a time she gave birth to a boy. When he could run about, this boy would go into the Indian camps and join in the games of the children, but would always mysteriously disappear in the evening. One day this boy told his mother that he intended to search among the camps for his father. Not long after this he was playing with the children in the camps as usual, and went into the lodge of a head man in company with a boy of the family. He told this head man that his father lived somewhere in the camp, and that he was anxious to find him. The head man took pity on the boy and sent out a messenger to call into his lodge all the old men in the camp.

When these were all assembled and standing around the lodge, the head man requested the boy to pick out his father. The boy looked them over, and then told the head man that his father was not among them. Then the head man sent out a messenger to call in all the men next in age; but, when these were assembled, the boy said that his father was not among them. Again the head man sent out the messenger to call in all the men of the next rank in age. When they were assembled, the boy looked them over as before and announced that his father was not among them. So once again the head man sent out his messenger to call in all the young unmarried men of the camp. As they were coming into the head man's lodge, the boy ran to one of them, and, embracing him, said, "Here is my father."

After a time the boy told his father that he wished to take him to see his mother. The boy said, "When we come near her, she will run at you and hook four times, but you are to stand perfectly still." The next day the boy and his father started out on their journey. As they were going along they saw a buffalo-cow, which immediately ran at them as the boy had predicted. The man stood perfectly still, and at the fourth time, as the cow was running forward to hook at him, she became a woman. Then she went home with her husband and child.

One day shortly after their return, she warned her husband that whatever he might do he must never strike at her with fire. They lived together happily for many years. She was a remarkably good woman. One evening when the husband had invited some guests, and the woman expressed a dislike to prepare food for them, he became very angry and, catching up a stick from the fire, struck at her. As he did so, the woman and her child vanished, and the people saw a buffalo-cow and calf running from the camp.

Now the husband was very sorry and mourned for his wife and child. After a time he went out to search for them. In order that he might approach the buffalo without being discovered, he rubbed himself with filth from a buffalo-wallow. In the course of time he came to a place where some buffalo were dancing. He could hear them from a distance. As he was approaching, he met his son, who was now, as before, a buffalo-calf. The father explained to the boy that he was mourning for him and his mother and that he had come to take them home. The calf-boy explained that this would be very difficult, for his father would be required to pass through an ordeal. The calf-boy explained to him that, when he arrived among the buffalo and inquired for his wife and son, the chief of the buffalo would order that he select his child from among all the buffalo-calves in the herd. Now, the calf boy wished to assist his father and told him that he would know his child by a sign, because, when the calves appeared before him, his own child would hold up its tail. Then the man proceeded until he came to the place where the buffalo were dancing. Immediately he was taken before the chief of the buffalo-herd. The chief required that he first prove his relationship to the child by picking him out from among all the other calves of the herd. The man agreed to this and the calves were brought up. He readily picked out his own child by the sign.

The chief of the buffalo, however, was not satisfied with this proof and said that the father could not have the child until he identified him four times. While the preparations were being made for another test, the calf-boy came to his father and explained that he would be known this time by closing one eye. When the time arrived, the calves were brought as before, and the chief of the buffalo directed the father to identify his child, which he did by the sign. Before the next trial the calf-boy explained to his father that the sign would be one ear hanging down. Accordingly, when the calves were brought up for the father to choose, he again identified his child. Now, before the last trial, the boy came again to his father and notified him that the sign by which he was to be known was dancing and holding up one leg. Now the calf-boy had a chum among the buffalo-calves, and when the calves were called up before the chief so that the father might select his child, the chum saw the calf-boy beginning to dance holding up one leg, and he thought to himself, "He is doing some fancy dancing." So he, also, danced in the same way. Now the father observed that there were two calves giving the sign and realized that he must make a guess. He did so, but the guess was wrong. Immediately the herd rushed upon the man and trampled him into the dust. Then they all ran away except the calf-boy, his mother, and an old bull.

These three mourned together for the fate of the unfortunate man. After a time the old bull requested that they examine the ground to see if they could find a piece of bone.

After long and careful search they succeeded in finding one small piece that had not been trampled by the buffalo. The bull took this piece, made a sweathouse, and finally restored the man to life. When the man was restored, the bull explained to him that he and his family would receive some power, some headdresses, some songs, and some crooked sticks, such as he had seen the buffalo carry in the dance at the time when he attempted to pick out his son.

The calf-boy and his mother then became human beings, and returned with the man. It was this man who started the Bull and the Horn societies, and it was his wife who started the Matoki.

(Blackfoot, Plains)

42
The Dog-husband

A long time ago, in a certain village there lived a young girl who had a dog of which she was very fond. She took the dog with her wherever she went; and at night, as was a common custom at that time with young girls, the dog slept at the foot of the bed. Every night he would change into human form and lie with the girl, and in the morning, before it was light, would turn back again into his dog shape: so no one knew anything about it. After a time she became pregnant; and when her parents found it out and knew that the dog was the cause, they were greatly ashamed, and, calling the people together, they tore down the house, put out all the fires, and moved away from the place, leaving the girl to die.

But Crow had pity on her, and, taking some coals, she placed them between two clamshells and told the girl secretly that after a time she would hear a crackling, and to go to the spot and she would find fire. So the girl was left alone, for the people had all gone a long way across the water. She sat still for a long time, listening for the crackling, and when she finally heard it she went to the place and found the fire as Crow had said.

Not long after this she gave birth to five dog pups, but as her father had killed the dog, her lover, she had to look after them by herself, and the only way she could live and care for them was to gather clams and other shellfish on the beach. There were four male pups and one female, and with the care their mother gave them, they grew very fast. Soon she noticed that whenever she went out, she heard a noise of singing and dancing, which seemed to come from the house, and she wondered greatly. Four times she heard the noise and wondered, and when, on going out again, she heard it for the fifth time, she took her clam-digger and stuck it in the sand, and put her clothes on it to make it look as if she were busy gathering clams. Then she stole back by a roundabout way, and creeping close to the house peeped in through a crack to see what the noise might be. There she saw four boys dancing and singing, and a little girl watching the place where the mother was supposed to be digging clams. The mother waited a moment and watched, and then coming in she caught them in human form, and scolded them, saying that they ought to have had that form in the first place, for on their account she had been brought to shame before the people. At this the children sat down and were ashamed. And the mother tore down the dog blankets which were hanging about, and threw them into the fire.

So they remained in human form after this; and as soon as they were old enough she made little bows and arrows for the boys, and taught them how to shoot birds, beginning with the wren, and working up to the largest. Then she taught them to make large bows and arrows, and how to shoot fur animals, and then larger game, up to the elk. And she made them bathe every day to try to get tamanous[1] for catching whales, and after that they hunted the hair seal to make floats of its skin. And the mother made harpoons for them of elk bone, and lines of twisted sinews and cedar, and at the end of the line she fastened the sealskin floats. And when everything was ready, the boys went out whaling and were very successful, and brought in so many whales that the whole beach stank with them.

Now, Crow noticed one day, from far across the water, a great smoke rising from where the old village had stood, and

---

[1] Power?

that night she came over secretly to see what it all meant. And before she neared the beach, she smelled the dead whales, and when she came up she saw the carcasses lying all about, and there were so many that some of them had not yet been cut up. When she reached the house, she found the children grown up; and they welcomed her and gave her food, all she could eat, but gave her nothing to take back, telling her to come over again if she wanted more.

When Crow started back, the girl told her that when she reached home, she was to weep so that the people would believe they were dead. But Crow, on getting home, instead of doing as she was told, described how the beach was covered with sea gulls feeding on the whales that had been killed by the boys.

Now, Crow had brought with her secretly a piece of whale meat for her children, and, after putting out the light, she fed it to them; and one of them ate so fast that she choked, and coughed a piece of meat out on the ground. And some of the people saw it, and then believed what Crow had told them, as they had not done before. Then the people talked it all over, and decided to go back; and they loaded their canoes and moved to the old village. And the boys became the chiefs of the village, and always kept the people supplied with whales.

(Quinault, North Pacific Coast)

43
The Girl Who
Married a Dog

A chief had a fine-looking daughter. She had a great many admirers. At night she was visited by a young man, but she did not know who he was. She worried about this and determined to discover him. She put red paint near her bed. When he crawled on her bed, she put her hand into the paint. When they embraced, she left red marks on his back.

The next day she told her father to call all the young men to a dance in front of his tent. They all came, and the whole village turned out to see them. She watched all that came, looking for the red marks she had made. As she turned about, she caught sight of one of her father's dogs with red marks on his back. This made her so unhappy and she went straight into her tent. This broke up the dance.

The next day she went into the woods near the camp, taking the dog on a string. She hit him. He finally broke loose. She was very unhappy, and several months later she bore seven pups. She told her mother to kill them, but her mother was kind toward them and made a little shelter for them. They began to grow, and sometimes at night the old dog came to them. After a time, the woman began to take an interest in them and sometimes played with them. When they were big enough to run, the old dog came and took them away.

When the woman went to see them in the morning, they were gone. She saw the large dog's tracks, and several little ones, and followed them at a distance. She was sad and cried.

She returned to her mother and said, "Mother, make me seven pairs of moccasins. I am going to follow the little ones, searching for them." Her mother made seven pairs of moccasins, and the woman started out, tracking them all the way. Finally, in the distance, she saw a tent. The youngest one came to her and said, "Mother, Father wants you to go back. We are going home. You cannot come." She said, "No! Wherever you go, I go." She took the little one and carried him to the tent. She entered and saw a young man, who took no notice of her. He gave her a little meat and drink, which did not grow less no matter how much she ate. She tied the little pup to her belt with a string. Next morning, she was left alone and the tent had vanished. She followed the tracks and again came upon them. Four times this happened in the same way. But the fourth time the tracks stopped.

She looked up into the sky. There she saw her seven pups. They had become seven stars, the Pleiades.

(Cheyenne, Southeast)

44
The Two Sisters

PERSONAGES

After each name is given that of the creature or thing into which the personage was changed subsequently.

Chuhna, spider; Haka lasi, loon; Hitchinna, wildcat; Jamuka, acorn worm; Juka, silkworm; Metsi, coyote; Tsanunewa, fisher (a bird); Tsore Jowa, eagle.

At some distance east of Jigulmatu lived old Juka. He had a great many sons and two daughters—a big house full of children.

Juka's two daughters were Tsore Jowa, the elder, and Haka Lasi, the younger. After a time Haka Lasi fell in love with her brother Hitchinna. One day she fell asleep and dreamed that he had married her.

Metsi lived, too, in Juka's house. He was no relative; he just lived as a guest there.

One day all the men were out hunting. It was then that Haka Lasi saw Hitchinna in a dream. She began to sing about him, and she sang: "I dream of Hitchinna; I dream that he is my husband. I dream of Hitchinna; I dream that he is my husband."

All the men came back from the hunt at night. At daylight next morning they went to swim, and Tsore Jowa made ready food for them. Haka Lasi took a very nice staff in her hand and went on top of the sweathouse. She looked in and sang:

"Where is my husband? Send him up here to me. I will

take him away. We must go on a journey. Where is my husband? Send him up here to me."

All knew that she had no husband.

"You have no husband," said they.

Hitchina was lying in one corner wrapped up in the skin of a wildcat.

"You have no husband in this house; all here are your brothers," said Juka.

"I have a husband, and I want him to come here to me," answered Haka Lasi.

"Well," said the eldest son, "I will go up to her. Let us hear what she will say." He went up.

"You are not my husband," said Haka Lasi. "Do not come near me."

She drove that one down, and called again: "Where is my husband? Send him up to me."

"Go you," said Juka to the second son.

"I don't want you," said Haka Lasi to the second son.

She refused one after another, and drove them away until none was left but Hitchinna. Juka went then to Hitchinna and said:

"My son, get up and go to her; it looks as though you were the one she wants."

"He is the one," said Haka Lasi; "he is my husband. I want him to go away with me."

Hitchinna said not a word, but rose, washed, dressed himself nicely, and went to the woman.

"The sun is high now," said Haka Lasi; "we must go quickly."

She was glad when taking away the one she wanted. They traveled along, and she sang of Hitchinna as they traveled, sang of him all the time. They went a long distance, and at night she fixed a bed and they lay down on it.

Young Hitchinna could not sleep; he was frightened. When Haka Lasi was asleep, he rose very quickly, took a piece of soft rotten wood, put it on her arm where she had held his head, covered it, and then ran away quickly, hurried back toward Juka's sweathouse with all his might. About daylight he was at the sweathouse.

Now Chuhna, Juka's sister, lived with him. She was the greatest person in the world to spin threads and twist ropes. She had a willow basket as big as a house, and a rope which reached up to the sky and was fastened there.

"My nephew," said she to Hitchinna, "I will save you and save all from your terrible sister. She will be here very soon; she may come any moment. She will kill all in this house; she will kill everyone if she finds us here. Let all go into my basket. I will take you up to the sky. She cannot find us there; she cannot follow us to that place."

"I will lie lowest," said Metsi. "I am a good man, I will go in first, I will go in before others; I will be at the bottom of the basket."

Metsi went in first; everyone in the sweathouse followed him. Then Chuhna ran up, rose on her rope, and pulled the basket after her.

The sweathouse was empty; no one stayed behind. Chuhna kept rising and rising, going higher and higher.

When Haka Lasi woke up and saw that she had a block of rotten wood on her arm instead of Hitchinna, she said:

"You won't get away from me; I will catch you wherever you are."

She rushed back to the sweathouse. It was empty; no one there. She ran around in every direction looking for tracks, to find which way they had gone. She found nothing on the ground; then she looked into the sky, and far up, very high, close to the sun, she saw the basket rising, going up steadily.

Haka Lasi was raging; she was so awfully angry that she set fire to the house. It burned quickly, was soon a heap of coals.

The basket was almost at the sky when Metsi said to himself, "I wonder how far up we are; I want to see." And he made a little hole in the bottom of the basket to peep through and look down.

That instant the basket burst open; all came out, poured down, a great stream of people, and all fell straight into the fire of the sweathouse.

Now, Tsore Jowa was outside on top of the basket. She caught at the sun, held to it, and saved herself.

Hitchinna went down with the rest, fell into the burning coals, and was burned like his brothers.

Haka Lasi was glad that they had not escaped her; she took a stick, fixed a net on it, and watched.

All were in the fire now and were burning. After a while one body burst, and the heart flew out of it. Haki Lasi caught this heart in her net. Soon a second and a third body burst, and two more hearts flew out. She caught those as well as the first one, She caught all the hearts except two—Juka's own heart and his eldest son's heart.

Juka's heart flew high, went away far in the sky, and came down on the island of a river near Klamath Lake. It turned into Juka himself there. He sank in the ground to his chin; only his head was sticking out.

The heart of the eldest son flew off to the foot of Wahkalu and turned to be himself again. He fell so deep into the earth that only his face was sticking out on the surface.

Now Haka Lasi put all the hearts which she had caught on a string, hung them around her neck, and went to a lake east of Jigulmatu. She wanted to live at the bottom of the lake, but could not find a place deep enough. So she went northwest of Klamath Lake to Crater Lake, where she could live in deep water.

Two Tsanunewa brothers lived near the lake with their old grandmother. One morning early these brothers were out catching ducks, and just at daybreak they heard someone call.

"Who is that?" asked the elder brother.

"I don't know," answered the younger.

Soon they saw Haka Lasi spring up on the water and call. She had a large string of hearts around her neck. Then she sank again in the water. Again she came up at some distance and called a second time.

Now Tsore Jowa came down from the sun and went to the old sweathouse, where she found nothing but a heap of bones and ashes. Putting pitch on her head and on her arms, and strips of deerskin around her neck with pitch on them, she cried and went around mourning. After a time she began to look for her sister. She went everywhere; went to Klamath Lake.

For some time the two Tsanunewa brothers had heard a voice singing:

*"Li-wa-éh, li-wa-há,
Li-wa-éh, li-wa-há."*

This was old Juka. He was lying in the ground where he had fallen, and was crying.

Tsore Jowa searched, inquired, asked everyone about Haka Lasi, and told what she had done—that she had killed her own brothers and father.

Tsore Jowa came at last to the house of the two Tsanunewa brothers one day about sunset, and spoke to their grandmother. "My sister, Haka Lasi, has killed all my brothers and my father," said she; and she told the whole story.

The old woman cried when she heard what Tsore Jowa told her. The two brothers were away hunting; they came home about dark with a large string of ducks. "This woman," said the grandmother, "is looking for her sister, who has killed all her people."

The two brothers cried when the story was told to them. When they had finished crying, they said to the old woman, "Cook ducks and let this woman have plenty to eat."

When all had eaten, the two brothers said to Tsore Jowa:

"Tell us what kind of a person your sister is. Which way did she go?"

"I don't know which way she went," said Tsore Jowa.

"Three days ago," said the elder brother, "just as daylight was coming, we saw a woman jump up in the lake where we were fishing. She seemed to have large beads around her neck. That woman may be your sister."

"Catch that woman for me. I will give you otter skins and beads. I will give bearskins. If you wish, I will stay with you here, if you catch her."

"We want no beads nor otter skins nor bearskins," said the brothers.

"What do you want?"

"We want red deer-bones and green deer-bones; small, sharp ones to stab fish with."

"You shall have all you want of both kinds," said Tsore Jowa.

Next morning she set out with a sack, went away to high mountains, gathered deer-bones, red and green leg-bones, and put them in her sack. At sunset she went back to the house with the sack full.

The two brothers were glad now. The elder took red, and the younger green bones. (The fat on the leg-bones of deer turns some red and others green.)

"You must catch her bad sister for Tsore Jowa," said the old woman to her grandsons.

All that night the brothers sat sharpening the bones and then fastening them to the spear shafts. They did not stop for a moment. "Let us go now; it is near daylight," said the elder brother.

They started. When they reached the lake, they went out on the water. Every morning at daybreak Haka Lasi sprang up to the surface and called from the lake. The elder brother took a stem of tule grass, opened it, placed it on the water, made himself small, and sat down in the middle of it. The younger brother fixed himself in another stem of tule in the same way. The two tule stems floated away on the water, till they came near the place where the brothers had seen Haka Lasi spring up the first time.

"Let me shoot before you," said the elder brother.

"Oh, you cannot shoot; you will miss her," said the younger. "Let me shoot first. You will miss; you will not hit her heart."

"I will hit," said the elder.

They watched and watched. Each had his bow drawn ready to shoot. Daylight came now. Haka Lasi rose quickly, came to the top of the water, and held out her arms before calling.

The younger brother sent the first arrow, struck her in the neck; the elder shot, struck her right under the arm. Haka Lasi dropped back and sank in the water.

The brothers watched and watched. After a time they saw two arrows floating, and were afraid they had lost her. She had pulled them out of her body, and they rose to the surface. After a while the body rose. Haka Lasi was dead.

The brothers saw that she had a great many hearts on a string around her neck. They drew her to the shore then and carried her home. They left the body hidden outside the house and went in.

"We did not see her," said the elder Tsanunewa to his grandmother.

All sat down to eat fish, and when they were through eating, the elder said to Tsore Jowa, "Come out and see what we caught this morning."

She ran out with them and saw her dead sister with a string of hearts on her neck. Tsore Jowa took off her buckskin skirt, wrapped up the body, and put it in the house. She counted the hearts.

"My eldest brother's heart is not here, and my father's is not here," said she.

"Every morning we hear someone crying, far away toward the north; that may be one of them," said the two Tsanunewas.

Tsore Jowa started out to find this one, if she could, who was calling. She left the body and hearts at the old grandmother's house and hurried off toward the north. She heard the cry soon and knew it. "That is my father," said she.

Tsore Jowa came near the place from which the cry rose; saw no one. Still she heard the cry. At last she saw a face; it was the face of Juka, her father.

Tsore Jowa took a sharp stick and dug. She dug down to Juka's waist; tried to pull him up, but could not stir him. She dug again, dug a good while; pulled and pulled, until at last she drew him out.

Juka was very poor, all bones, no flesh at all on him. Tsore Jowa put down a deerskin, wrapped her father in it, and carried him to the old woman's house; then she put him with Haka Lasi's body, and carried them home to the old burned sweathouse east of Jigulmatu.

She was crying yet, since one brother was missing. She put down the basket in which she had carried them, hid it away, covered it carefully.

At the foot of Wahkalu lived a certain Jamuka, an old man who had a wife and two daughters.

"Bring in some wood," said the old man one day to his daughters.

The two girls took their baskets and went to bring wood. Soon they heard someone singing:

"I-nó i-nó, I-no mi-ná
I-nó i-nó, I-no mi-ná."

"Listen," said the younger sister; "someone is singing."
They listened, heard the singing; it seemed right at the foot

of Wahkalu. They went toward the place from which the sound came.

"That is a nice song," said the younger sister. "I should like to see the one who sings so."

They went near, saw no one yet. "Let us take the wood home," said the elder sister, "then come back here; our father may be angry if we stay away longer."

They took the wood home, put it down, and said nothing. Both went back to the place where the singing was and listened. At last the younger sister came to the right place and said, "I think this is he who is singing."

There was a head sticking out of the ground, and the face was covered with water. The man had cried so much that he looked dirty and ugly.

The sisters took sharp sticks and dug all around the head, dug deeply. They could not pull out the person; they had only dug to his waist when night came and they had to go.

"Why did you stay out so late?" asked their father.

"We heard someone singing and wanted to know who it was, but were not able. We will go back in the morning and search again."

"That is well," said Jamuka. He had heard how Juka's sons had been killed. "Perhaps one of these people is alive yet," said he; "you must look for him."

They went early next morning to dig, and drew the man out. They took off their buckskin skirts then and wrapped him up carefully. He was nothing but bones, no flesh at all on his body. The younger sister ran home to get wildcat skins to wrap around him.

"We have found a man, but he is all bones," said she to her father.

"Take good care of the stranger, feed and nurse him well," said Jamuka; "he may be Juka himself, and he is a good man."

They wrapped the man in wildcat skins. A great stream of water was running from his eyes, and deer came down the hill to drink of that water.

The girls lay on each side of the man, and gave him food; stayed all night with him. Next morning they went home for more food.

"Feed him, give him plenty," said Jamuka; "he may get health and strength yet."

The sisters went back and stayed a second night. The man began to look better, but he cried all the time, and many deer came to drink the water that flowed from his eyes. The girls went home the second morning. "The man looks better," said they to their father.

"I have heard," said old Jamuka, "that Juka's sons were killed. This must be one of them."

They went back right away and stayed another day and night with the stranger. The man looked as though he might get his health again. He began to talk. "Has your father a bow and arrows?" asked he of the sisters.

"He has; he has many."

"Bring me a bow and arrows; many deer come near me to drink; I may shoot one."

They took the man's words to their father. Jamuka gave them a bow and some arrows, and they went back to the sick man.

"You may go home tonight," said he. "I wish to be alone."

The girls left him. At sundown a great buck came and drank of the tears; he killed him. Later another came, he killed that one. At midnight a third came; he killed the third; now he had three. At daylight a fourth buck was killed; he had four now. "That is enough," thought he.

When the girls came and saw four great bucks lying dead near the stranger, they were frightened; they ran home and told their father. Old Jamuka was glad when they told him. He sharpened his knife, hurried out to the woods, and looked at the stranger. "That is Juka's son," said he; "take good care of him, daughters."

Jamuka dressed the deer, carried them home, and cut up the venison for drying. Next evening Juka's son sent the girls home a second time and killed five great deer that night. Next morning the girls came to see him and ran home in wonder.

Their father was very glad. He dressed the five deer as he had the four, and cut up the venison.

Tsore Jowa was hunting everywhere all this time to find her brother. She had left the hearts, her sister's body, and her father hidden away carefully; had done nothing yet to save them.

The night after Juka's son killed the five deer the two girls took him home to their father. He was well now and beautiful, in good health and strong. He cried no more after that. A salt spring was formed in the place where he had fallen and shed so many tears. The spring is in that place till this day, and deer go in herds to drink from it. People watch near the spring and kill them, as Juka's son did. Tsore Jowa went to every house inquiring about her brother. At last she came to Jamuka's house, and there she found him. She was glad now and satisfied. She left her brother with his two wives and hurried home.

Tsore Jowa made in one night a great sweathouse, prepared a big basket, and filled it with water. When the second night came, she dropped hot stones into the water; put all the hearts into the basket. Opening her sister's body, she took out her heart and put it in with the others. At this time the water in the basket was boiling. She covered the basket and placed it on top of the sweathouse. Then she went in, lay down and slept.

The water was seething all night. At daybreak the basket turned over, and there was a crowding and hurrying of people around the sweathouse. They began to talk briskly.

"We are cold, we are cold!" said they. "Let us in!"

Soon broad daylight came. Tsore Jowa opened the door, and all crowded into the sweathouse. Tsore Jowa said not a word yet. All the brothers came; behind them Haka Lasi. She looked well, she was good. Her heart was clean; there was nothing bad now in it.

"Where is our eldest brother?" asked all.

"He is well; I have found him. He has two wives," said Tsore Jowa.

Juka was in good health and strong. She had washed him and given him good food.

All were happy, and they went hunting.

"I think your husband would like to go home," said Jamuka one day to his daughters.

Juka's son and his two wives set out to visit his father. Juka saw his son coming; took a big blanket quickly, caught him, placed him in it, and put him right away.

Now the wives of Juka's son came in and sat down in the house. Two other brothers took them for wives. They stayed a long time, never saw their first husband again. Old Juka kept him secreted, made him a Weänmauna, a hidden one.

After a time the two women wished to go home to visit Jamuka. They took beads and blankets, nice things of all kinds, and went to their father at the foot of Wahkalu.

"We have never seen our husband," said they, "since we went to his father's. We have new husbands now."

"I think that is well enough," said Jamuka. "His father has put him away. His brothers are as good for you as he was."

The sisters agreed with their father and went back and lived at Juka's house after that.

◈

(Wintun, California)

45
Rolling Skull

The people were living at Matsaka. A young man was a great hunter. He went every day after deer. One day he was far from home at sunset, and it was dark and raining. He saw smoke from a house in Halona and thought to himself, "I will go and get shelter there." He climbed to the top of the roof and looked down the hatchway. Inside a fine-looking woman was sitting by the fireplace tying her daughter's hair. He went into the house, and the woman said, "Sit down." He sat down, and the girl brought out food and the man ate. When he had finished he said, "Thank you." The woman said to him, "Where were you going?" He answered, "My home is in Matsaka, and I was hunting deer." She said, "It is too dark for you to find your way now. Stay here tonight." "All right." The old woman said, "Will you have my daughter tonight?" "I think so." The girl was beautiful. When the bed was made in the inner room, the girl and the hunter went in to sleep.

Next morning at daybreak the hunter woke. The house was an old ruin, and all the good blankets he had gone to sleep on were bits of rag. The girl was a skeleton. Her arm lay over the hunter's shoulder, and when he jumped the bones rattled as he threw it off. He was terrified. He ran to the ladder and started off as fast as he could. He could hear the old woman's skull rolling after him.

At Hawiku they were dancing the yaya dance. The hunter ran among them, and cried, "Somebody is chasing me. Save me." They said, "Go into the circle and dance with the girls." He danced the yaya. The skull came rolling into the plaza. It called out, "Where is my daughter's husband? She is crying for her husband." The skull rolled right into the dance. The girls screamed and the men ran in every direction. The hunter ran off as fast as he could.

He came to a Navaho camp. They were dancing the war dance. He called out, "Save! Save me! Someone is chasing me." They said, "We will." They took off his clothing and put on Navaho costume and did his hair Navaho fashion and hung a quiver over his shoulder. The skull came. It called out, "Where is my daughter's husband? Have you seen my daughter's husband?" It rolled right up to the hunter, and he ran off as fast as he could.

He came to Laguna. They were dancing the harvest dance. He cried out, "Save me. Save me. Someone is chasing me." They said, "Dance with us. Take this bow in your hand." He went into the dance. The skull came. It cried, "Where is my daughter's husband? Have you seen my daughter's husband? She is crying for him." It rolled right among the dancers. They scattered, and the hunter ran as fast as he could.

He came to bluebirds in a piñon tree. Bluebird Chief said to the hunter, "Why are you running?" He answered, "Someone is chasing me. Save me!" "Come up here and climb under my wing." He climbed up the piñon and hid under the bird's wing. The skull came. It called out, "Where is my daughter's husband? Have you seen my daughter's husband?" The bluebirds tittered, "Ha, ha, ha, ha! We haven't seen your daughter's husband." The skull called again, "Where is my daughter's husband? Have you seen my daughter's husband?" The bluebirds tittered, "Ha, ha, ha, ha. We haven't seen your daughter's husband." The skull came right up the tree and up to Bluebird Chief. The hunter jumped out from under his wing and ran off as fast as he could.

He came to a large lake with sunflowers growing around it. The biggest sunflower said to him, "Why are you running?" He said, "Someone is chasing me. Save me." "Come up on my ear." The hunter climbed up and sat on the big leaf of the sunflower. The skull came. It called, "Where is my daughter's husband? Have you seen my daughter's husband?" The sunflowers said, "No, we didn't see your daughter's husband." The skull called, "Sunflowers, you have seen my daughter's husband." "No, we didn't see your daughter's husband." The skull shook the biggest sunflower, and the hunter fell down and ran as fast as he could to the east.

He came to Porcupine. He cried, "Save me. Someone is chasing me." Porcupine said, "Come into my house. Get piñon gum and put it a hand deep inside the door." When he had done this, he sat down by the Porcupine. The skull came. "Where is my husband? [*sic*] Have you seen my husband?" Porcupine said, "No, I have not seen your husband." "Yes, his tracks went in here. Send out my husband." "Come in and get him." "Send him out to me." "No, if you want him, come in and get him." The fourth time Skull came into Porcupine's house. It stuck fast in the piñon gum, and Porcupine set fire to the gum and burned Skull and destroyed it. The hunter stayed with Porcupine and married Porcupine Girl.

(Zuni, Southwest)

46
Water Jar Boy

The people were living at Sikyatki. There was a fine-look-ing girl who refused to get married. Her mother made water jars all the time. One day as she was using her foot to mix some clay, she told her daughter to go on with this while she went for water. The girl tried to mix the clay on a flat stone by stepping on it. Somehow some of it entered her. This made her pregnant, and after a time she gave birth. The mother was angry about this, but when she looked she saw it was not a baby that had been born, but a little jar. When the mother asked where it came from the girl just cried. Then the father came in. He said he was very glad his daughter had a baby. When he found out that it was a water jar, he became very fond of it.

He watched it and saw it move. It grew, and in twenty days it had become big. It could go about with the other children and was able to talk. The children also became fond of it. They found out from his talk that he was Water Jar Boy. His mother cried, because he had no legs or arms or eyes. But they were able to feed him through the jar mouth.

When snow came the boy begged his grandfather to take him along with the men to hunt rabbits. "My poor grandson, you can't hunt rabbits; you have no arms or legs."

"Take me anyway," said the boy. "You are so old, you can't kill anything." His grandfather took him down under the mesa where he rolled along. Pretty soon he saw a rabbit track and followed it. Then a rabbit ran out, and he began to chase it. He hit himself against a rock. The jar broke, and up jumped a boy.

He was very glad his skin had been broken and that he was a big boy. He had lots of beads around his neck, earstrings of turquoise, a dance kilt and moccasins, and a buckskin shirt. He was fine-looking and handsomely dressed. He killed four jackrabbits before sunset, because he was a good runner.

His grandfather was waiting for him at the foot of the mesa, but did not know him. He asked the fine-looking boy, "Did you see my grandson anywhere?"

"No, I did not see him."

"That's too bad; he's late."

"I didn't see anyone anywhere," said the boy. Then he said, "I am your grandson." He said this because his grandfather looked so disappointed.

"No, you are not my grandson."

"Yes, I am."

"You are only teasing me. My grandson is a round jar and has no arms and legs."

Then the boy said, "I am telling you the truth. I am your grandson. This morning you carried me down here. I looked for rabbits and chased one, just rolling along. Pretty soon I hit myself on a rock. My skin was broken, and I came out of it. I am the very one who is your grandson. You must believe me." Then the old man believed him, and they went home together.

When the grandfather came to the house with a fine-looking man, the girl was ashamed, thinking the man was a suitor. The old man said, "This is Water Jar Boy, my grandson." The grandmother then asked how the water jar became a boy, and the two men told her. Finally, the women were convinced.

The boy went about with the other boys of the village. One day he said to his mother, "Who is my father?"

"I don't know," she replied. He kept on asking, but it just

made her cry. Finally he said, "I am going to find my father, tomorrow."

"You can't find him. I have never been with any man so there is no place for you to look for a father," she said.

"But I know I have one," the boy said. "I know where he lives. I am going to see him."

The mother begged him not to go, but he insisted. The next day she fixed food for him, and he went off toward the southwest to a place called Horse Mesa Point. There was a spring at this place. As he approached he saw a man walking a little way from the spring. He said to the boy, "Where are you going?"

"To the spring," the boy answered.

"Why are you going there?"

"I want to see my father."

"Who is your father?"

"He lives in this spring."

"Well, you will never find your father," said the man.

"Well, I want to go to the spring. My father is living in it," said the boy.

"Who is your father?" asked the man again.

"Well, I think you are my father."

"How do you know that?"

"I just know, that's all."

Then the man stared hard at the boy, trying to scare him. The boy just kept on saying, "You are my father." At last the man said, "Yes, I am your father. I came out of the spring to meet you." He put his arms around the boy's neck. He was very glad his boy had come, and he took him down to the spring.

There were many people living there. The women and the girls ran up to the boy and put their arms around him, because they were glad he had come. This way he found his father and his father's relatives. He stayed there one night.

The next day he went to his own home and told his mother he had found his father.

Soon his mother got sick and died. The boy thought to himself, "It's no use for me to stay with these people," so he went to the spring. There he found his mother among the other women. He learned that his father was Red Water Snake. He told his boy that he could not live over at Sikyatki, so he had made the boy's mother sick so she would die and come to live with him. After that they all lived together.

(Tewa, Southwest)

47

The Storytelling Stone

In a Seneca village lived a boy whose father and mother died when he was only a few weeks old. The little boy was cared for by a woman, who had known his parents. She gave him the name of *Poyeshao^n* [Orphan].

The boy grew to be a healthy, active little fellow. When he was old enough, his foster mother gave him a bow and arrows, and said, "It is time for you to learn to hunt. Tomorrow morning go to the woods and kill all the birds you can find."

Taking cobs of dry corn the woman shelled off the kernels and parched them in hot ashes; and the next morning she gave the boy some of the corn for his breakfast and rolled up some in a piece of buckskin and told him to take it with him, for he would be gone all day and would get hungry.

Poyeshao^n started off and was very successful. At noon he sat down and rested and ate some of the parched corn, then he hunted till the middle of the afternoon. When he began to work toward home he had a good string of birds.

The next morning *Poyeshao^n*'s foster mother gave him parched corn for breakfast and while he was eating she told him that he must do his best when hunting, for if he became a good hunter, he would always be prosperous.

The boy took his bow and arrows and little bundle of parched corn and went to the woods; again he found plenty of birds. At midday he ate his corn and thought over what his foster mother had told him. In his mind he said, "I'll do just as my mother tells me, then some time I'll be able to hunt big game."

Poyeshaoⁿ hunted till toward evening, then went home with a larger string of birds than he had the previous day. His foster mother thanked him, and said, "Now you have begun to help me get food."

Early the next morning the boy's breakfast was ready and as soon as he had eaten it he took his little bundle of parched corn and started off. He went farther into the woods and at night came home with a larger string of birds than he had the second day. His foster mother praised and thanked him.

Each day the boy brought home more birds than the previous day. On the ninth day he killed so many that he brought them home on his back. His foster mother tied the birds in little bundles of three or four and distributed them among her neighbors.

The tenth day the boy started off, as usual, and, as each day he had gone farther for game than on the preceding day, so now he went deeper into the woods than ever. About midday the sinew that held the feathers to his arrow loosened. Looking around for a place where he could sit down while he took the sinew off and wound it on again, he saw a small opening and near the center of the opening a high, smooth, flat-topped, round stone. He went to the stone, sprang up onto it, and sat down. He unwound the sinew and put it in his mouth to soften, then he arranged the arrow feathers, and was about to fasten them to the arrow when a voice, right there near him, asked, "Shall I tell you stories?"

Poyeshaoⁿ looked up expecting to see a man, not seeing anyone he looked behind the stone and around it, then he again began to tie the feathers to his arrow.

"Shall I tell you stories?" asked a voice right there by him.

The boy looked in every direction, but saw no one. Then he made up his mind to watch and find out who was trying to fool him. He stopped work and listened and when the voice again asked, "Shall I tell you stories?" he found that it came from the stone, then he asked, "What is that? What does it mean to tell stories?"

"It is telling what happened a long time ago. If you will give me your birds, I'll tell you stories."

"You may have the birds."

As soon as the boy promised to give the birds, the stone began telling what happened long ago. When one story was told, another was begun. The boy sat, with his head down, and listened. Toward night the stone said, "We will rest now. Come again tomorrow. If anyone asks about your birds, say that you have killed so many that they are getting scarce and you have to go a long way to find one."

While going home the boy killed five or six birds. When his foster mother asked why he had so few birds, he said that they were scarce; that he had to go far for them.

The next morning *Poyeshao^n* started off with his bow and arrows and little bundle of parched corn, but he forgot to hunt for birds; he was thinking of the stories the stone had told him. When a bird lighted near him he shot it, but he kept straight on toward the opening in the woods. When he got there he put his birds on the stone, and called out, "I've come! Here are birds. Now tell me stories."

The stone told story after story. Toward night it said, "Now we must rest till tomorrow."

On the way home the boy looked for birds, but it was late and he found only a few.

That night the foster mother told her neighbors that when *Poyeshao^n* first began to hunt he had brought home a great many birds, but now he brought only four or five after being in the woods from morning till night. She said there was something strange about it, either he threw the birds away or gave them to some animal, or maybe he idled time away, didn't hunt. She hired a boy to follow *Poyeshao^n* and find out what he was doing.

The next morning the boy took his bow and arrows and

followed *Poyeshao^n*, keeping out of his sight and sometimes shooting a bird. *Poyeshao^n* killed a good many birds; then, about the middle of the forenoon, he suddenly started off toward the east, running as fast as he could. The boy followed till he came to an opening in the woods and saw *Poyeshao^n* climb up and sit down on a large round stone; he crept nearer and heard talking. When he couldn't see the person to whom *Poyeshao^n* was talking he went up to the boy, and asked, "What are you doing here?"

"Hearing stories."

"What are stories?"

"Telling about things that happened long ago. Put your birds on this stone, and say, 'I've come to hear stories.' "

The boy did as told and straightway the stone began. The boys listened till the sun went down, then the stone said, "We will rest now. Come again tomorrow."

On the way home *Poyeshao^n* killed three or four birds.

When the woman asked the boy she had sent why *Poyeshao^n* killed so few birds, he said, "I followed him for a while, then I spoke to him, and after that we hunted together till it was time to come home. We couldn't find many birds."

The next morning the elder boy said, "I'm going with *Poyeshao^n* to hunt, it's sport." The two started off together. By the middle of the forenoon each boy had a long string of birds. They hurried to the opening, put the birds on the stone, and said, "We have come. Here are the birds! Tell us stories."

They sat on the stone and listened to stories till late in the afternoon, then the stone said, "We'll rest now till tomorrow."

On the way home the boys shot every bird they could find, but it was late and they didn't find many.

Several days went by in this way, then the foster mother said, "Those boys kill more birds than they bring home," and she hired two men to follow them.

The next morning, when *Poyeshao^n* and his friend started for the woods, the two men followed. When the boys had a large number of birds they stopped hunting and hurried to the opening. The men followed and, hiding behind trees, saw them put the birds on a large round stone, then jump up and sit there, with their heads down, listening to a man's voice; every little while they said, "$\hat{U}^n$!"

"Let's go there and find out who is talking to those boys," said one man to the other. They walked quickly to the stone, and asked, "What are you doing, boys?"

The boys were startled, but $Poyeshao^n$ said, "You must promise not to tell anyone."

They promised, then $Poyeshao^n$ said, "Jump up and sit on the stone."

The men seated themselves on the stone, then the boy said, "Go on with the story; we are listening."

The four sat with their heads down and the stone began to tell stories. When it was almost night the stone said, "Tomorrow all the people in your village must come and listen to my stories. Tell the chief to send every man, and have each man bring something to eat. You must clean the brush away so the people can sit on the ground near me."

That night $Poyeshao^n$ told the chief about the storytelling stone, and gave him the stone's message. The chief sent a runner to give the message to each family in the village.

Early the next morning everyone in the village was ready to start. $Poyeshao^n$ went ahead and the crowd followed. When they came to the opening each man put what he had brought, meat or bread, on the stone; the brush was cleared away, and everyone sat down.

When all was quiet the stone said, "Now I will tell you stories of what happened long ago. There was a world before this. The things that I am going to tell about happened in that world. Some of you will remember every word that I say, some will remember a part of the words, and some will forget them all—I think this will be the way, but each man must do the best he can. Hereafter you must tell these stories to one another—Now listen."

Each man bent his head and listened to every word the stone said. Once in a while the boys said "Ûⁿ!" When the sun was almost down the stone said, "We'll rest now. Come tomorrow and bring meat and bread."

The next morning when the people gathered around the stone they found that the meat and bread they had left there the day before was gone. They put the food they had brought on the stone, then sat in a circle and waited. When all was quiet the stone began. Again it told stories till the sun was almost down, then it said, "Come tomorrow. Tomorrow I will finish the stories of what happened long ago."

Early in the morning the people of the village gathered around the stone and, when all was quiet, the stone began to tell stories, and it told till late in the afternoon, then it said, "I have finished! You must keep these stories as long as the world lasts; tell them to your children and grandchildren generation after generation. One person will remember them better than another. When you go to a man or a woman to ask for one of these stories carry something to pay for it, bread or meat, or whatever you have. I know all that happened in the world before this; I have told it to you. When you visit one another, you must tell these things, and keep them up always. I have finished."

And so it has been. From the Stone came all the knowledge the Senecas have of the world before this.

(Seneca, Iroquois)

48
How Chipmunks
Got Their Stripes

A grandmother and granddaughter were living together. They had a skin blanket, but it was old and a good deal of the hair was worn off.

The two women went to the forest to camp and cut wood, and they carried the blanket to cover themselves with at night. They had been in the forest only a few days when they found that their skin blanket was alive and was angry. They threw the blanket down and ran toward home as fast as they could go. Soon they heard the skin following them.

When it seemed very near the grandmother began to sing and her song said, "My granddaughter and I are running for our lives, My granddaughter and I are running for our lives."

When the song ended, the women could scarcely hear the skin following them, but not long afterward they heard it again. When they reached home the skin, now a bear, was so near that as they pushed open the door it clawed at them and scratched their backs, but they got in.

The old woman and her granddaughter were chipmunks. Since that time chipmunks have stripes on their backs, the result of the scratches given by the bear.

(Seneca, Iroquois)

49
Bat

Once there was a war between beasts and birds. Bat was on birds' side. In the first battle, the birds were badly beaten. As soon as Bat saw that the battle was going against them, he crept away, hid under a log, and stayed there till the fight was over.

When the animals were going home, Bat slipped in among them.

After they had gone some distance, they saw him and asked one another: "How is this? Bat is one of the men who fought against us?"

Bat heard them, and he said: "Oh, no! I am one of you; I don't belong to the bird people. Did you ever see one of those people who had double teeth? Go and look in their mouths and see if they have. If you find one bird with double teeth, you can say that I belong to the bird people. But I don't; I am one of your own people."

They didn't say anything more; they let Bat stay with them.

Soon after, there was another battle; in that battle birds won. As Bat's side was getting beaten, he slipped away and hid under a log. When the battle was over and birds were going home, Bat went in among them.

When they noticed him, they said: "You are our enemy; we saw you fighting against us."

"Oh, no," said Bat, "I am one of you; I don't belong to those beasts. Did you ever see one of those people who had wings?"

They didn't say anything more; they let him stay with them.

So Bat went back and forth as long as the war lasted. At the end of the war, birds and beasts held a council to see what to do with him. At last they said to Bat: "Hereafter, you will fly around alone at night, and will never have any friends, either among those that fly, or those that walk."

(Modoc, California)

50
Strong Man Who
Holds Up the Sky

Ages ago, when all the Tsimshian were living at Metlakatla
Passage and at Gadu, on the present cemetery site at
Metlakatla stood the Gitzarhlaehl village. The chief had four
sons. Three of them were very active, but the fourth, the
youngest, appeared to be very lazy and also indifferent to everything. Nothing seemed to interest him. His brothers were
very industrious and were foremost in all activities. In wrestling they overcame everybody, and in rock-putting they also
outdid all competitors. In hunting they were unsurpassed. At
all times they made fun of their young dirty brother, who was
lazy and dirty and always slept in the ashes beside the fire. He
would never take a cleansing bath but would be content to lie
by the fire in what looked like filth. Everyone in the house
made fun of him and rebuked him for his laziness, but he
never paid any attention to what they said.

It was now the time when the people would go and hunt
the sea lions at an island away out to sea. Only the strongest
and quickest could take part. The island was a bare one. A
high sea always ran, and one mistake by the hunter would
mean his death. He must be able to climb and grasp the huge
sea lion or be struck by the beast. A sea-lion hunter had to be
not only strong, but quick and smart. The lazy man's brothers
were now training for this event. Every morning, they would
go down to the water to bathe. Then they would return to the
house, where the chief, their father, would whip them with

shrub branches and rub them with a brew of roots.[1] Then they drank in large quantities a brew of devil's-club. All the brothers were treated alike, except the youngest, who was seemingly too lazy and was satisfied to lie by the fire in ashes and filth. He was never seen even to go out to urinate or excrete. Every day the other brothers were being trained. They tested their strength by pulling off the branches of the nearby trees.

Each morning, the inmates of the chief's house would rebuke the lazy brother, saying, "Why do you not bathe sometimes to keep clean?" Others would say, taunting him, "You will be the one whom we will have to depend on to feed us when we starve." To all these insults and taunts, the lazy brother paid no heed.

Now, unbeknown to the others, the lazy brother would arise and go out and bathe when all were asleep in the house, and he would also massage his body with roots, just as his brothers did. When he had finished, he would return to his ragged robes and lie on the dirt and ashes and would pay no attention to the others.

Every day his brothers were gaining in strength and cleverness. Now they were able to break off the spruce-tree branches with apparent ease. And they increased their insults and taunts to their lazy indifferent brother. Finishing their ablutions, they would go off to rest in comfort. At night, again and again, the lazy brother would come out to bathe and massage himself and then would slip back into the house unobserved and would lie in the ashes and filth, to the shame and disgust of his father and all the rest of the household. Among those who ridiculed him more than anyone else was an uncle, his oldest uncle, who was very much ashamed of him. But a younger uncle and his wife used to befriend him by secretly giving him food. They would rebuke those who ridiculed him.

---

[1] The roots of a very strong poisonous plant.

The uncle would say, "Cease your taunts; the time for my nephew to improve his strength has not yet come. When he is ready, he will prove to you that he is worthy." This only served to bring on more taunts. The eldest brother was most sarcastic. He would say, "He likes the odor of his own urine and excrement. How can he ever be a hunter?" Instead of becoming angry, the lazy brother paid no heed. Every night he went to bathe and massage himself, and every night he would test his strength.

One night when he came to bathe in the cold water, he saw a loon swimming towards him and calling out, as if to speak to him. When it came close to where he was bathing, the young man spoke to the loon, saying, "What is it, supernatural one?" The loon then spoke, "Brother, I feel sorry for the way your haughty brothers taunt you. I will give you strength that will overcome them all. Take hold of my feet, and I will dive underwater with you." So the young man took hold of the loon's feet, and it dove down with him. When they reached the bottom, a cavern opened, and the loon led the young man in, and said, "At the end of the cave, you will find a spring. Bathe in this, and then return to your village. Partake of devil's-club to cleanse yourself, and lie by the fire as you have always done, as if nothing had happened. The young man, having finished his bathing, returned to his father's house, and soon all in the household were up and awake. The young man's brothers went into the water to bathe. They went out to a spruce tree and broke off the limbs. They were now much improved in strength. When they came back into the house, they heaped more taunts and abuses at their lazy brother. All in the house were bitter against him, but the youngest uncle and his wife took the lazy brother's part, as they pitied him. They themselves did not know of his secret training; they only felt pity for him.

Every day the brothers were training, and every night when all were asleep the younger brother went down for his training. So one night the loon said to him, "Now you must go to the large spruce tree and tear its branches from it, and then bend the tree until its top touches the ground." The young man went to the spruce tree and pulled a large branch from it. Then he took hold of the trunk and pushed it over until its top touched the ground, as he had been directed. Then he went to lie down by the fire, as he had always done, as if asleep. Here he rested all day.

The young brothers now had nearly finished their training. Soon they would be ready for the sea-lion hunt, and, as ever, they taunted their lazy brother, "Come, you who lie in your own excrement! Make yourself ready to help the slaves when we bring back canoe-loads of sea lion! You should be able to carry the small pieces of meat from the canoes to the house when we return." Thus they taunted the younger brother before they completed their massaging with roots and retired to rest.

It was now time for them to go for their sea-lion hunt. They were divided among the uncles. There were only three brothers who were trained, but there were four uncles, each having his own canoe. So there was no one for the youngest uncle. They were making preparations, and the young man who was always lying by the fire came to his youngest uncle's wife and said, "My aunt, prepare me a new shirt and some provisions. I will go with my uncle in his canoe." When the other brothers heard this, they all laughed and told him, "What can you do? You will be in the hunters' way. Besides, you are so filthy that even the sea lions will go away from you, and we may not get anything. Do not let him come!" Thus they cried out, and the elder uncles said, "Why did you not train, if you wanted to go along? You will be only a hindrance and delay us." The elder uncles refused to have him. The youngest uncle then said, "Come into my canoe; you can help in many ways and then you can always stay in the canoe." So the unclean brother who had apparently disregarded all the training ways went along in the canoe of his young uncle.

It was very early in the morning and still dark, just before daybreak, when they set out to go to the place where sea lions gathered in herds. While the hunters were still a long way off, they could hear the roaring of these large beasts. There were so many of them. The island, which stood alone, away out to sea, was shaped like a huge sea lion. The hunters now had arrived at this sea-lion island, where it was always stormy and difficult to approach and where there were always high seas running. It was necessary to jump from the canoe on the crest of a wave, and if the hunter missed his jump he would perish in the water or be jumped upon by the sea lions. So there must be no mistake.

The first canoe to reach there was that of the oldest uncle with several of his kinsmen who had trained faithfully. The uncle stood at the bow of his canoe, ready to jump to where the sea lions were. As the canoe rose on top of the wave, he jumped, and as he did, another wave crashed the canoe against the rock and broke it. All in the canoe perished. As soon as the oldest uncle landed on the island, he was attacked by a huge sea lion and thrown into the air; his back was broken. Then the next uncle came and stood ready. When the canoe rode on the crest of the wave, he jumped, but failed to land. His canoe was smashed, and all perished. It was then that the youngest brother said to his uncle, "I will jump onto the rock, and you will guide the canoe, and we will overcome the sea lions." The others in the canoe would not heed what the younger brother wanted. They said, "Why should you overcome the sea lions, while those who have observed all training ways have failed. This will only belittle us the more. It is well we should now go back rather than perish like the rest." But the young man was insistent, saying, "Are you old women or little children that you cannot do what men can do?" They were all embarrassed, and the young uncle headed the canoe toward the rock. The young brother, whom all others had been making fun of as being lazy and useless, stood up in the canoe and, as the canoe rose on the crest of the wave and was at its highest, he jumped safely onto the island. As he landed, a huge sea lion, the chief of the sea lions, approached him. Without any effort the young man seized the monster, threw it over, and broke its back. He did the same with many more sea lions. Seeing that they were being overcome, the other beasts jumped into the water.

As the rock was now bare (all sea lions and many carcasses remained on the island), the young man called his youngest uncle. Each time the canoe rose on the crest of the waves, the young man placed in it the carcass of a sea lion, until the canoe was full. Then he himself jumped into the canoe, and they returned to their village. Those that had survived were very much ashamed, because they had made taunting and belittling remarks about the youngest brother.

Landing below the house of the youngest uncle, the young man went up. Instead of going to his usual sleeping place, he made himself a place to sleep alongside the fire. There he slept while the slaves brought up the sea-lion carcasses.

The next day he arose and called upon his uncle, saying, "Come, we must go for more sea lions." So they went out every day, and at nightfall they would return with a canoeload of sea lions. This they did for a long while. Now the youngest uncle's house was full of sea-lion meat, and he was the only one that had a plenteous supply. He began trading with all the other tribes. Soon he became very wealthy, to the embarrassment of the elder uncles who now had to come to the young man for food.

It was now time for the competitions of the various tribes from all over to find out who were the strongest contestants in their midst. Many young men began to train and fast; they went through long periods of training. Again the young man seemingly paid no heed and would sleep in the dirt. Whenever he did rise, the people saw a pool of water where he had slept. So they said, "Why does he not go out to urinate?" To all this he, as formerly, paid no heed, but when all were asleep he would go quietly to the beach and bathe and train himself. As soon as he had finished, he would go into the forest at the rear of the village and tear off the limbs and the large branches of trees. Finally he began uprooting first whole small trees and then large ones. He would carry them out and throw them into the sea. Every night he did this secretly, unbeknown to the people in the house. And while he was training the large loon would always swim about him, advising him what to do.

Again the people began to make fun of his lazy ways. Some said, "Why does he not train as the others do, so that at least he may be strong?" Others said, "How can one train and be unclean? We are ashamed of him." And as before, only the wife of his younger uncle had compassion for him and shielded him. When the others would have thrown him out, she said, "Do not forget that he once put you all to shame."

For a while the people kept quiet while the other young people trained for the athletic combats, which were wrestling and weight-throwing. They would wrestle among themselves and throw heavy boulders. After this, they would cleanse themselves by bathing and drinking devil's-club juice. Then they would retire by themselves to their sleeping places and would have no contact with anything impure. No women were allowed even to look at them, except their aged paternal aunts, who were allowed to prepare their food or to assist them in any way. Sexual indulgence was prohibited, and above all absolute cleanliness was the rule. The trainee was made to swim great distances, and this even in freezing weather. As they came from the water, the chief would whip their bare backs. Then they would go to the chief's house to be fed and advised. This training period was a hard one for all. But the young brother seemed to pay no attention to the taunts directed at him. Nobody knew that he was secretly training and as a result was in very good condition. He was able to uproot big trees with ease and to throw large boulders a long distance.

The day on which tribal contests were to take place was near, and distant tribes began to gather. All the strong men from these were picked for the stone-throwing contest. Large stones were gathered together. Each contestant took his turn at throwing, and the one who could throw the farthest was a winner. All the tribes were the spectators. As each contestant heaved the heavy-weighted boulder, should it fall short of other contestants' he would be jeered by such remarks as, What a mess! Among the contestants was a great man and a warrior from Gitrhahla. He was the contestant who so far had outthrown all the others. The Gitrhahla were very happy and began challenging others, "Come, bring down your strong men; do not send women as if they were men!" These taunts aggravated the other Tsimshian tribes. While they were thus excited, the young brother who they thought had not trained came down from his uncle's house and proceeded to where the other contestants stood. As soon as his own people saw him, they cried out, "Call him back, we have had enough shame now! He will further belittle us. He has never trained, and those who have trained were overcome. What does he expect to accomplish, he who has such filthy habits!" The people tried to get him to return, but he would not listen to anybody. He went to the boulder which the contestants were using and said, "Why use so small a stone? This is only fit for children to use." He went to where a huge boulder was and, without any effort, picked it up and raised it on the palm of his hand. He gave a mighty throw, and the boulder traveled much farther than those of the other contestants who were using smaller ones. A great murmur of approval went up among the Tsimshian, and the Gitrhahla who had been so boastful were now much embarrassed. The young man, after he had accomplished this, went back to his uncle's house, to the spot where he had always slept. He was unconcerned at what he had done and did not take any part in the happy dancing that followed, when the Tsimshian had overcome all competitors by his stone-throwing. The stone-throwing had taken many days, as the competitors were many and came from all the different tribes, not only Tsimshian, but also the Git'amat, the Gitlawp, the Wudstae, the Niskae, the Gitrhahla, and all the nearby nations.

When the wrestling began, it took a long while. The winner of the first match would be challenged by another, until he would be defeated. This kept on until finally there was an outstanding contestant. He was a large man, a Git'amat, a giant. As fast as competitors came forward, he would grasp them and throw them down with such violence that their backs would break. He was now openly challenging everybody to come and meet him. "Where are the brave and strong men of the Tsimshian? Come, I want you to try me and overcome me." This he called out, and the Tsimshian tribes were now crestfallen. There was none among them who could answer the challenge. But behold, the young man whom they had always ridiculed as the "Filthy One" came down the beach toward the giant monster, to meet him. They were astounded. Some said, "Do not let him shame us further! Stop him!" But the young man went on down the beach. Taking off his robe, he began to make preparations to meet his opponent. There were a great many spectators, all making fun of the Tsimshian because of the "Filthy One." The giant ran at the young man, who at once turned about and grasped his attacker. The huge man went up into the air and fell back to the ground, his bones broken. The Git'amat, who had been very happy, were now very much embarrassed. Such a simple-looking fellow had defeated their champion so thoroughly that every bone in his body was smashed. Again the Tsimshian were jubilant. But the young man, quite unconcerned, went up the beach, as no further competitors came forward. He returned to his uncle's house and went to his sleeping place alongside the fire. The people no longer made fun of him; they now recognized that he was no ordinary being. All now had respect for him.

The wrestling competitions once over, it was now a competition of complete strength, in which the competitor was called to go up into the woods and to uproot a tree and drag it down to the beach. The one who could bring down the largest tree would be the winner. This was the final test of the athletes, and it was in this that the young man had been training. A tree nearby had been selected, and one competitor went to it. After a long struggle, he gave it up. Then the next, and so on until finally one was able to uproot this tree and drag it down. This man was a Wudstae. This tribe was now outstanding, and as each following competitor went to another tree to try and uproot it but failed, he was jeered by the Wudstae, who all felt that their man would not be defeated. When it seemed that no one would come forward to challenge him, the Wudstae were even more outspoken in their jeers. They called out, "Where is he that sleeps in his own urine?" meaning the young man who had won the first and second contests. The people were startled to see the young man walking from his uncle's house and going to where the competition was taking place. Arriving there, he looked at the tree that they were endeavoring to uproot, and said, "Why do you strong men play with a sapling? Why not a large spruce tree, that one?" pointing to a large tree standing on a hill. As soon as he had finished speaking, he walked up to this tree and began shaking it. Then he pulled out the lower branches without breaking them. Next he grasped the tree trunk, and began shaking it. He gradually lifted it out of the ground, roots and all. Then he packed it down to the water's edge. A great murmur of approval arose from all the people, excepting the Wudstae, who were now crestfallen. The young man not only had overcome their strong man but had brought down a much larger tree.

The young man's fame spread to all the other countries. Various animals began to hear of it. They, in their separate turns, came to attack him, first the Howhow [mountain lion], the Medeek [grizzly], the Gibaeo [wolves]. But all these he overcame. The forests themselves began to crowd down upon the village where the champion lived, but he uprooted the trees as fast as they came. The mountains began to crowd down, and he pushed them back, one by one, to where they now stand. So now this young man had overcome everything in the world.

At this time, there was a man who was holding up the world on the end of a stout hemlock pole. Ever so often, the bluebill duck used to go to where he was and grease his joints. Every time he moved, he caused an earth tremor. When he changed hands, he caused an earthquake. This man was now very old, and he wanted to rest.

The young champion who had acquired his strength and power from the loon was sleeping by the fireside, and as usual he bothered nobody and spent most of the time asleep. He was now again beginning to be made fun of by his people, even though he had saved them from shame and embarrassment. But the people were forgetful.

One night at a time when all were asleep, a large canoe came to the beach below the house in which he was staying. When landing, those in the canoe kept saying to each other— there were many in the canoe—"This is the place; this is where he lives." Then the steersman jumped ashore, saying, "I will go up and see him. You await us here!" The strange man walked up directly to the house in which the young man was staying with his uncle and went straight to the young man who was sleeping. He shook him, saying, "Well, dear man, we have come for you. Your grandfather is now very weak, and he wants you to take his place." The champion woke up, and, without saying anything to anyone in the house, he followed the stranger down into the canoe. There he seated himself in the stern, and the steersman said, "Let us be on our way!" Without any paddling the canoe moved away as if it were alive, and it traveled fast. This canoe was alive. It was a black fish, and the canoeman sat on its back. When they were away out to sea, out of sight of land, they came to a rocklike island. Here they landed, and the crew, which was human-like, changed into loons. Only the steersman kept his human shape. He said to the young man, "Your grandfather feels very ill. That is why he sent for you, as it is now time that you should replace him. He has trained you these many days, and now you have overcome everything and everybody. You must take up the work which he has prepared you for. Follow me!" So without anything more being said, they went down a path which led inside this rocklike island. The trail all along was guarded by ducks and loons. Finally they came to the end of the trail. Then the loon, who was still in human form, stooped down and pulled the lid off an opening in the ground. A long ladder was seen by the young man. They climbed down this ladder. Finally they came to a small platform, all four sides of which were steep. No bottom was visible. In the middle of this platform sat a very aged man who was holding between his legs a huge hemlock pole. This he held against what appeared to be a flat floor. Then the loon man spoke, "Your grandfather has been holding up the world since it was made; now he has become weakened with age. You will take his place, after he has told you what you shall do. The aged one, seeing the young man, said, "I have been waiting a long while for you, but I wanted to be certain that you would be strong enough to carry on this work. That is why I wanted you to train and win all competitions in strength. This you have done, and now I will further instruct you. The ducks and loons will be your messengers, and they will supply you with food. They also will constantly oil your joints, in order that they may not grow stiff. They will know where to find me after I leave here. Now remember, you must always stay very still, as every time you move or change your position, no matter how slightly, it will be the cause of earthquakes. Should you collapse, this would cause the destruction of the world. All would perish." When he had finished, he very slowly arose, still holding the huge hemlock pole, and the young man sat down in his stead. The aged one placed the pole in his hand, and said, "Now I am going to sleep and rest. I am confident you can carry my burden."

The young man, it must be said, had been under the influence of the old man right from the start. He had made it so that he did not crave for the company of others, but was always satisfied to be by himself. Thus he would be accustomed to the loneliness of his new duties. He had shunned all companions and had never shown any desire to meet any woman. Yet, after he had accomplished his great feats of strength, they made many attempts to tempt him, but he always held himself aloof. Thus when he took his new duties he was contented.

When, next morning, the people of his uncle's house arose and saw that his sleeping place was vacant, they felt that a secret raid had come upon them and he had been taken away. But the uncle and his wife said, "I am certain no harm can happen to him, for he is a supernatural being. He is not like us. That is why he was always able to accomplish those wonders which we witnessed. Now we may see him again, but whatever he is doing, you may be sure that it is something worthwhile." The people searched for him, but he had left no trace anywhere.

(Tsimshian, Northwest Coast)

51
The Faster

There was once a man who had an only child. One day he said, "My child, you must know that you are all alone in the world, with no one from whom to hope for anything. Only the spirits can help you." Thus he spoke to his child.

Then the son fasted. After he had been fasting for some time his father came to him and said, "My dear son, you have now been fasting for a very long period. Surely you have obtained some gift from the spirits. You had better stop now." "Father," answered the boy, "you are quite right, but still I should like to continue. All that you have told me to fast for, all that I have now obtained. I have received the gift of killing an enemy at will; I have obtained the gift of old age. Indeed, the spirits came to me and took me to a doctor's lodge and there they brought me to a person who was dead and told me that I could restore him to life again. It was then they told me not to fast any longer. Yet in spite of their request I continued. Then the spirits from below came, from the creation lodge they came, and they bestowed all things upon me—victory in war, the ability to cure the sick, success in hunting, a long and complete life—all this they gave me. Indeed every spirit to whom Earthmaker had given power, each one bestowed something upon me. 'You have fasted enough,' they said. But, Father, what I most desire is that I shall not die. That is why I do not want to stop. So let me continue. Indeed, only when I have obtained that gift shall I stop."

So the youth continued. The spirits came to him and said, "Young man, you have fasted enough. Earthmaker has bestowed upon you the gift of living to extreme old age, of obtaining everything you wish." "I am grateful," said the boy, "but what I desire is never to die." The spirits could not dissuade him. "Indeed, I shall never be satisfied until I obtain the gift of immortal life," continued the boy. He was unable to face the thought of death; he dreaded it very much.

In the council lodge of the spirits it was accordingly decided that he should die. So they looked down upon the place where the boy was fasting and there he lay, dead. Then the spirits spoke to the father and said, "All that we promised your son, you shall have. Do not think about this matter [your son's death] any more and bury him."

Then the father dug a grave and buried him. "I wonder how it all happened," he thought to himself. "They told me they were unable to dissuade him, and it was for that reason that they killed him; they told me not to think of the matter any more."

Sometime after, when the father went to the grave, he noticed a tree growing at its head. That was his son. Only a tree lives forever, and that is why the spirits transformed him into a tree. The father realized it and was happy. He lived contented and prosperous thereafter.

Now this is what the father himself reported and it is because of this [the fate of the youth] that young people are told not to fast for too long a period.

(Winnebago, Central Woodland)

52
Who Is the Strongest?

Once upon a time it was raining, and the first little red ant came out in Halona. There was still snow, and he froze his foot. He said, "Snow, you are stronger than I am. Are you the strongest thing there is?" The Snow answered, "No, I am not the strongest thing there is. The Sun is stronger than I am, for when the Sun shines, I melt."

The little red ant went to the Sun. He said, "Sun, you are stronger than the Snow. Are you the strongest thing there is?" The Sun said, "No, I am not the strongest thing there is. The Wind is stronger than I am, for when I am shining the Wind blows clouds across my face." The little red ant went to the Wind. He said, "Wind, you are stronger than the Sun. Are you the strongest thing there is?" The Wind answered, "No, I am not the strongest thing there is. A house is stronger than I am, for I run against a house, and it kills me."

The little red ant went to House. He said, "House, you are stronger than Wind. Are you the strongest thing there is?" The House answered, "No, I am not the strongest thing there is. Mouse is stronger than I am. He makes holes in my body and kills me."

The little red ant went to Mouse. He said, "Mouse, you are stronger than House. Are you the strongest thing there is?" Mouse answered, "No, I am not the strongest thing there is. Cat is stronger than I am. Cat can overtake me and kill me."

The little red ant went to Cat. He said, "Cat, you are stronger than Mouse. Are you the strongest thing there is?"

Cat answered, "No, I am not the strongest thing there is. Stick is stronger than I am. If you hit me with Stick, it kills me."

The little red ant went to Stick. He said, "Stick, you are stronger than Cat. Are you the strongest thing there is?" Stick answered, "No, I am not the strongest thing there is. Fire is stronger than I am. If you throw me in the fire, it kills me."

The little red ant went to Fire. He said, "Fire, you are stronger than Stick. Are you the strongest thing there is?" Fire answered, "No, I am not the strongest thing there is. Water is stronger than I am. If you pour water on me, it kills me."

The little red ant went to Water. He said, "Water, you are stronger than Fire. Are you the strongest thing there is?" Water answered, "No, I am not the strongest thing there is. Cow is stronger than I am. When cow drinks me, it kills me."

The little red ant went to Cow. He said, "Cow, you are stronger than Water. Are you the strongest thing there is?" Cow answered, "No, I am not the strongest thing there is. Stone Knife is stronger than I am. When Stone Knife cuts me in the heart, it kills me."

The little red ant went to Stone Knife. He said, "Stone Knife, you are stronger than Cow. Are you the strongest thing there is?" Stone Knife answered, "No, I am not the strongest thing there is. Big Stone is stronger than I am. When I am thrown down upon Big Stone, it kills me."

This is what happened long ago, and that is why we are afraid of the rock.[1]

(Zuni, Southwest)

---

[1] Children say when they are frightened, "Oh, I am afraid! I shall be killed like the stone knife."

Bibliography

I. BASIC SOURCES

Barbeau, M. *Tsimsyan Myths.* ("National Museum of Canada Anthropological Series," No. 51, Bulletin No. 174.) Ottawa: 1961.

Benedict, R. *Zuni Mythology.* 2 vols. N.Y.: Columbia University Press, 1935.

Clark, E. E. *Indian Legends of the Pacific Northwest.* Berkeley: University of California Press, 1933.

Coffin, T. P. *Indian Tales of North America.* Philadelphia: American Folklore Society, 1961.

Curtin, J. *Creation Myths of Primitive America.* Boston: Little, Brown and Co., 1898.

——. *Myths of the Modocs.* Boston: Little, Brown and Co., 1912.

——. *Seneca Indian Myths.* N.Y.: E. P. Dutton & Co., 1923.

Grinnell, G. B. *Blackfoot Lodge Tales.* N.Y.: Charles Scribner's Sons, 1892.

Radin, P. *Primitive Man as a Philosopher.* N.Y.: Dover Publications, Inc., 1957.

——. *Winnebago Hero Cycles.* ("Indiana University Publications in Anthropology and Linguistics," Memoir No. 1.) Bloomington: Indiana University Press, 1948.

Swanton, J. R. *Tlingit Myths and Texts.* Washington: Smithsonian Institution, 1909.

Thompson, Stith. *Tales of the North American Indians.* Cambridge, Mass.: Harvard University Press, 1929.

II. ADDITIONAL SOURCES

The greater bulk of American Indian tales have appeared in sci-
entific journals and in certain series of learned publications. The
following is a list of the most important of these:

American Anthropologist.

Bulletin of the American Museum of Natural History.

Bulletin of the Bureau of American Ethnology.

Publications of the Carnegie Institution.

Columbia University Contributions to Anthropology.

Field Museum of Natural History, "Anthropological Series."

Geological Survey of Canada, "Anthropological Series."

Journal of American Folklore.

Publications of the Jessup North Pacific Expedition.

Memoirs of the American Folklore Society.

Anthropological Papers of the American Museum of Natural History.

Report of the Bureau of American Ethnology.

University of California Publications in American Archaeology
and Ethnology.

University of Pennsylvania, The University Museum Anthropological Publications.

University of Washington, "Publications in Anthropology."

Due to the great number of collections, only a few of the most
representative works are given for each cultural area:

General:

Curtis, E. S. *The North American Indian.* 20 vols. Cambridge, Mass.:
Harvard University Press, 1908–30.

Eskimo:

Rasmussen, K. *Eskimo Folk Tales.* London: Gyldendal, 1921.

Rink, H. *Tales and Traditions of the Eskimo.* Edinburgh: W. Black-
wood and Sons, 1875.

Mackenzie:

Lowie, R. H. *Chipewyan Tales.* ("American Museum of Natural
History Anthropological Papers.") N.Y.: 1912.

Plateau:

Boas, F. *Folk-Tales of Salishan and Sahaptin Tribes.* N.Y.: 1917.

Teit, J. A. *Mythology of the Thompson Indians.* ("American Museum of Natural History Memoirs," Vol. 12, No. 27.) N.Y.: 1912.

North Pacific:

Boas, F. *Bella Bella Tales.* N.Y.: American Folklore Society, 1932.

——. *Kwakiutl Tales.* ("Columbia University Contributions to Anthropology.") N.Y.: Columbia University Press, 1935.

——. *The Mythology of the Bella Coola Indians.* ("American Museum of Natural History Memoirs," Vol. 2, Part 2.) N.Y.: 1898.

——. *Tsimshian Texts.* ("American Ethnology Bureau Bulletin," No. 27.) Washington: 1916.

Swanton, J. R. *Haida Texts and Myths.* ("American Ethnology Bureau Bulletin," No. 29.) Washington: 1905.

California:

Barrett, S. A. *Pomo Myths.* ("Public Museum of the City of Milwaukee Bulletin," No. 15.) Milwaukee, Wis.: 1933.

Dixon, R. B. *Maidu Texts.* ("American Ethnology Society Publications," Vol. 4.) N.Y.: 1912.

Gayton, A. H. and S. S. Newman. *Yokuts and Western Mono Myths.* Berkeley: University of California, 1940.

Plains:

Beckwith, M. W. *Mandan-Hidatsa Myths and Ceremonies.* N.Y.: American Folklore Society, 1938.

Dorsey, G. A. *The Pawnee Mythology.* Part I. Washington: Carnegie Institution, 1906.

Duvall, D. C. *Mythology of the Blackfoot Indians.* N.Y.: 1909.

Lowie, R. H. *Myths and Traditions of the Crow Indians.* N.Y.: The Trustees of the American Museum of Natural History, 1918.

Sapir, E. *The Southern Paiute.* Boston: Little, Brown, and Co., 1931.

Central Woodland:

Bloomfield, L. *Menomini Texts.* N.Y.: G. E. Stechert & Co., 1928.

Iroquois:

Barbeau, C. M. *Huron and Wyandot Mythology.* Ottawa, Canada: Government Printing Bureau, 1915.

Northeast Woodland:

Rand, S. T. *Legends of the Micmacs.* N.Y.: Wellesley Philo. Publications, 1894.

Southwest:

Boas, F. *Keresan Texts.* N.Y.: American Ethnological Society, 1928.

Bunzel, R. *Zuni Texts.* N.Y.: G. E. Stechert & Co., 1933.

Goddard, P. E. *Navajo Texts.* ("American Museum of Natural History Anthropological Papers.") N.Y.: 1933.

Opler, M. E. *Myths and Tales of the Jicarilla Apache Indians.* N.Y.: American Folklore Society, 1938.

Voth, H. R. *The Traditions of the Hopi.* ("Field Columbian Museum Publications," No. 96, "Anthropological Series," Vol. 8.) Chicago: 1905.

III. SUGGESTED READING

Alexander, H. B. *North American Mythology.* N.Y.: Cooper Square Publishers, 1963.

Boas, F. "The Mythology and Folktales of the North American Indians," in *Race, Language and Culture.* N.Y.: Macmillan Co., 1940.

Bloomfield, L. *Sacred Stories of the Sweet Grass Cree.* ("National Museum of Canada Bulletin," No. 60, "Anthropological Series," No. 11.) Ottawa, Canada: 1930.

Lowie, R. H. "The Test Theme in North American Mythology," *Journal of American Folklore,* Vol. XXI, No. 97.

Rasmussen, K. *The Intellectual Culture of the Iglulik Eskimos.* Copenhagen: Gyldendalske Boghandel, Nordisk Forlag, 1929.

———. *Observations on the Intellectual Culture of the Caribou Eskimos.* Copenhagen: Gyldendalske Boghandel, Nordisk Forlag, 1930.

Thompson, Stith. "The Folktale in a Primitive Culture: North American Indian," in *The Folktale.* N.Y.: The Dryden Press, 1946.